Alfred Durand

Catholic ceremonies and explanation of the ecclesiastical year

From the french of the abbe Durand

Alfred Durand

Catholic ceremonies and explanation of the ecclesiastical year
From the french of the abbe Durand

ISBN/EAN: 9783742837653

Manufactured in Europe, USA, Canada, Australia, Japa

Cover: Foto ©Andreas Hilbeck / pixelio.de

Manufactured and distributed by brebook publishing software (www.brebook.com)

Alfred Durand

Catholic ceremonies and explanation of the ecclesiastical year

ST. PATRICK'S CATHEDRAL, NEW YORK.

CATHOLIC CEREMONIES

AND

Explanation of the Ecclesiastical Year.

FROM THE FRENCH OF THE ABBÉ DURAND.

WITH 96 ILLUSTRATIONS OF ARTICLES USED AT CHURCH CEREMONIES AND THEIR PROPER NAMES.

NEW YORK, CINCINNATI, CHICAGO:
BENZIGER BROTHERS
PRINTERS TO THE | PUBLISHERS OF
HOLY APOSTOLIC SEE | BENZIGER'S MAGAZINE

Nihil Obstat.
> Thos. L. Kinkead,
>> *Censor Librorum.*

Imprimatur.
> ✠ Michael Augustine,
>> *Archbishop of New York.*

New York, July 23, 1896.

PREFACE.

THIS volume, it is hoped, will be the handbook of all those who love to inform themselves upon those ceremonies of which they are too often blind and unappreciative spectators.

Mass, Vespers, and the feasts, that is to say, the ordinary offices at which the faithful assist—these are the compass of its pages. In order to explain them the use of symbolism has been chosen, which is the soul, the perfume, the marrow of worship, and the nourishment of Christian piety.

The word symbol, in its widest acceptation, answers to sign, image, figure, to the representation of an idea or a sentiment, something not to be reached by the senses. "From a liturgical point of view a symbol is a sign which, under the veil of words or things, represents mysteries above our nature, and which it is important for us to know. Among these symbols the most excellent are the sacraments of the Church, because to the sign they join an effect." (*Spicil. de Solesmes*, t. iii. l. v.) To symbolize an idea is to give it a physiognomy, a body, in order to make it more easily apprehended by all. All peoples have employed the mysterious language of symbols. If we see them more frequently used in divine worship, it is because, on the one hand, the teachings of religion are most difficult to understand, and, on the other, it is necessary to bring them within the grasp of all. Symbolism is thus the form of teaching which responds most thoroughly to the needs of the people in the religious life.

The great traditions of the liturgy begin to revive. For a long time they have been buried in the tomb of disdain or forgetfulness which Protestantism, Jansenism, and philosophy have prepared for them; they have burst their bonds, and the world salutes their glorious triumph with hope. May they contribute to bring back among us the golden age of Christian piety! The fervent generations of past centuries loved to come often into the holy place; in spite of the long hours consecrated to prayer they never wearied in the house of God.

To-day the sacred offices are abandoned by a great number; those who still frequent them find them too long, and, for the majority, the sanctification of Sunday is limited to a simple Low Mass. Whence comes this difference? The former understood the beauties of the worship, the mysteries of the liturgy, and the latter, like the idols of which the prophet speaks, "have eyes, but see not, and ears, yet hear not." If he who has written these pages attains his end, Sion shall see her ways less deserted upon her solemn feasts; the sacred offices will be better understood; and then, in the holy place, each look shall become a prayer.

CONTENTS.

PART I.—THE SACRIFICE OF THE MASS.

	PAGE
CHAPTER I.—THE ALTAR	9
CHAPTER II.—SACRED VESTMENTS	14
1. Priestly Vestments	14
2. Colors and Ornaments	16
3. Vestments of the Deacon, Subdeacon, and Acolytes	18
CHAPTER III.—THE VESSELS, LINENS, BREAD AND WINE OF THE SACRIFICE.	21
1. Vessels of the Sacrifice	21
2. Sacred Linens	22
3. The Bread and Wine of the Sacrifice	23
CHAPTER IV.—CEREMONIES OF THE MASS	24
First Part:	
1. The Preparation at the Foot of the Altar	26
2. The Introit, or the Incarnation	27
3. The Kyrie, or the Cry of Fallen Humanity	29
4. The Gloria in Excelsis, or the Cry of Bethlehem	30
5. The Dominus Vobiscum, or the Effusion of the Seven Gifts of the Holy Ghost	32
6. The Collect, or the Prayer of the Hidden Life	34
7. The Epistle, or the Mission of the Precursor	36
8. The Gradual and Tract, or the Sighs of Penitence	37
9. The Alleluia, or the Canticle of the Celestial Country	38

Contents.

		PAGE
10.	The Gospel, or the Preaching of Christ	39
11.	The Credo, or Profession of Faith in the Doctrine Preached by Jesus Christ	42

Second Part:

1.	The Offertory, or Last Supper	43
2.	The Incensing, or the Perfumes of Mary Magdalen	45
3.	The Secret, or the Prayer in the Garden of Olives	46
4.	The Preface, or the Chant of Triumph	46
5.	The Canon, or the Passion	47
6.	The Imposition of Hands, or the Crucifixion	49
7.	The Elevation, or Our Lord raised upon the Cross	49
8.	The Memento for the Dead, or the Just raised again by Jesus Christ	51
9.	The Nobis Quoque Peccatoribus, or the Prayer of the Good Thief	52
10.	The Second Elevation, or the Death of Our Saviour	52

Third Part:

1.	The Pater Noster, or the Prayer of Jesus Christ upon the Cross	53
2.	The Libera Nos, or the Mysteries of the Burial	54
3.	The Breaking of the Host, or the Side of Jesus opened by the Lance	55
4.	The Agnus Dei, or the Resurrection	56
5.	The Communion, or the Eucharistic Repasts of Jesus Christ arisen with His Apostles	58
6.	The Chants of the Communion, or the Joy of the Apostles in the Resurrection of Jesus Christ	60
7.	The Post-Communion, or the Forty Days of the Glorious Life	61

		PAGE
8.	The Ite Missa Est, or the Ascension	62
9.	The Benediction, or the Descent of the Holy Ghost	64
10.	The Last Gospel, or the Preaching of the Apostles and their Successors	65

CHAPTER V.—PONTIFICAL MASS ... 66
    1. The Bishop's Ornaments ... 66
    2. Ceremonies of the Pontifical Mass ... 71
CHAPTER VI.—MASS FOR THE DEAD ... 76
CHAPTER VII.—HOLY WATER, BLESSED BREAD, AND THE SIGN OF THE CROSS ... 80
    1. Holy Water ... 80
    2. Blessed Bread ... 83
    3. The Sign of the Cross ... 86
CHAPTER VIII.—PROCESSIONS ... 89
CHAPTER IX.—CHURCHES ... 93
    1. The Catholic Temple a Symbol of the Church ... 93
    2. The Catholic Temple a Symbol of the Cross ... 97
    3. The Bells ... 98

PART II.—VESPERS.

CHAPTER I.—THE DIVINE OFFICE ... 101
    1. Origin and Division ... 101
    2. Assistance at the Divine Office ... 102
    3. Vestments of the Celebrant of the Office ... 103
    4. The Chant ... 107
CHAPTER II.—VESPERS ... 111
    1. Mysteries of this Office ... 111
    2. Method of Assisting Piously at Vespers ... 112
CHAPTER III.—THE PSALMS OF VESPERS ... 115
    1. Preliminaries of the Office ... 115
    2. The First Psalm ... 121
    3. The Second Psalm ... 124
    4. The Third Psalm ... 128

		PAGE
5. The Fourth Psalm		133
6. The Fifth Psalm		137
7. The Little Chapter		145

CHAPTER IV.—HYMN, MAGNIFICAT, AND ANTHEM OF
THE BLESSED VIRGIN............... 146
    1. Hymn.................................. 146
    2. The Magnificat......................... 147
    3. The Anthem of the Blessed Virgin........ 157

CHAPTER V.—COMPLINE AND THE BENEDICTION OF
THE BLESSED SACRAMENT............. 159
    1. Compline.............................. 159
    2. The Benediction of the Blessed Sacrament... 163

PART III.—THE LITURGICAL YEAR.

CHAPTER I.—DIVISION OF TIME IN THE CHURCH..... 168
CHAPTER II.—THE TIME OF ADVENT AND OF CHRISTMAS................................... 178
    1. Advent Time........................... 178
    2. Christmas Time........................ 183

CHAPTER III.—SEPTUAGESIMA AND LENT.......... 196
    1. Septuagesima.......................... 196
    2. The Time of Lent...................... 198

CHAPTER IV.—HOLY WEEK....................... 206
    1. Palm Sunday........................... 206
    2. Office of Tenebræ..................... 206
    3. Holy Thursday......................... 207
    4. Good Friday........................... 210
    5. Holy Saturday......................... 214

CHAPTER V.—PASCHAL TIME AND PENTECOST....... 220
    1. Paschal Time.......................... 220
    2. Pentecost Time........................ 227

THE ORDINARY OF THE MASS..................... 246
VESPERS..................................... 268
BENEDICTION OF THE BLESSED SACRAMENT......... 282

CATHOLIC CEREMONIES.

Part I.—The Sacrifice of the Mass.

CHAPTER I.—THE ALTAR.

Form of the Altar.—The Catholic altar has always been a table or a tomb. This double form has perpetuated through the ages the remembrance of the institution of the Eucharist and of the burial of Our Lord. The cloth that covered the table at the last supper, the winding-sheet of the Saviour's embalming, are recalled to our love by the white linens spread upon it. The altar, the eucharistic table, the mystical tomb, is, above all, the holy mountain where Jesus Christ transfigures and immolates Himself at the same time; raised as it is above the ground, it appears to us always as a Thabor and a Calvary. Happier we than the apostle, for we can make for ourselves there a perpetual dwelling-place, even in the heart of the divine Saviour.

The Sacred Stone.—During the Mass the priest often kisses the middle of the altar. In this spot is a stone become, by the consecration of the bishop, a figure of

Jesus Christ. Like the Word of God, it *has received the sacred unction;* like Him, it bears the mark of five wounds, and these are also made by the hammer and iron; like the Lamb of God, of Whom "not one of the bones was broken" (Exod. xii. 46), the sacred stone is entire, cut from a single piece. He who loves Our Lord will understand these kisses so often repeated; the Church wishes to make reparation during the holy sacrifice for all the outrages of the passion—the derisive genuflections of the Jews replaced by the genuflections of the priest; the perfidious kiss of treason by the respectful kiss of love. In the sacred stone is enclosed a little tomb, sealed by the arms of the bishop; with the relics of the saints is laid herein three grains of incense. Here again is a reminder of the burial, and the different perfumes which Jesus Christ then received from the piety of His disciples—the aromatic herbs of Joseph of Arimathea, of Magdalen, and the holy women.

Relics in the Altar.—In his marvellous vision St. John saw "under the altar the souls of them that were slain for the Word of God." (Apoc. vi. 9.) The Church militant, heir of their holy relics, and following the steps of her sister in heaven, has placed them under the altar of sacrifice. This custom, observed from the earliest days of Christianity, teaches us how we should receive Jesus Christ in holy communion.

Our heart becomes an altar where Our Lord consummates His sacrifice, and upon this living altar He wishes to see the blessed wounds of a martyr. The saints have tasted in communion ineffable sweetness; recompense, we may be sure, of the immolation which they made of themselves each day. It is easy for us to experience this; let us prepare ourselves for such a solemn act by the sacrifice of our tastes, of our passions, as the Hebrews ate the paschal lamb with bitter herbs. The Eucharist will then bear in us the most abundant fruit ; it will be the grain of wheat sown in our hearts, to grow there till the resurrection, the day of blossoming and of harvest ; the heavenly wine, which maketh virgin those hearts inclined to evil ; the divine fire, which will give to the weak the courage of the lion.

The Tabernacle.—The rich materials which cover the place where the Blessed Sacrament rests, even the name given it, recall the tabernacle of the Old Law, in which the ark of the covenant was kept, one of the prophetic figures of the sacrament of our altars. Its most ordinary form is that of a *tower;* this symbol of strength could not be more suitably employed than in sheltering Him Whom St. Augustine so well calls "the bread of the strong."

The Cross.—Above the tabernacle is the cross. Its presence alone in this place speaks simply and eloquently : " It is here that Jesus Christ renews the sacrifice of Calvary. The cross raised by deicidal hands remains always laden ; love forever fastens to it the divine victim. His arms extended call the sinner to return and to pardon ; His lips never cease to utter the great prayer of mercy: 'Father, forgive them ;' grace flows from His heart in torrents." Christian souls, all these things the crucifix, by its wounds, says to you each day.

Candles.—Doubtless they recall to us that the catacombs were the cradle of the Church and her first temple ; that the divine mysteries were there celebrated by the light of torches. This touching reminder of the persecuted Church should not be lost sight of.

But if it were merely as a reminder of the bloody period of the Church's martyrdom that candles were used, why demand wax for the altar-lights? The anxiety of the Church on this point shows us that there is here some mystery. "Wax," says Mgr. de Cony, summing up the teaching of all the liturgists, "is one of the most expressive symbols furnished the Church by nature to express allegorically the holy humanity of Jesus Christ. The earliest doctors dwell on *the virginity of the bees*, and the *purity* of that substance drawn from the nectar of the most exquisite flowers, and compare these things to the conception of the Saviour in the pure womb of Mary. The whiteness of the wax, laboriously obtained, signifies again the glory of Jesus Christ, the result of His sufferings; then the flame, mounting from that column of wax which it consumes, is the divinity of Jesus Christ, manifesting itself by the sacrifice of His humanity, and illuminating the world." (*Cérém. Rom.*, l. i. c. 6.) "It is not, then, to lighten the darkness of the sanctuary, let us say with St. Isidore, that the altar-candles are lighted, because the sun is shining, but this light is a sign of joy, and it represents Him of Whom the Gospel says: "He is the true light." (*Orig.*, l. i. c. 12.)

During the holy mysteries, when thick darkness clouds our soul, let us beg God, the eternal light, to scatter this gloomy night. If at the foot of this new Calvary our heart is indifferent and frozen, let us pray God, infinite love, to melt it in His fires. There will come a day when this blessed light will be, for those who have despised it, the fire of justice ; O Lord, inspire my heart with such a profound horror of sin that I may escape the flames of Thy vengeance.

The Sanctuary-lamp.—In honor of Jesus Christ a lamp burns perpetually before the altar. The Christian soul longs to remain in constant adoration at the feet of Our Lord, there to be consumed by gratitude and love. In heaven alone will this happiness be given to us, but here below, as an expression of our devout desires, we place a lamp in the sanctuary to take our place. In this little light St. Augustine shows us an image of the three Christian virtues. Its *clearness* is faith, which enlightens our mind ; its *warmth* is love, which fills our heart ; its *flame*, which, trembling and agitated, mounts upward till it finds rest in its centre, is hope, with its aspirations toward heaven, and its troubles outside of God. (*Serm.* lxvii., *de Script.*)

May our heart watch in the sanctuary under the eye of God ! During the labors of the day nothing is easier than to fly there in thought, to offer to Jesus Christ our pain, our weariness, our actions.

At night let us place ourselves at the feet of Jesus, and say : While I sleep I wish to love Thee and bless Thee always ; here would I take my rest. If many Christians were faithful to this pious practice, it would not be merely a faint and solitary lamp which would illumine the holy place, but thousands of hearts would shed there their sparkling rays of light.

Altar-candlesticks.—The heavenly Jerusalem has her sacrifice, and also her altar. St. John thus describes it : "The altar of gold had seven golden candlesticks, and in the midst was the Son of man, shining like the snow by the whiteness of His garments, and more brilliant than the sun by reason of the splendor of His face." (Apoc. i.)

It is, then, reminders of heaven which the Church constantly places before the eyes of her children ; how can we help thinking of it when all around us speaks of it: the altar, the candlesticks, the Eucharist ?

The Missal.—Upon the altar in heaven was also a mysterious book, sealed with seven seals, and which no man could open. The lion of the tribe of Juda, Jesus Christ, came, and His triumphant hand broke the seals. The resemblance here is easily traced. The book which contains the prayers of the liturgy is placed upon the altar before the sacrifices, but it remains closed; only the priest, representing Jesus Christ, has the right to open it.

In the West Latin is the language of the liturgy of the Church. However, certain Greek words, such as *Kyrie eleison*, and some Hebrew expressions, like *alleluia, amen, sabaoth,* have been enshrined in this rich casket, that the language of the Christian sacrifice may recall the inscription placed above the Saviour's cross, which was written, says the evangelist, in Hebrew, in Greek, and in Latin.

CHAPTER II.—SACRED VESTMENTS.

1. PRIESTLY VESTMENTS.

The Amice.—This is a white linen cloth with which the priest covers his head, and then allows to fall upon his shoulders. Ancient customs teach us that the head of the criminal sentenced to death was enveloped in linen. The sentence was thus framed: "Go, lictor, bind his hands; cover his head; scourge him, and fasten him upon the cross." The amice reminds us that a shameless servant in the house of Herod filled this office to Jesus even before His condemnation.

The Alb.—At the sight of the white linen robe which covers the entire body of the priest, recollections of Thabor, of heaven, and of the passion should be presented to our mind. On the mount of the transfiguration, and in the vision of St. John, Our Lord showed Himself in garments white as the snow and shining like the sun; in the court of Herod, abused by madmen, He was clothed with the white robe of innocence.

The Girdle.—Here is again a memorial at once of glory and of humiliation. The shining robe of Our Lord in the vision of St. John was bound by a girdle of gold, emblem of virginity; in the scourging we see the divine body of Jesus lashed to the column by cords.

The Maniple.—The maniple, worn on the left arm of the priest, is an eloquent preacher, teaching him what he should expect from man. The servant is not greater than his master; now what was the recompense of Jesus Christ? Because He had dried tears, fed the poor, cured the blind and the dumb, caressed the children, raised the dead, His divine hands were covered with chains during the passion. They are bound by love when He could chastise. The priest also, who wears each day this maniple, should have his hands always open for kindness, but closed to vengeance; tied when he could punish, but open to absolve.

The Stole.—The stole worn around the neck of the priest, and falling before him, takes the place of the rope which was used to lead the divine victim through the streets of Jerusalem to Calvary.

The Chasuble.—This vestment, worn over all the others, has a meaning not less touching. The soldiery, in Pilate's house, wished to mock Jesus with a caricature of a royal coronation. A scarlet cloak for a mantle, a reed for a sceptre, a crown of thorns for a diadem— these were the insignia of that derided majesty. Those murderers, tired at last of striking and torturing Him, threw a cross upon the torn shoulders of the Saviour, and led Him forth to Calvary.

See the priest at the altar : the chasuble recalls the mantle at the prætorium ; the tonsure, the crown of thorns. Nothing is wanting, not even the cross ; see it, drawn large upon the chasuble ; the celebrant, like his Master, carries it upon his shoulders.

This cross is formed of our iniquities. Let us not forget it when the priest comes forth to offer the sacrifice ; let us say to him who stands in the place of Jesus Christ : "It belongs to me to carry that cross, which love has made you bear in my stead. I know that my weakness is too great for such a burden. But at least I will fill the place of Simon the Cyrenean, and will help you with the feeble aid of my prayers." How few Christians pray for the priest as he goes to the altar, yet not culy charity but justice renders this a duty.

2. COLORS AND ORNAMENTS.

The colors are : White, red, green, purple, and black.

White, emblem of purity, is consecrated to the feasts of Our Lord, except those which commemorate His sufferings. What color could be more suitable to Him Who

INTERIOR OF A CHURCH.

is infinite sanctity, and Who showed Himself to His apostles on Thabor, and to St. John in heaven, "clothed in a robe whiter than the snow"?

This color is also that of the feasts of Mary. After God there is nothing purer than the Blessed Virgin. The Holy Spirit compares her to a lily shining in whiteness, to a spotless dove, to a tower of ivory, and to a limpid fountain.

White is worn on the solemnities of the angels because of their purity, and on the feasts of virgins, "sisters of angels in their innocence," says Peter de Blois.

Red is the figure of blood and of fire. The Church clothes herself in it for those feasts which have connection with the passion of Our Lord, and on those days recalls to us that Jesus Christ has not feared for love of us to be reddened in His own blood, shed in torrents on the pavement of the prætorium, on the road to Calvary, and on the wood of the cross. At Pentecost the Church wears red to figure forth the mystery of the tongues of fire on the heads of the apostles, and the effusion of that other interior fire with which the hearts of those generous messengers of good tidings were filled. Red, the color of blood, is also used on the feasts of martyrs.

Green, in the liturgy as in nature, is a symbol of hope; it is the emblem of good things to come. The Church uses it on the simple Sundays during the time called "of pilgrimage," because it recalls the militant life of the Church, from the descent of the Holy Ghost to the end of the world.

This time comprehends the Sundays and weeks from Pentecost to Advent. From the octave of the Epiphany to Septuagesima we find green in use among the altar-ornaments. Says Dom Guéranger: "This choice shows that in the birth of Our Lord, Who is the flower of the fields, is born also the hope of our salvation, and that after the winter of paganism and Judaism the green springtime of grace has begun in our hearts." (*The Liturgical Year*, vol. ii., "Christmas.")

Purple, the color of the mortification of the flesh by penitence, is reserved to the following periods: Advent, Lent, ember-days, vigils and rogations, and the procession of St. Mark, to teach us that we should then expiate our sensual lives by fasting and mortification.

Black.—It is hardly necessary to explain the signification of this color of death; even without speaking, the priest who mounts to the altar clad in these sad vestments is a preacher sufficiently eloquent. Let us listen to the voice of grace which cries: "Remember, man, that dust thou art, and unto dust thou shalt return."

3. VESTMENTS OF THE DEACON, SUBDEACON, AND ACOLYTES.

The Deacon.—This word means servitor. One of the principal duties of this sacred minister is to assist the priest during the holy mysteries. He is always at his side, and, by the place of honor which he occupies, he reminds us of the beloved disciple leaning on the heart of Jesus during the last supper, and standing under the cross on Calvary.

The deacon chants the gospel, and dismisses the people at the end of Mass by intoning: "*Ite, Missa est.*"

His vestments are the amice, alb, girdle, stole, and dalmatic; except the latter all are already understood.

The dalmatic was originally worn in Dalmatia, whence it was brought to Rome. It is a long and ample garment, with very large sleeves, but short, descending only to the elbow. From the second century among the Romans it was the vestment of the emperors; the Church adopted it for the Sovereign Pontiff and the bishops. The deacons received it from Pope Sylvester, but the privilege of wearing it was confined to the deacons of the church at Rome, and for them only granted on festival-days as a sign of joy; consequently it was laid aside during Advent, Lent, and fast-days, periods of sadness and mourning in the Church.

The dalmatic is of the same color as the chasuble of the priest.

The bands of rich stuff, or even of gold or silver, which are laid perpendicularly on each side, were, in ancient times, reserved to persons of distinction. We find them again upon the chasuble of the priest, the dalmatic of the deacon, and the tunic of the subdeacon because of the elevated rank which these sacred ministers hold in the hierarchy; their duties bring them near to Our Lord in the Eucharist, and by the chastity which they have irrevocably sworn they are become like heavenly spirits. The short sleeves of the dalmatic, allowing the deacons to move more easily, remind us that, according to the etymology of their name of servitor, they assist, not only the priest at the altar, but the poor, the widows, and orphans. They find also in the large sleeves of their vestment a lesson of liberality toward the poor. The deacon does not wear the stole in the same manner as the priest; he places it on the left shoulder, and brings the extremities under the right arm. The stole being formerly a robe, the deacon necessarily had to roll it up under the right arm in order more easily to serve the priest at the altar.

The Subdeacon.—This minister is charged with the preparation of the sacred vessels, the bread and wine of the sacrifice, giving the water to the celebrant when he washes his hands, and reading the epistle. His vestments are the amice, alb, girdle, maniple, and tunic. The tunic was formerly distinguished from the dalmatic by its form and material; now it is in all respects like it, hence it is unnecessary to speak of it.

The Acolytes.—The ministers who carry the candles, prepare the incense, and serve the subdeacon and deacon at the altar are called acolytes. Samuels of the new law, they always wear in their functions a linen robe. Are they not also angels upon the earth? Their white vestments; the flowing sleeves with which they are adorned, like two wings; the censer swinging in their hands; their comings and goings in the sanctuary—do they not recall the celestial spirits around the throne of the Lamb? The white vestment of the acolyte is called a surplice, and covers a cassock generally black.

This striking contrast has not escaped the interpreters of our ceremonies, who have given us its meaning. Nearly all the religious Orders have adopted for their habit black or white, in remembrance of the glorious or sorrowful mysteries of the life of Jesus Christ. These two colors, united in the costume of the young levite, illustrate the great motto of Christianity: To die to one's self, and live again in Jesus Christ.

CHAPTER III.—THE VESSELS, LINENS, BREAD AND WINE OF THE SACRIFICE.

1. VESSELS OF THE SACRIFICE.

The Chalice and the Paten.—To seal an alliance the ancients at the end of the banquet caused to be passed from one to another of the guests a cup to which each touched his lips. Our Lord followed this custom at the last supper. The chalice used at the altar is made upon the model of the one from which Jesus Christ drank on the eve of His death. While the chalice receives the blood of Jesus Christ, the paten is reserved for His divine body. It is a large plate, of gold or silver like the chalice, but always golden in that portion which comes in contact with the holy species. Like the chalice, before it is used in the sacred mysteries it is consecrated by chrism, and special prayers said by the bishop. Let us receive from the gold, the holy chrism, and the particular benediction of the prelate given to those vessels upon which the Holy of holies rests but an instant the lesson which the Church teaches us. In communion our hearts become living chalices; our tongue is another paten upon which the priest lays Jesus Christ. May Our Lord always find our tongue and heart bright with the gold of charity; let us consecrate this mystical chalice and paten with the unction of Christian sweetness and the perfume of prayer.

The Ciborium.—Above the primitive altars was raised a canopy held up by columns, the base resting on the pavement of the sanctuary. Silken curtains adorned the space between these columns, which were drawn during a part of the holy mysteries, the priest finding himself then completely concealed from the gaze of the people, as if in a mysterious cloud. This top of the altar received, because of its shape, the name of *ciborium*, a kind of cup in use among the Egyptians; the upper part in fact resembled a reversed cup; the whole was surmounted by a cross. In the middle of these ciboriums were hung doves of gold or silver, upon which the host was laid. Toward the twelfth century the ciboriums were done away with; they were replaced by little domes built in the middle of the altar, held up by four columns; they received the vessels containing the consecrated species, which ceased to be suspended, as they had been formerly. The name of ciborium passed then to the vessel itself; the upper part, half spherical and surmounted by a cross, and also the curtains of velvet or silk hung around it, recalls the ancient ciborium.

2. SACRED LINENS.

The corporal is the linen upon which the priest places the chalice and the host during the Mass. The name *shroud*, which it formerly bore, and the white linen of which it is made, remind us of the winding-sheet used at the burial of Our Saviour. The learned author of the *Rational* says that the reason it is spread out upon the altar is because the winding-sheet of Our Lord was found unrolled in the tomb.

The burse, in which the corporal is enclosed after the Mass, was not known to the early Church.

The purificator is the linen which the priest uses to dry his fingers and lips, as well as the chalice, after the communion. The Greeks use a sponge, in memory of the one filled with gall which the soldier presented to Our Saviour.

The pall is the white linen, most frequently covering a card, which the priest lays over the chalice during Mass to preserve the precious blood which it contains from all accident.

The veil is not classed among the sacred linens. We will speak of it here because the matters of which we treat lead us to do so. Up to the time of the offertory it covers the chalice, the paten, and the pall; then it is raised, to recall to us the stupidity and ignorance veiling the great mystery of the Eucharist from the eyes of the apostles. Our Lord announced it to them often, but their faith remained wavering and blind; only at the last supper was this darkness completely dispelled.

The finger-towel is the linen with which the priest dries his fingers at the *lavabo*. It represents that other white linen mentioned in the Gospel used at the washing of feet before the last supper.

3. THE BREAD AND WINE OF THE SACRIFICE.

Bread.—The circular form was very early adopted for the eucharistic bread; the circle being the emblem of infinity, this form was peculiarly suitable to Him Who has no beginning and no end.

The whiteness of the sacramental bread should be to us an image of the sanctity of the Saviour, and a reflection of His glory.

The Latin Church uses the bread of the *azyme*, or unleavened bread, and this for two reasons. In the first place, she wishes to imitate Our Lord, Who used this kind of bread in instituting the new Pasch; the Jewish law forbidding, under pain of death, to have leavened bread in the house during the paschal time. (Exod. xii. 15.) In the second place leaven was considered a sign of corruption, as St. Paul distinctly states (I. Cor. v. 6), and so leavened bread would not be suitable for consecration of the virginal body of Jesus Christ. What care on the part of the Church to withdraw from the Holy of holies, in the sacrament of His love, even the shadow of that which could recall sin! May we all learn in this elevated school the respect due to Jesus Christ.

Wine.—Ecclesiastical history teaches us that the fruit of certain renowned vineyards was reserved for the service of the altar. For making the sacrificial wine the Greeks chose the fairest and purest of the grapes; they were not trodden by the feet, but the hands were used to express the juice.

Red wine has always been preferred by the Church; its color represents better the mystery wrought by the words of consecration. Besides which it cannot be mistaken for water, and so by its use many mistakes are avoided. It was principally this reason which called forth in several councils the prohibition of white wine for the Mass. Now it is permitted to use either.

CHAPTER IV.—CEREMONIES OF THE MASS.

THE venerable Curé d'Ars loved to repeat that if one knew what the Mass was he would die. Yes, we should die of love and gratitude. That which was the desire of

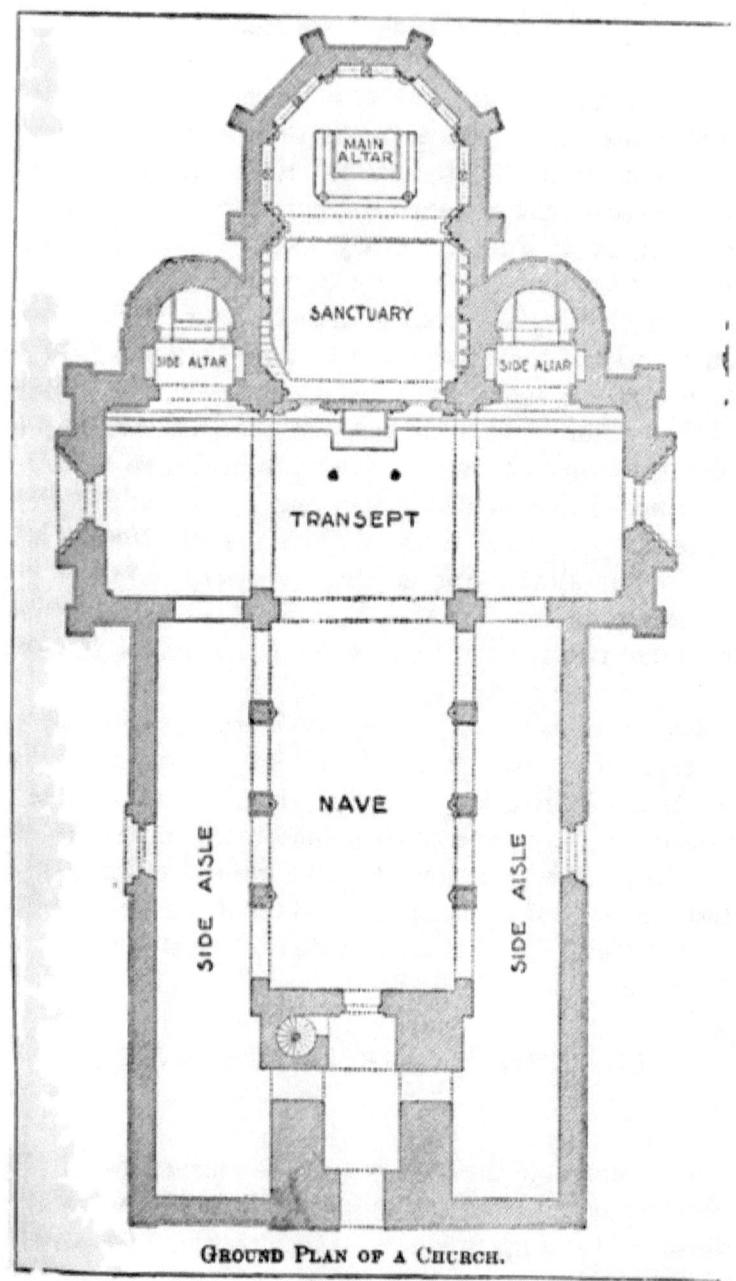

GROUND PLAN OF A CHURCH.

the patriarchs, and was foreseen by the prophets; that of which the shepherds at Bethlehem, the apostles at the last supper, Mary and the holy women on Calvary and at the holy sepulchre, the disciples after the resurrection, were witnesses, we see ourselves every day. In the person of the priest, and under the eucharistic veils, Our Lord renews on the altar all the mysteries of His life. "The order of the Mass," says Pope Innocent III., in his admirable treatise on the sacrifice, "is arranged upon a plan so well conceived that everything done by Jesus Christ, or concerning Him, from His incarnation to His ascension, is there largely contained, either in words or in actions, wonderfully presented."

We have divided the Mass into three parts, corresponding to the three epochs in the life of Our Saviour. The first, from the *Introit* to the *Credo*, comprises the thirty-three years of the life of Our Lord up to the institution of the Eucharist. The second, from the *Credo* to the *Pater*, retraces the different scenes of His sufferings. The third, from the *Pater* to the end of the last gospel, embraces all His glorious life.

It is from this magnificent point of view that the greatest doctors of the Church have seen the august sacrifice. Thus considered, the holy mysteries cannot fail to inspire the Christian soul with respect and love. As we leave our houses to go to the church let us consider the pious haste of the shepherds and the Magi going to adore the Saviour in the stable; the sorrow which filled the holy women ascending Calvary, their loving ardor in going to the sepulchre. Their happiness is to be ours; let us have in our hearts something of their faith and of their piety.

First Part.

1. THE PREPARATION AT THE FOOT OF THE ALTAR.

In the earthly paradise the first man enjoyed familiar conversations with God. He fell, and was driven far from the face of the Lord, and sentenced to live in a vale of tears. He was not, however, left without hope: a redeemer was promised to him and to his children. And for four thousand years all the echoes of this poor earth carried up to heaven cries of anguish and of confidence, claiming the fulfilment of the divine promise. The Church places before our eyes at the beginning of the sacrifice the reminder of this fall. Between Eden and Calvary there are many connections; is not one the explanation of the other? The priest, as he descends the steps of the altar, represents man fallen, and driven from paradise. The preparatory prayers which he then recites recall those of the world of antiquity. Is there not in these prayers, as in those of the patriarchs and prophets, confidence and sorrow, joy and tears by turns?

"I will go unto the altar of God, to God Who rejoiceth my youth.

"Judge me, O God, and distinguish my cause from the nation that is not holy.

"To Thee, O God, my God, I will give praise upon the harp: why art thou sad, O my soul; and why dost thou disquiet me?"

These are surely the utterances of sinful man; fear and hope are always side by side; the heaven in his heart is never without a cloud. A redeemer has been promised to the guilty world; toward this divine victim all eyes are turned. The cross, foreseen by the prophets, will be the hope, at the same time that it is the support and consolation, of humanity. The priest indicates this thought to us as he traces the sacred sign several times upon his brow during the preparatory prayers.

2. THE INTROIT, OR THE INCARNATION.

The Kiss on the Altar.—The prayers ended, the priest ascends the steps of the altar, and, resting his hands upon the sacred table, kisses it respectfully. This ceremony, so simple in appearance, is filled with mystery; it represents the infinite love of the Son of God in His incarnation. (St. Bernard and St. Melito, *Spicil. de Solesmes*, t. iii. p. 29.) God pursued humanity, which, since the time of Adam, had tried to escape from the yoke of obedience and love. But there was a day, a day fixed from all eternity in the decrees of God, for which He waited: *apprehendit*, thus St. Paul expresses it. What would He do to this guilty, fleeing humanity? He embraced it in the clasp of an infinite charity; He clothed Himself with the mantle of its miseries: the Word was made flesh.

The anthem at the *Introit*, by the chant, and not by the meaning of its words, is the expression of the ardent longing which made "the clouds rain the just" (Is. xlv. 8); so says Innocent III. "It is repeated to show the ardor of these sighs" (*De Sacro Alt. Myst.*, l. ii. c. 28); and in solemn Masses its chant, grave and slow, reminds us how long it was before heaven granted the Messias, only after forty centuries of tears and waiting. Why is it that this anthem is preceded by the sign of the cross? The deicidal cries have not yet been uttered:

why show already the sign of the humiliations and agony of Calvary?

Theology answers us. From the first instant of His incarnation Jesus Christ saw the rods, the thorns, the blows, the nails, the lance, the cross, and He suffered in His heart all the torments of His sorrowful passion. "Even in sleeping," says Bellarmin, "the heart of Jesus saw the coming cross." Christian art has transformed this teaching into an allegory as beautiful as it is touching. The child Jesus sleeps upon a cross, and His little hands press to His heart a crown of thorns.

From whom has the mystery of the Word made flesh received its first adoration? When God revealed it to the heavenly spirits, they chanted its praise before the throne of the Eternal; then one of their princes, the archangel Gabriel, in the humble house of Nazareth, had first the privilege of adoring with Mary the Word Incarnate. For this reason the *Gloria Patri*, the chant of the angels, divides the *Introit*.

The Incensing of the Altar.—Before the *Introit* in solemn Masses the altar is incensed. Ecclesiastical tradition has seen in incense the symbol of the sweet odor of Jesus Christ. To the name of Jesus has been added another, that of Christ, meaning *anointed* or *sacred*, for He has received from His Father a mysterious unction, of which the world has caught the blessed perfume. And, even in our day, in the atmosphere of corruption and error in which we live, what is the secret charm that draws souls to God? The odor of Thy sweetness, O Jesus, Thy miracles, Thy doctrine, and Thy goodness.

It is the nature of our heart to render honor to all which recalls a beloved person. Jesus Christ is all in all to His Church; thus we see the spouse of Christ pouring out incense, the expression of her respect and love, upon all the objects which speak to her of her divine spouse—upon the altar, the symbolical figure of the cross, His glorious standard; upon the holy relics of the saints, His living temples; upon the priest, His visible representative; upon the faithful, the members of His mystical body. In union with the Church let us love to honor Jesus Christ wherever faith shows us traces of His presence; certainly in the Eucharist, but also in the priest, the poor, in little children, the sick, in those whom we employ.

3. THE KYRIE, OR THE CRY OF FALLEN HUMANITY.

Why is it said before the *Gloria?* The prayer of mankind since its fall has become a profound sigh; indeed, in Latin both *sorrow* and *prayer* are expressed by the same word. The oldest and the widest-spread prayer—the prayer of the adult as of the child, of the sick, the poor, and the despairing—is short as a sigh: " Have pity on me."

Nature herself sympathizes with the misfortune of her fallen king. Everywhere arise voices which join with that of man in the note of melancholy and of pain, thus forming a universal harmony, of which St. Paul said : " For we know that every creature groaneth, and travaileth in pain even till now." (Rom. viii. 22.)

The *Kyrie* is, then, the cry of humanity at all the periods of its history, but above all at the coming of the Messias. Said before the *Gloria*, it expresses the profound misery of the old world, and the immense need that it had of redemption. In this place, too, the *Kyrie* has another signification: "The seventy weeks are shortened," said the angel to Daniel (Dan. ix. 24), and the doctors believe that the time of the incarnation was hastened in the designs of God as a recompense to the prayer of the patriarchs, the prophets, and of Mary above all. During this chant let us not forget the power of prayer; it will abridge for us the bitter days of trial and God's abandonment; for the Church the time of persecution and tears.

The Kyrie is Repeated Nine Times.—Nine times the Church repeats this cry, in memory of the nine heavenly choirs. While the rebel angels tried to prevent the accomplishment of the divine plan, the good angels implored God for the incarnation with all their strength. They united their prayers to those of earth. God had chosen human nature, but this consideration of a mean jealousy could not affect them. They saw but one thing: the glory of God. God must be glorified; by whom, where, or how? What did it matter to true love? What a lesson and what memories for us in this ninefold repetition of the *Kyrie!*

4. THE GLORIA IN EXCELSIS, OR THE CHANT OF BETHLEHEM.

Intonation of the Gloria.—To represent the journey from Nazareth to Bethlehem the priest returns to the middle of the altar, while the last *Kyrie* carries to God the supplications of earth.

Borrowing from the angels the words sung beside the cradle of the infant God, he announces to the world the supreme joy: "*Gloria in excelsis Deo, et in terra pax hominibus bonæ voluntatis.*"

In solemn Masses the choir continues the celestial chant, for the Gospel says that an angel proclaimed the good news to the shepherds: "And suddenly there was with the angel a multitude of the heavenly host, praising God." (Luke ii. 13.) The hands of the priest raised toward heaven at the word *gloria* seem to try to return to God all the glory. "Not to us, O Lord, but to Thy name be the glory," sings the psalmist. (Ps. cxiii. 9.) To God be the glory of all our works; to us the humility, but also the peace which is their assured fruit. It is in order to receive this divine peace that the priest again joins his hands at the words: *Pax in terra.*

During this chant let us represent vividly to our faith Jesus Christ present in the tabernacle, the new stable of His eucharistic life.

The ciborium is His manger; the species of bread and wine His swaddling-bands. He is cold, for it is winter about Him, the winter of forgetfulness and indifference. Let us fall at His feet, with the angels, to praise Him, with the shepherds to glorify Him, with the Magi to adore Him. Let us also offer Him gifts—the gold of a heart that loves Him, the incense of a heart that prays, the myrrh of a heart that is resigned.

The Sign of the Cross.—Persecution quickly attacked the child in the crib, but He escaped the fury of Herod by flight. The sign of the cross at the end of the joyous canticle of Bethlehem should recall to us the massacre of the innocents, the flight into Egypt, the anxieties of exile, and also the blood shed under the knife of the circumcision.

5. THE DOMINUS VOBISCUM, OR THE EFFUSION OF THE SEVEN GIFTS OF THE HOLY GHOST.

The Kiss on the Altar.—The venerable Olier has so well explained this ceremony that we cannot resist the pleasure of quoting him. "It is necessary to remark," he says, "that the priest does not say, '*Dominus vobiscum*,' or, '*Oremus*,' without first kissing the altar, and even before the *Orate fratres* he kisses it again, to show that it is from the bosom of God that he draws the spirit of prayer which he wishes to give to the people. It is the same case in the benedictions which he gives the people, or to the host, or to himself; they are often preceded by a kiss upon the altar, to show that he gets from God the blessings for the people and himself, having of himself neither graces nor blessings, except in God, Who has, as St. Paul says, 'blessed us with all benediction in His Son.'"

Meaning of the Dominus Vobiscum.—What touching reminders are in this salutation: The Lord be with you!

One of the greatest joys of Christianity, the greatest surely, is to know that since His birth God has made Himself our Emmanuel, and remains always among us. When He died, He did not leave us, He stayed with His children in the sacrament of His love. The Lord be with you, says the priest before the prayer; let us not fear; let us pray with confidence; He has drawn near us to hear our prayers.

He is with us; may He be also in us, in our hearts. May He unite us all in a common bond of charity. The open and wide-spread arms of the priest give Him to us all; his arms closed tell us why He gives Himself: "that

ALTAR.

we may be made perfect in one." (St. John xvii. 23.) The goodness of God inspires Christians with a loving boldness. Lord, Thou art with us to listen to our prayers, but " we know not what we should pray for as we ought." (Rom. viii. 26.) Give us, then, Thy spirit, " the spirit of prayer, which shall help our weakness, and make supplication for us with unutterable groaning."

"*And with Thy Spirit.*"—This is the meaning of the response of the faithful. (Isidore Pelus., l. i. *epist.* 122.)

The Seven Repetitions of Dominus Vobiscum.—Seven times the priest salutes the faithful by the *Dominus vobiscum;* seven times is the same response heard : "*Et cum spiritu tuo*"—at the Collect, the Gospel, the Offertory, the Preface, the *Agnus Dei*, the Post-communion, and the *Ite, Missa est.* Seven is the number of the Holy Spirit, called *septiform* in the chants of the Church ; the faithful beg for His seven divine gifts at each salutation of the priest : 1st, after the *Gloria*, for the gift of wisdom, which the incarnate Wisdom has merited for us, triumphing over pride in the humiliations of the stable. 2d, before the *Gospel*, for the gift of understanding, to comprehend the word of God. 3d, at the *Offertory*, for the gift of counsel, which makes us prefer the joys of sacrifice to the pleasures of the world, after the example of the Saviour, immolating Himself for us at the last supper. 4th, at the *Preface*, for the gift of fortitude, which sustained Our Lord in the anguish of His agony in the Garden of Olives. 5th, at the *Agnus Dei*, for the gift of knowledge, the divine light which enlighteneth each soul admitted to the banquet of angels. 6th, at the *Post-communion*, for the gift of piety, so necessary for him who has become the living tabernacle of Jesus Christ. 7th, at the *Ite, Missa est,* for the gift of the fear of the Lord, which should inspire us with a holy terror at the thought of the Last Judgment. Five times only does the priest turn toward the people in addressing them with the salutation of peace. The Church has so arranged it to figure in this sacrifice commemorative of the death, resurrection, and ascension of Jesus Christ, the five apparitions of Our Saviour on Easter Day. The *Gospel* mentions Magdalen, the holy women, St. Peter, the disciples at Emmaus, and the apostles as having enjoyed this favor.

6. THE COLLECT, OR THE PRAYERS OF THE HIDDEN LIFE.

Return to the Epistle Side of the Altar.—Before the storm of persecution raised by Herod Our Lord fled into Egypt. The severe trials of exile in an idolatrous land were succeeded by hard tasks in the workshop until He was thirty years old. But during the days passed in Egypt and in Nazareth the divine Saviour silently wrought the work of our redemption by labor and prayer. When the priest leaves the middle of the altar to go to the epistle side, let us think of Jesus as a child, journeying into exile; let his hands raised to heaven remind us of the manual labors of Nazareth, and the *Collect* the prayers which sanctified it.

The Priest's Hands Raised and Joined.—The hands raised during the *Collect,* the *Secret,* and the *Post-communion* have another mysterious meaning. Tertullian tells us that in his time it was customary for Christians to pray with the arms extended in the form of a cross; later the hands only were raised; but the profound meaning of this ceremony remains the same. Jesus

Christ alone has the right to be heard; if man, then, wishes to obtain grace from on high, he must identify himself with his Redeemer, become another self by sacrifice, resignation, and the cross. God looks lovingly upon those who suffer; at their prayer His heart overflows, pouring down torrents of mercy. If the Lord does not listen to our prayers, we are to blame. Do we bear with Christian resignation the marks of the cross printed by sorrow on our hearts, or on our bodies by illness? The secret of the power with God which the saints possessed is in their spirit of generous sacrifice: "For when I am weak, then am I powerful." (II. Cor. xii. 10.) These words, addressed to the Corinthians by the Apostle, have been many times verified; each page of the lives of the saints bears witness to their truth. The priest himself has become a man of trials and sorrow because he has made himself our mediator in prayer; this is why God has constituted the priesthood a Calvary, and not a Thabor. But the priest does not pray alone. "Let us pray," he says, pray together; let us put ourselves in those good dispositions which obtain everything from God. His raised hands when he says these words remind us what these dispositions are: to accept the cross without murmuring, to carry it resignedly.

Often the priest joins his hands. This position has its meaning; we shall find it in the answer of Nicholas I. to the Bulgarians:

"It is very suitable during prayer," says the Pope, "to bind one's hands, so to speak, before God, and to conduct ourselves in His presence like criminals prepared for punishment, in order to escape condemnation, such as the wicked receive in the parable of the Gospel."

7. THE EPISTLE, OR THE MISSION OF THE PRECURSOR.

Before the *Gospel*, and under the name of *Epistle*, the Church reads certain extracts from the Old or New Testament. This reading recalls to us the mission confided to the prophets and disciples of preparing the world for Our Lord's preaching the Gospel. It was for this end that the divine Master sent before Him some of His chosen ones before He came to preach. Among those thus sent there is one greater than all the others; he came like the dawn, proclaiming the rising of the Sun of justice, and it is he whom the Church has especially in view in the ceremonies which accompany the reading of the *Epistle*. Thus, contrary to the manner of reading the *Gospel*, the *Epistle* is read, or sung, with the face turned toward the east, because St. John the Baptist always had his eyes fixed upon the Messias, Whom the Scriptures and the Church style "the true Orient." In solemn Masses, the chant of the *Epistle* is an echo of the voice of the precursor "crying in the wilderness," and the absence of lights around the subdeacon is an illustration of those words applied to John: "He was not the light." (St. John i. 8.) The faithful remain seated during the chanting of the *Epistle*, to figure the sad state of the old world—"them that sit in darkness and the shadow of death" (St. Luke i. 79) —before Jesus Christ came to bring them truth and life.

St. Alphonsus Liguori recommends us to listen to the *Epistle* as if God spoke to us by the means of His prophets and apostles; let us lend a willing ear to the words which are "the spirit and life." (St. John vi

84.) Was it not in reading an epistle of St. Paul that St. Augustine found the truth, and the grace of conversion? Who can say what rich treasures God has hidden there for us?

8. THE GRADUAL AND TRACT, OR THE SIGHS OF PENITENCE.

The Gradual and the Tract, always analogous to the truths contained in the *Epistle*, are the response of the faithful, the protestation of their good will and their disposition to conform to the precepts which they have just heard. The crowd assembled by the preaching of St. John the Baptist returned to their homes converted and penitent; it is of this page in the Gospel story that we should think during this part of the Mass. The commentators on the liturgy have observed that the chant of the *Gradual* presents greater difficulties in its execution than the other liturgical chants. Why has the Church thus arranged it if not to show her children that the observance of the Lord's law is hard to fallen nature, and that one cannot "love the good God even a little," as St. Vincent de Paul has so well said, "except by the sweat of his brow."

Let us respond to the call with which God has for so long summoned us to perfection and penitence. Let us say with David: "My heart is ready, Lord, my heart is ready."

Not to-morrow, not to-night, not soon, but this moment, now, let us begin the work. If there are difficulties and pains, there are also consolations and joys, in the service of God, and the flowers grow thicker than the thorns.

9. THE ALLELUIA, OR THE CANTICLE OF THE CELESTIAL COUNTRY.

If the labors of the service of God affright our soul, at least the sight of the reward arouses our courage. "They who sow in tears shall reap in joy." (Ps. cxxv. 6.) The *Alleluia*, the joyous chant of heaven, following the *Gradual* and *Tract*, arouses in our poor hearts, so easily discouraged, this consoling thought. "We shall rejoice more than we can express," says St. Gregory the Great.

"We prolong indefinitely the heavenly song, that the ecstatic soul may fly toward those blessed regions where life shall have no end, the light no cloud, and happiness be unmixed with sorrow." This unending bliss is a happiness which even the tongue of St. Paul himself could not describe, and the Church, by this long series of inarticulate tones which accompany the *Alleluia*, has but one thought—to show to her children that words fail her when she thinks of the splendors prepared for the elect of God. This is the interpretation of St. Bonaventure.

"When we pause so long on the last letter of the word *alleluia*," says this holy doctor, "we seem to say: The happiness of the saints in heaven shall have no end, and we are powerless to speak suitably of its bliss." In the Christian solemnities, figures as they are of the eternal joys, we delight to prolong the *Alleluia*, adding to it a certain number of notes. The words thus added were called *sequences*, that is to say, the prolongation of the *Alleluia*; they are also called the *Prose*.

10. THE GOSPEL, OR THE PREACHING OF JESUS CHRIST.

Preparation.—The time to begin His mission had come; Our Lord left Judea to go into Galilee. His choice was Capharnaum, a city wherein lived many gentiles. But previously to beginning His public life He prepared Himself for preaching the Gospel by forty days of penance and prayer in the desert. How does the Church recall to us these divers circumstances? The priest withdraws from the epistle side of the altar, as Our Lord left ungrateful Judea; then, pausing in the middle of the altar, still like his divine Master, he recollects himself, and prays. Let him not pray alone. Let us beg God for a good and docile heart to receive the divine seed. If those lips which proclaim the Gospel needed purifying, ought not the heart which is to receive it be prepared?

Changing the place of the book before the Gospel shows us, says St. Bonaventure, that "the nations, figured by the left side of the altar, have received the doctrine of Jesus Christ from the Jews. For the Jews, with the exception of a small number, have rejected the teaching of the Saviour, and driven out the apostles. And they have deserved to hear the words: 'Because you have refused the word of God, we will carry it to the gentiles.'" (*Expositio Missæ.*)

The same book brought back to the right side toward the end of Mass prophesies the return and pardon of the children of Israel. (*Rational*, l. iv. c. 27.) There shall come a day when Our Lord will reunite the dispersed tribes, to receive them into the fold of the Church; then they will accept the truth rejected by their fathers. As to us, let us feel a salutary fear. When a people closes its eyes obstinately to the light of faith, God sends the blessed torch to nations more grateful, and when a soul resists grace the despised grace is offered to souls who will accept it. Lord, we implore Thee, stay with us always.

Turning toward the North.—The preaching of the Gospel is the invincible weapon which God has always used to conquer the demon ; it is this which the Church desires to teach in ordering that the priest shall turn toward the north in reading the Gospel. Why the north? On that side the rebel angel has established his throne, says Isaias. (xiv. 18.) And Jeremias adds : "From the north shall an evil break forth upon all the inhabitants of the land." (i. 14.) The only thing that can stem the venom which Satan pours forth upon the world is the word of God.

The Faithful Standing.—Having been seated during the *Epistle*, the faithful rise at the *Gospel*, to show that the old world, shaking off the dust of the tomb, was raised to life by the word of Jesus Christ. This is also to recall the other miracles wrought by the voice of Our Saviour : the sick healed and rising up and walking ; the dead brought back to life and falling at His feet; the crowd leaving all to follow Him. On reflection we shall find in this ceremony teaching proper to ourselves. If we are sitting in discouragement and torpor, let us rise ; the voice of the Master calls: "Arise." Perhaps, like another prodigal, we live far from God, far from the sacred banquet, far from the joys of the Christian family, plunged in the mire of vice. May this ceremony not be

PORTABLE ALTAR.

Contains vestment, corporal for chalice, altar-cloth, alb, cincture, and all the necessary linens, chalice, oilstock, pyx, altar bell, cruets, bread box, wine flask, candlesticks, crucifix, altar cards, and missal. It is used by priests on the mission.

to us a lie; let us rise, and go to God, our Father, Who calls us.

Signs of the Cross.—The sign of the cross made by the priest on the sacred text reminds us that Jesus Christ has confirmed the truth of His teaching by His death the cross has been the seal of the Gospel. The priest then makes the sign of the cross upon his brow, his lips, and his heart. "This triple sign of the cross," says Father Lebrun, "prints the memory of Jesus Christ and His holy words in our mind, that we may be filled with the holy lessons which Jesus Christ came upon earth to teach; and in our hearts, that we may give all our love to carrying them out; and on our lips, that we may love to speak of them, and make them known."

Kissing the Book.—Let us kiss the gospel with the priest. We cover the letter of a father who is gone with kisses and tears, and the gospel remains with us as the legacy of God to His children. By this respectful and filial kiss we ask Him to pardon all offences and irreverences committed against His divine Word.

In solemn Masses the chanting of the Gospel is accompanied with other ceremonies. The deacon, before fulfilling his duty, asks the celebrant's blessing; no one can preach who is not sent by God, or those who hold his place. The subdeacon goes with him, to show the harmony between the two Testaments, the prophets and the apostles.

The Church gives to the gospel the same honors as to the Eucharist. She fills its way with the perfume of incense; she accompanies it with the light of tapers; she incenses it three times, and the deacon who carries the

Gospel, as well as the priest who bears the Eucharist, receives this testimony of respect. When we read or hear the sacred word, we are like children of the household seated around the Lord's table, where we eat the heavenly bread. "Let us not lose a word of it," Origen warns us. "For, as in receiving the Eucharist we are careful, and rightly so, not to let the smallest crumb fall, why should we not believe it a crime to neglect even a single word of Jesus Christ, as it is to be careless of His body?" (*Hom.* xiii. *in Exod.*)

The priest is also a gospel, but a living gospel; by his conduct he should preach to the people. That he may not forget this duty so important, the Church bestows upon him the honor of incense, as to the sacred book itself.

11. THE CREDO, OR PROFESSION OF FAITH IN THE DOCTRINE PREACHED BY JESUS CHRIST.

The word of the humble workman of Nazareth has transformed the world; it has abolished slavery, exalted poverty, consoled sorrow, consecrated sacrifice. As it is impossible to attack Jesus Christ, glorious and immortal, the devil has combated His doctrine, and, after the murderers of the prætorium and Calvary had taken from Him His mortal life, Satan inspired heretics whose constant aim was to destroy the spiritual life of Jesus Christ, His life in souls by faith. But Jesus Christ dies but once; heresies are always vanquished, and upon their tomb the Catholic Church chants her joyous and triumphal *Credo*. Let us say it in these pious sentiments; let us also thank God for the inestimable gift of faith. Let us be ready to defend this faith against all who deny it, even unto death, if need be, for we have solemnly promised to do this in making the sign of the cross at the end of the Creed.

By the genuflection at the words: "And the Word was made flesh," we honor the humiliations of the incarnate Word.

Second Part.

1. The Offertory, or the Last Supper.

The Offering of the Bread and Wine.—Like his divine Master, the priest takes bread in his hands and offers it to God. The bread here takes the place of the Church and Christian people, for, as bread is the nourishment and life of man, when he offers it at the altar it is as if he offered himself to God to be sacrificed to His glory, like Jesus Christ, our head. As the bread is to be changed into the body of Jesus Christ, may our hearts also be transformed into Him, till it may be "no more we who live, but Jesus Christ Who lives in us."

The sign of the cross, after the oblation, shows us how we can attain this glorious transformation: by mortification and sacrifice.

Our Lord also offered wine mixed with water. The wine represents Jesus Christ, "the true vine"; and water, the Christian people.* St. Cyprian, in a letter to Cecilius, teaches this formally. This image is a vivid figure of the ineffable union of God with man wrought by the incarnation, and of that other union in the Eucharist, and again of that third union which will be

---

* This last comparison is familiar to sacred writers, who often represent the faithful under the image of water.

consummated in glory. It is, then, the Church united with Jesus Christ, the members to their head, the bride to her bridegroom, which the priest offers to God in the oblation of the chalice.

In the drop of water, which is the figure of the faithful, what an admirable lesson of humility! Is it not a striking image of our annihilation in the presence of the God of the Eucharist?

"Behold," says Isaias, "the gentiles are as a drop in a bucket." (Is. xl. 15.) And again, ah, what a terrible lesson! This drop of water reminds us of the small number of the saved.

Washing of the Hands.—Our Lord, before giving His body and blood to the apostles, washed their feet, thus showing us what purity He required in those who would sit down at the sacred banquet. Equally privileged with the disciples, the priest is about to partake of the same mysteries; it would be a closer imitation of Our Lord if he washed his feet, but, as St. Thomas says, "it is sufficient to wash the hands; besides, it is more convenient, and it is enough to show perfect purity, especially as it is to our hands that all works are ascribed." (l. iii. quæst. 88, art. 5.) During this ceremony we will enter into the intentions of the Church, praying Our Lord to purify our souls by the virtue of the tears which He must have shed on the feet of the traitor Judas as He washed them for the last supper.

The paschal supper over, the Saviour said a hymn as an act of thanksgiving, and, the hymn being finished, went out to the Garden of Olives. The priest also ends the Offertory with a hymn: "*Lavabo inter innocentes manus meas*," and returns to the middle of the altar, in remembrance of the way of Our Lord from the chamber of the last supper to Gethsemani.

2. THE INCENSING, OR THE PERFUMES OF MARY MAGDALEN.

Triple Incensing.—Three times, by pouring out her perfumes, the penitent of Bethany wished to honor the person of the adorable Saviour: first in the house of Simon the Pharisee, again in the house of Simon the leper, and at the holy sepulchre. Faithful to fulfil the words of Jesus Christ: "Wheresoever this gospel shall be preached in the whole world, that also which she hath done shall be told in memory of her," the priest three times incenses the bread and wine of the sacrifice, destined so soon to become the divine body and blood; then he incenses the altar, the figure of Jesus Christ.

The Form of the Cross and of the Crown.—The incensing of the sacred species is done three times in the form of a cross, to recall the passion of Our Saviour, foreshadowed by Magdalen. "This woman," Jesus Christ said to His disciples, "in pouring this ointment upon My body has done it for My burial." (St. Matt. xxvi. 13.) Following this, the incense is offered three times in the form of a crown, because, in His sacred humanity, the humiliations of Jesus Christ were followed by His triumphant coronation. During this ceremony let us think of the mercy of Jesus toward sinners. Were we a thousand times more guilty than Magdalen, He would receive us tenderly and sweetly. If we are poor prodigals, come back to God after long wandering, let us shed upon the feet of Our Lord the perfumes of a heart broken by repentance and burning with the fire of divine love.

3. THE SECRET, OR THE PRAYER IN THE GARDEN OF OLIVES.

Our Lord, being come into the Garden of Olives, began to pray, but His sorrow soon became so profound that He fell with His face prostrate upon the ground in agony. And see the priest, come to the middle of the altar, pray also, but leaning forward, his hands joined, in a position of humiliation and prostration.

A little later Jesus Christ came to seek His apostles, but found them heavily sleeping. "What," He said to them, "could you not watch with Me one hour? Watch ye and pray." (St. Matt. xxvi. 40, 41.) The priest also raises himself, interrupts his prayer, and, turning to the faithful, says: "*Orate, fratres.*" "It is Our Lord, in the Garden of Olives, exhorting His disciples to pray, that they may not fall into temptation," says St. Bonaventure.

In the person of the priest, then, we should see Jesus Christ Himself, Who looks at us with affectionate compassion, and says: "My brothers,—for this you are through My incarnation,—pray and increase your recollection; the solemn moment of My sacrifice and yours draws near."

4. THE PREFACE, OR THE CHANT OF TRIUMPH.

The Preface and Sanctus.—We have entered into the way of the cross. Already the clamor of the multitude reaches us, the threatening of the tempest. Only a few hours now, and the Son of God will be "bound, scourged, buffeted, put to death, and reckoned among the guilty."

The Church opposes the chant of love to the deicidal shouts, for the *Preface* is the reparation for the blasphemies hurled against the divinity of Jesus Christ in the hour of His passion. It is for us He suffered, and drained the chalice of anguish; the Church in our name thanks God for the blessed sign of the redemption, and for all the mercies of which it has been the source. The *Preface*, the chant of triumph, is also a canticle of thanksgiving. But when we would praise and thank God we can but stammer like infants, and this is why the Church calls upon the angels, the thrones and dominations, and all the heavenly powers to come with their celestial harps, and chant the *Sanctus* of eternity. The priest says it with them, and, like them, prostrated.

The Sign of the Cross and the Hosanna.—After the hymn of heaven comes that of earth, the chant of the Hebrew children at the triumphal entry of Jesus Christ into Jerusalem. This last canticle is accompanied by the sign of the cross: the joys of triumph were of short duration; a few days afterward the same people loudly clamored for the death of this same Jesus Whom they had received as a king, chanting hosannas. Our piety will find reminders of an unparalleled ingratitude in the sign of the cross mingling with the *Hosanna* and *Benedictus*.

5. THE CANON, OR THE PASSION.

The Silence of the Canon.—The sacred chants are followed by the profoundest silence—silence in the priest; silence among the faithful. Are not the latter the figure of the timid apostles at the hour of the passion? None among them dared raise his voice in favor of their divine Master, although all had sworn with Peter: "Though I should die with Thee, I would not deny Thee."

What tender emotions are awakened in the soul by the silence of the priest! The divine Lamb in the hands of His enemies uttered not a word, not a complaint. In the house of Herod, when He was buffeted, He was silent; in the prætorium, under the rods and the thorns, He was silent; on Calvary, confronted with blasphemies, He was silent. His silence, more eloquent than all words, teaches the pardon of injuries, sweetness in the face of persecution.

During the three hours of His agony upon the cross Our Lord prayed in silence; His dying lips uttered but seven words, treasured by the evangelists as the testament of His heart. How touching it is to see His representative at the altar praying in a low voice from the Offertory to the Communion, that is to say, during the sacrifice properly so called, and interrupting this mysterious silence but seven times, namely: 1st, at the *Orate fratres;* 2d, at the *Preface;* 3d, at the *Nobis quoque peccatoribus;* 4th, at the *Pater Noster;* 5th, at the *Pax Domini;* 6th, at the *Agnus Dei;* 7th, at the *Domine non sum dignus.*

From the *Sanctus* to the *Elevation* our minds, and our hearts above all, should accompany Our Lord on the road to Calvary with Mary and the holy women. With confidence we draw near to Him with Veronica, and beg Him to remember us upon His cross. Let us recommend to His mercy also at this moment the persons who are dear to us.

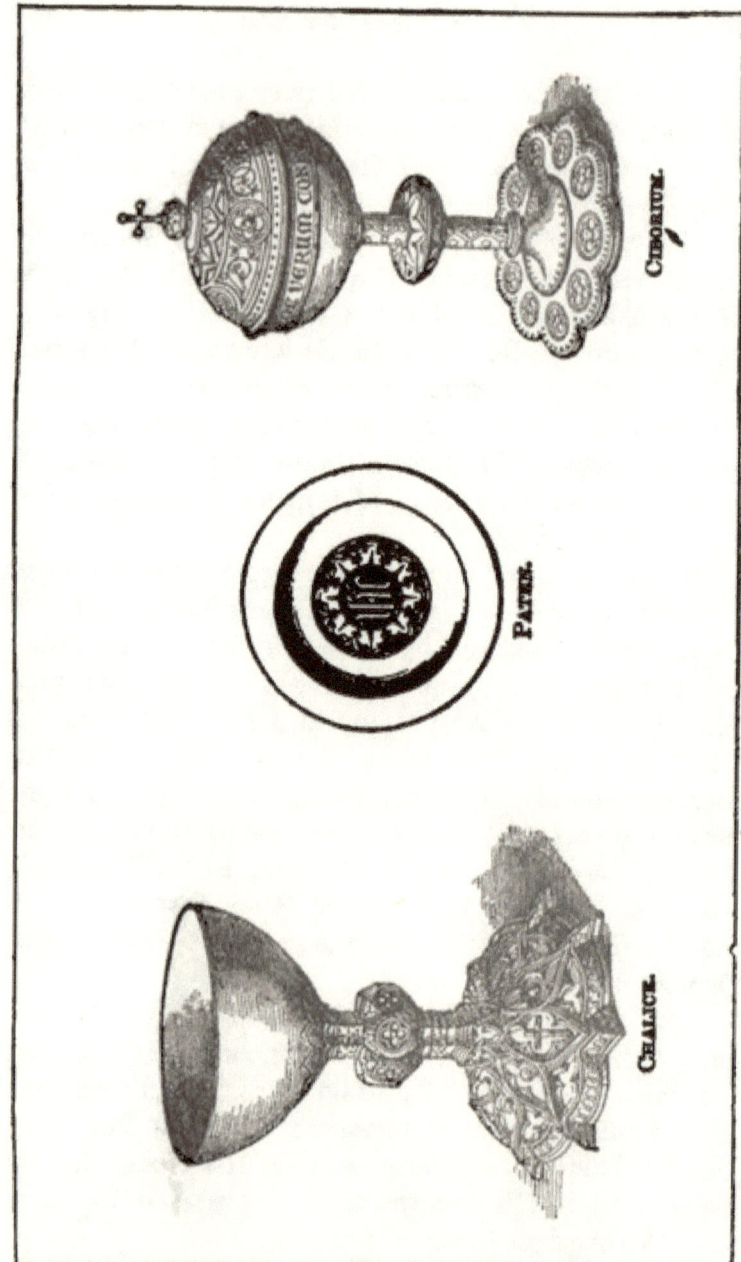

6. THE IMPOSITION OF HANDS, OR THE CRUCIFIXION.

The priest's hands held over the bread and the wine which are about to be changed into the body and blood of Christ, the sign of the cross so often repeated, represent vividly the scene of the crucifixion. History tells us that formerly it was the custom to impose hands upon the head of one condemned to death, to pour upon him all the odium of the crimes of which he was guilty, but this ceremony renewed at our altar reminds us that the innocent One took upon Himself the guilt of sinners, and that it is in the name of sin-stained humanity that the priest lays upon the august victim the sins of all people, that they may be expiated in His blood. This is done, too, in the name of God the Father, Who, says Isaias, "hath laid on Him the iniquity of us all."

7. THE ELEVATION, OR OUR LORD RAISED UPON THE CROSS.

The Elevation of the Host.—"Remember," says Father Nouet, "the elevation of Jesus Christ upon the cross each time that you adore Him during the elevation of the host ; see Him as if He bowed His head to give you the kiss of peace ; as if He opened His arms to embrace you ; as if His hands were pierced to give you the bounty of His gifts ; as if His feet were nailed in order to stay with you." (*Meditation on the Passion.*) Let us adore Him, bending our knees to expiate the derisive genuflections of the Jews ; let us bow our heads lowly, in respect for our divine head crowned with thorns.

The Elevation of the Chalice.—The priest, taking the

chalice, places it at the feet of Jesus, as if to catch the blood bursting in torrents from all His wounds, and after the consecration he adores it, and the faithful prostrate adore with him. The olive-trees of Gethsemani, the rods of the scourging, the thorns in the crown, the wood of the cross, the lance of the soldier, were all reddened with this blood enclosed in the chalice raised above our heads. This blessed chalice also holds the sweat which bathed the workshop of Nazareth, the roads of Judea, the mountain of Calvary. It contains the tears shed in the crib, at the tomb of Lazarus, gazing at Jerusalem, and over each one of us. Let us adore it with love and faith.

An ancient custom was to sound the trumpet at the moment of the execution of one who had been condemned to death, to drown the cries or words of the sufferer, the tears or murmurs of the crowd.

Tradition says that this custom was followed at the crucifixion of the Saviour; we love to remember this when the sound of the sanctuary bell floats through the arches.

Genuflections, and Signs of the Cross.—Calvary, the cross, the Redeemer, what memories are vividly present to us during the Canon!

Everything at the altar is of a nature to recall them to us.

The priest often bends the knee before Jesus Christ, in reparation for the hypocritical adoration rendered by the Jews on Calvary. Each time that he pronounces the name of the body or blood of the Saviour he makes the sign of the cross upon the host and the chalice, to confess that he has before him the body and blood of

Jesus *crucified*, and he makes it five times, in memory of the five wounds of the adorable victim, while the kiss he gives the altar is the figure of the reconciliation between heaven and earth wrought by the redemption. (Steph. Eduens, *De Sacrif. Alt.*, c. xvii.; Florus, *Exposit. Missæ.*)

The Five Prayers of the Canon.—From the Elevation to the *Pater* there are five prayers in the Canon. In order to say them well let us place ourselves in each one of the wounds of Our Lord. If our piety leads us to unite ourselves at this time with those privileged witnesses of Our Saviour's death, let us recite the first one with Mary, the mother of sorrows, standing at the foot of the cross; the second with the beloved apostle; during the third let us shed tears of penitence with Magdalen on the feet of Jesus; at the fourth let us unite ourselves with the holy women; and at the fifth, with the good thief let us beg for mercy.

8. THE MEMENTO OF THE DEAD, OR THE JUST RAISED AGAIN BY JESUS CHRIST.

Our Lord upon the cross remembered the just who had died in His grace: "And the graves were opened: and many bodies of the saints that had slept arose." (St. Matt. xxvii. 52.)

This same God, the sovereign master of life and death, is upon the altar. The priest recommends to Him the souls of those "who have preceded us, and sleep in the sleep of peace." He implores Him to drop upon them the blessed dew of His blood, and to give them "a place of refreshment, light, and peace."

At the Memento let us all pray for those whom we

have lost; faith shows them to us in purgatory, with their guardian angels descending into its abysses, bringing to them the precious blood.

How consoling to the heart is the thought that many of these poor souls so dear to us receive help in their sufferings. Some of them, we will gladly believe, entirely purified, come around the altar to join with us, the angels, and the saints in adoring their Redeemer.

9. THE NOBIS QUOQUE PECCATORIBUS, OR THE PRAYER OF THE GOOD THIEF.

At these words of the Canon: "*Nobis quoque peccatoribus*," the priest raises his voice, and strikes his breast, representing the repentance, the confession, and the prayer of the thief crucified on the right hand of Our Lord. He openly acknowledged himself guilty: "We receive the due reward of our deeds." Then, recommending himself to the Saviour, he added: "Lord, remember me when Thou shalt come into Thy kingdom." (St. Luke xxii. 42.) Encouraged by this example, the priest dares to ask a place in heaven with the apostles, the martyrs, the virgins, and all the saints. Who, then, should fear or despair? God has put into the guiltiest hands the two keys which will infallibly open heaven: confidence and repentance.

10. THE SECOND ELEVATION, OR THE DEATH OF OUR SAVIOUR.

The three signs of the cross made with the host raised above the chalice, and the two others outside of the chalice recall the three hours passed on the cross by the Saviour (St. Thomas) and the separation of His soul and His body.

The body is here represented by the host; the soul by the blood enclosed in the chalice.* (St. Thom.) The sound of the bell is a symbol of the convulsion of nature in this supreme hour (Benedict XIV.); and the louder voice of the priest, interrupting the long silence of the Canon, recalls the words of the sacred text: "Jesus uttered a loud cry, and bowing His head He gave up the ghost." (St. Matt. and St. John.)

At this second elevation let us bow our heads devoutly, and adore Jesus Christ bowing His head, and breathing out His last sigh.

Third Part.

1 THE PATER NOSTER, OR THE PRAYER OF JESUS CHRIST UPON THE CROSS.

Our Lord had just breathed His last sigh. His blessed Mother, the beloved disciple, Magdalen, and the holy women were at the foot of the cross. What was that faithful and devoted little band doing? The Gospel is silent on this point. But if we ask our hearts, their ardent love and the liveliness of their faith in Jesus Christ, the Redeemer, we seem to see them falling upon their knees, with their eyes, wet with tears, fixed upon the blood-stained body of Jesus, and praying that the blessed fruits of the redemption would save the guilty world which the Saviour had loved so much.

The same victim is there, immolated before us. At the sight of the bitter chalice presented to His lips He

---

* It is commonly said that the soul abides in the blood, because it is indispensable to life. This observation is from St. Thomas.

said: "Father, not My will but Thine be done." (St. Luke xxii. 22.) And from the cross He called down only benedictions upon His murderers: "Father, forgive them, for they know not what they do." (St. Luke xxiii. 34.) Let us enter into the spirit of the Master, and lay at the foot of the cross a heart which is resigned to suffering, and pardons all injuries.

Formerly the people said the *Pater Noster* together. This custom still prevails among the Greeks, and existed in France until the time of Charlemagne. A trace of this practice is found in the faithful having the honor of saying aloud the last request of this prayer.

2. THE LIBERA NOS, OR THE MYSTERIES OF THE BURIAL.

"The chalice," says St. Bernard, "represents to us the sepulchre, and the pall the stone which sealed its mouth; the corporal is the figure of the winding-sheet, and the host, which we see, is no longer bread, but is the flesh of Jesus Christ fastened to the cross for the salvation of mankind." (Sermon on the dignity of the priest.)

The priest taking the body of his Saviour, laying it in the chalice, which he then covers with the pall, carries us to the holy sepulchre. There let us keep as close as possible to Jesus Christ; let us press our lips affectionately to the wounds in His feet and hands: behold the perfumes which He asks of us for His burial.

The silence which follows the *Pater* is an image of the silence of the tomb. It also recalls the recollection and the sorrow of the holy women kept in their homes by the observance of the Sabbath. (Innocent III., l. v. c.

28.) While the friends of Our Saviour on earth were rendering to His body the last duties of love, where was His divine soul? The souls of the just of the old law were in limbo, sighing as they awaited His coming; His soul went down to them to announce the nearness of their hour of deliverance. The prayer *Libera nos* is the lively expression of their sighs.

There are still souls who sigh in the hope of heaven; at this part of the sacrifice Our Lord goes to them to console them. Let us recommend them to His tender love.

3. THE BREAKING OF THE HOST, OR THE SIDE OF JESUS OPENED BY THE LANCE.

Our Lord had died, and a soldier armed with a lance opened His right side, from which flowed water and blood. At that moment, springing from the open side of the new Adam, sleeping on the tree of the cross, came the spouse whom He had chosen, the holy Catholic Church.

This solemn circumstance of the formation of the Church upon Calvary should have its place in the sacrifice of the Mass. We shall find it under a thrilling form. The priest holds above the chalice the body of his God; he divides the holy species, and then, from the right side of the host, he breaks a fragment, marvellously figuring the wound in the side of Our Lord. The host is divided into three parts, by their number and their nature symbolizing the Church coming from the open side of Jesus Christ. For Jesus Christ is not divided except in appearance, and under each of the three parts He remains entire.

Is not this a symbolic image of the Catholic Church, divided into three branches: the Church triumphant, the Church militant, and the Church suffering, all three making, however, only one and the same Church? (St. Thomas.)

After breaking the host the priest makes three times the sign of the cross with the body of Jesus Christ on the chalice, in memory of the three days in the sepulchre (St. Thomas); then, fixing his eyes respectfully upon that sacred flesh, covered with the kisses of Mary, and watered by the tears of John and the Magdalen, like another Joseph of Arimathea, as an early writer calls him, he lays it in the chalice, become another tomb on this new Calvary.

4. THE AGNUS DEI, OR THE RESURRECTION.

The Part Laid in the Chalice.—"In the Mass," says Benedict XIV., "the passion and death of Jesus Christ are represented by the separation of His body and His blood. Although this separation can only be in a mystical manner, because the body could not be apart from the blood, nor the blood from the body, however, by this entirely mystical separation of the body from the blood, and the blood from the body, the passion and death of Our Lord are perfectly represented. It remains, then, but to express in the sacrifice His glorious resurrection; it could not be done more perfectly than by putting into the chalice a fragment of the host, and thus showing the reunion of the body and blood of Jesus Christ." (*De Sac. Missæ*, l. ii. c. 20.)

Pax Domini, and Agnus Dei.—The words of the liturgy now join themselves to the ceremonies to reiter-

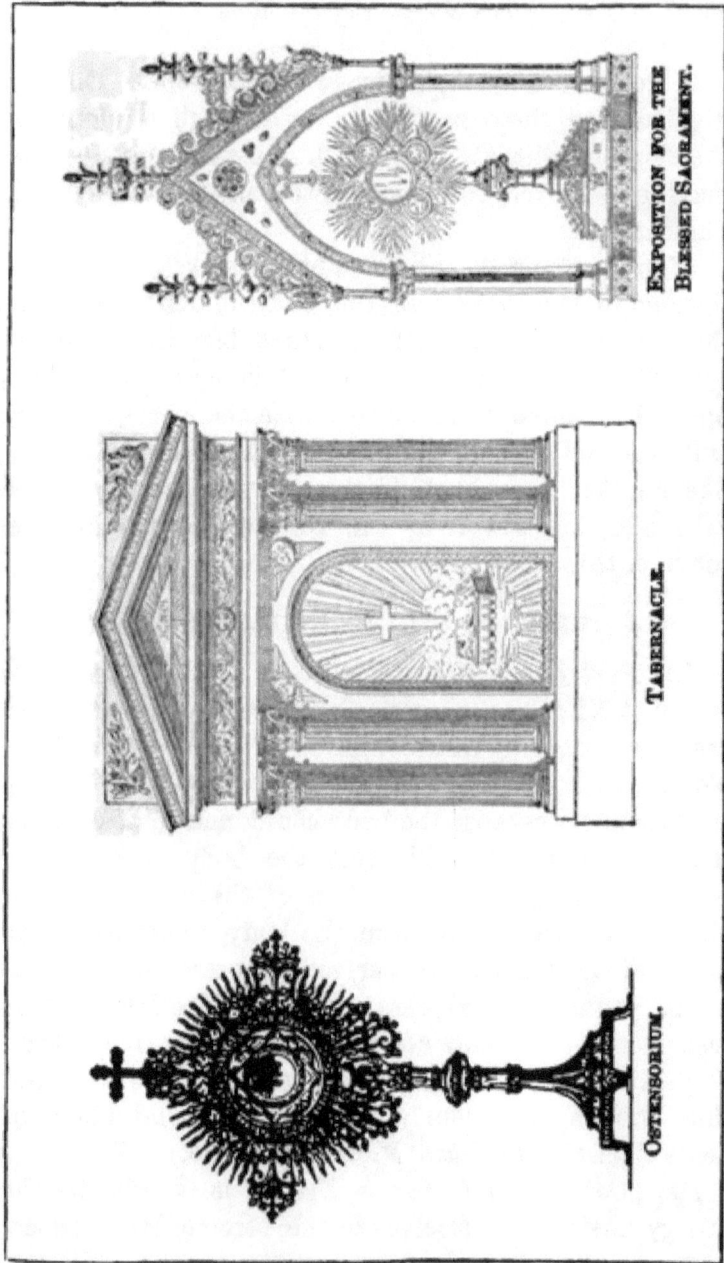

EXPOSITION FOR THE BLESSED SACRAMENT.

TABERNACLE.

OSTENSORIUM.

ate the holy joys of the resurrection. The *Pax vobiscum* is an echo of the salutation of peace given by Our Lord on Easter to the assembled disciples. "*Pax vobiscum*" ("Peace be unto you"), He said to them. (*Micrologus*, c. xx.)

On that day the walls of the chamber of the paschal supper heard the solemn words which gave to the apostles the power to remit sins; in memory of this the Church repeats three times the suppliant cry of the *Agnus Dei*, asking mercy and pardon for her numerous family. (Innocent III., l. iv. c. 4.) Scarcely has the *Agnus Dei*, which is called the chant of the resurrection, been heard in the sanctuary than the choir, until that time upon its knees, in a posture of humiliation and sorrow, rises up, in token of the victory over death of Jesus Christ arisen.

The Kiss of Peace.—During the first six centuries the salutation of the priest: "May the peace of the Lord be always with you," was the signal for the Christians giving one another peace by embracing.

The men gave to men this holy kiss, women gave it to women, and then the people, a family of brothers, drew near joyously to the banquet of the Lamb, at which, according to the language of the doctors, the peaceful alone had the right to sit down. The Church has preserved something of this custom. In the solemn Masses the deacon gives to the subdeacon the kiss of peace which he has just received from the celebrant; the latter, to show us that he has drawn this peace from the very heart of the Saviour, first kisses the altar. Formerly he kissed the sacred host. (Benedict XIV., *De Sac. Missæ*. l. ii. c. 20.)

Should not this ceremony have had its origin in the chamber of the last supper? The Gospel does not say so, but Jesus Christ has taught us too much of the compassionate tenderness of His heart for us to doubt that He reassured His terror-stricken apostles by embracing them.

5. THE COMMUNION, OR THE EUCHARISTIC REPASTS OF JESUS CHRIST ARISEN WITH HIS APOSTLES.

Communion of the Priest.—After the intermingling of the body and blood the priest, with the eyes of faith, sees before him upon the altar Jesus Christ, but Jesus Christ arisen. He knows Him; it is the same Jesus Christ Who, after His resurrection, appeared to the holy women; like them, he bows down to adore Him. He speaks to Him with a sweet confidence, for Our Lord has said to him, to him also, "It is I: fear not." (St. John vi. 20.) It is the same Jesus Christ Who gave Himself in food to the disciples at Emmaus; like them, the priest knows Him in the broken bread, laid there before him upon the paten. It is the same Jesus Christ Who said to St. Thomas: "Bring hither thy hand and put it into My side." (St. John xx. 28.) Oh, the ineffable happiness of a priest! He takes into his hand the glorious and immortal body of Jesus Christ arisen; he covers with his finger the open wound in the side of the Saviour, and, under the fragile species recognizing with the apostle his "Lord and his God," he strikes his breast three times, and humbly says: "*Domine, non sum dignus,*" etc. ("Lord, I am not worthy that Thou shouldst enter into the house of my soul, but only speak one of those almighty words which have created the world, controlled the elements, death, and the demon, and my soul shall be healed ").

He raises to his lips the bread of angels, lays it on his trembling tongue, thus become the throne of the Most High—the union is consummated, and it is no more the priest who lives, but Jesus Christ Who lives in him. The sign of the cross made with the chalice, as it was made before with the sacred host, should recall to the priest, if he could ever forget it, that he is about to drink the blood of his *crucified* God. Filled with this thought, he raises it to his lips with love, as if he pressed them to the side of his divine Master.

Thus watered with this divine dew, bear fruit, O my soul! And may thy fruits endure; may this redeeming blood heal thy wounds, render thee invulnerable to sin, and preserve thee unto eternal life.

Of what event of the glorious life of Our Lord should the communion of the priest remind us? Of the eucharistic banquets of Jesus Christ arisen with His apostles.

The Gospel makes us assist, even the very night of the resurrection, at the breaking of bread in the village of Emmaus. Later it shows us the divine Master, on the seashore, eating broiled fish and a honeycomb. Now the fathers have seen in the broiled fish a figure of the body of Jesus Christ crucified, and in the honeycomb a symbol of His blood, "sweeter than the most fragrant honey."

Communion of the Faithful.—The disciples at Emmaus had part in the breaking of bread, and, in the repast beside the sea, Jesus Christ, having taken a piece of the broiled fish and of the honeycomb, gave the rest to His disciples. Following the steps of the Saviour's friends, come, holy souls, sit down at the sacred banquet. At Emmaus He concealed His glory under the garb of a pilgrim; at the altar He hides within the person of the priest. His hands have broken the bread of heaven; draw near, come and eat the bread of angels, the mystical fish, the heavenly honey. Has your heart contracted in the dust of the roadside one of those stains from which we cannot entirely preserve our poor nature? Let it rise up in confidence; Jesus Christ Himself asks pardon for it. "May Almighty God have mercy upon you, forgive you your sins, and bring you to eternal life. May the almighty and merciful Lord give you pardon, absolution and full remission of all your sins. Amen." Let us recite the Confiteor, that prayer of repentance and hope, with sorrow and humility, and, bending beneath the consecrated hand raised above our heads to call down pardon, let us have unlimited confidence; the voice which invokes mercy upon us is powerful in heaven with the heart of God.

6. THE CHANTS OF THE COMMUNION, OR THE JOY OF THE APOSTLES IN THE RESURRECTION OF JESUS CHRIST.

In the beautiful days of the youthful Church psalms were sung during the Communion in accord with that holy action. In the East it was the canticle: "As the hart panteth after the fountains of waters, so my soul panteth after Thee, O God." In the West it was the thirty-third psalm: "I will bless the Lord at all times, His praise shall be always in my mouth." The hymns sung now during the communion are the revival of this pious custom. "What is more beautiful?" says

Mgr. Gaume. "The festivals of kings and the great ones of the earth are accompanied by songs and music; should not harmonious chants arise during the sacred feast to which God Himself, at once the host, the food, and the guest, invites His children? And while the arches of the temple resound with the chants of our love, the angels present at the divine banquet repeat upon their golden harps the goodness of God and the happiness of man." (*Catechism*, l. xxiii.) The ancient psalm of the Communion has been reduced to a versicle called the *Communion*. Like the chant of the first centuries, this versicle represents the joy of the apostles at the tidings of the resurrection. (Innocent III., l. iv. c. 8.)

7. THE POST-COMMUNION, OR THE FORTY DAYS OF THE GLORIOUS LIFE.

After the Communion the priest turns to the people twice to wish them peace: our thoughts should turn to Our Lord repeating twice within the walls of the chamber of the last supper the *Pax vobis* of pardon, and in these salutations the priest, extending his hands and showing his heart, recalls to us principally Jesus Christ showing the wounds of His hands and that of His side to His disciples. (Innocent III., l. iv. c. 8.)

Post-communion.—During the days of the glorious life Our Lord continued by prayer His office of divine mediator, and in heaven His wounds intercede for us. The hands of the priest, raised toward heaven during the Post-communion, represent this mystery of mercy.

This prayer is said for the communicants. During Lent the spirit of humility and of penitence withdrawing from the holy table some of the faithful, the Church, in order not to deprive them of such an efficacious prayer in this part of the sacrifice, established for their benefit a special prayer. This is the one said last in Lent, and preceded by the words: "*Humiliate capita vestra Deo*" ("Bow down your heads to God"). On Sunday this is omitted, because on this day all the faithful communicating, or being about to communicate, have a part in the prayers of the Post-communion.

8. THE ITE, MISSA EST, OR THE ASCENSION.

The details of the ascension, as told in the Scriptures, are: the benediction given to the disciples, the words of the angel bidding them to go back to Jerusalem, and the joyous return of these same disciples—three circumstances reproduced in the liturgy at the end of the Mass.

The Last Dominus Vobiscum.—The priest going back to the middle of the altar represents Our Lord going to Bethany upon the Mount of Olives. Like his divine Master, he blesses the faithful, and for the last time wishes them peace. Our Saviour said to His followers in order to console them: "Behold I am with you all days, even to the consummation of the world." At the last *Dominus vobiscum* let us not forget this promise; it must have been the cause of great joy to the apostles' hearts in the hour of separation. We are going back to our houses, to separate ourselves from Jesus Christ. But no; there is no more separation; God is with us, in our hearts, above all if we have had the happiness to communicate.

The Ite, Missa Est.—In Low Masses the priest, or if it is a High Mass the deacon, filling the office of the angels, dismisses the faithful with these words: "*Ite, Missa* est," that is to say: "Go now, for Jesus Christ, our one advocate, has left this altar to enter into His glory." "*Deo gratias*" ("Thanks be to God"), answer the people, uniting their gratitude to the disciples', who "went back to Jerusalem with great joy, praising and blessing God." Ah, yes, let us lovingly say: "Thanks be to God, ["*Deo gratias*"], for heaven and earth are reconciled." Thanks be to God that the august victim, awaited for four thousand years, came to immolate Himself for us. Thanks to God the Father, Who has delivered anew His Son to be sacrificed upon the altar. Thanks to the Son, Who renewed among us the mysteries of His mortal life. Thanks to the Holy Spirit, Who formed the victim in the womb of Mary, and Whose fruitful power has formed Him again upon our altar. Thanks to the Blessed Trinity for all His goodness, of which the sacrifice which has just been offered is the wonderful epitome:

The Benedicamus Domino.—During Advent and Lent our fathers not only assisted at Mass, but at the Canonical Hours with which it was followed. In those days of longer and more fervent prayers, instead of dismissing the congregation with the words: "*Ite, Missa est,*" they were invited to bless the Lord by the sacrifice of praise: "*Benedicamus Domino*" ("Let us bless the Lord"). These words have been preserved in the Church to remind us that it is necessary to sanctify the holy time of penitence by prayer.

9. THE BENEDICTION, OR THE DESCENT OF THE HOLY GHOST.

The Placeat.—The prayer of the apostles assembled in that upper room, and that of Our Saviour asking His Father to send the Consoler, are figured by the prayer *Placeat*, placed between the last *Dominus vobiscum*, the meaning of which we have already seen, and the benediction, regarded by the greatest liturgists as the symbol of the descent of the Holy Ghost on the apostles. (Inn. III., vi. 14.) Seven times during the Mass the prayer "*Et cum spiritu tuo*" rises from the hearts of the faithful to Our Lord, imploring the coming of the divine Paraclete. These devout aspirations are about to be answered.

The Words and Form of the Benediction.—The priest first kisses the altar, the figure of Jesus Christ, to show that it is the Son of God Who sent the Holy Spirit of consolation upon the earth. Then he blesses: "In the name of the Father, and of the Son, and of the Holy Ghost," for, says Innocent III., although the Holy Spirit especially was sent, the works of the Trinity being indivisible, the three divine Persons have co-operated in this mystery: it is for this reason, he adds, that the benediction is given in the name of the august Trinity. (Inn. III., vi. 14.) The sign of the cross which accompanies this blessing recalls to Christians that the mercies of Pentecost are the fruits of the merits of the passion. Jesus Christ has said this: "It is expedient to you that I go, for if I go not the Paraclete will not come to you." (St. John xvi. 7.)

We have received the Holy Spirit in Confirmation.

FERETORY.
A very rich style of Reliquary.

The darkness of our minds, the faltering of our wills, the wrong in our hearts, prove that the Spirit of light, of strength, of piety, no longer reigns in us.

With bowed heads, as on the day when we were enrolled in the army of Christ, let us beg the Holy Spirit to vouchsafe once more to be the guest of our hearts.

10. THE LAST GOSPEL, OR THE PREACHING OF THE APOSTLES AND THEIR SUCCESSORS.

After Pentecost the apostles, filled with the Holy Spirit, went into all parts of the known world to sow the seed of the Gospel. Other laborers have carried on the divine work, and even to the end of time the Christian apostolate will be continued upon the earth. This preaching is figured by the reading of the last gospel. The authority of the apostles was that of their Master: "He who hears you hears Me," Our Lord said to them; upon the lips of God or upon those of an apostolic laborer the Gospel is the same; for which reason the two gospels are read at the same side of the altar.

Because of this, too, they are always accompanied by the same salutation, the same signs of the cross. However, as the greatest honor is due to the preaching of the Master, for the first gospel only, which symbolizes this there is chanting, lights carried, the sacred text is incensed and kissed.

For a long time the Mass ended at the blessing of the priest. Pope Pius V. obliged all priests to add to it the Gospel of St. John. In some churches it was recited in going to the sacristy; in others it was said within the sacristy. The usage of the Roman Church is to read it at the altar. This observation leads us to another. The preparatory prayers of the Mass, now said at the foot of the altar, were also said for a long time in the sacristy; consequently the Mass upon which the liturgists commented commenced at the Introit, and ended at the benediction.

Before leaving the altar at which so many graces have been given us, let us love to say, with the Maronite priest, this prayer which he says as he kisses the altar at the end of Mass: "Rest in peace, holy and divine altar of the Lord. Shall I return to thy feet, or will death prevent me? I know not. May God grant at least that I see thee again in the celestial church of the first-born of heaven. I will rest in this hope which God has given me. Remain in peace, holy and propitious altar. May the sacred body, may the blood which has just been offered, wash away my stains, destroy my sins, and give me confidence before the throne of our God, the immortal Lord. Remain in peace, holy altar, life-giving table. Pour down upon me the mercy of Jesus Christ, and may I keep thy memory in my heart, now and forever and ever. Amen."

CHAPTER V.—PONTIFICAL MASS.

1. THE BISHOP'S ORNAMENTS.

WHEN the bishop celebrates pontifically, besides the sacerdotal vestments of which we have spoken, he wears the hose, the sandals, the tunic, the dalmatic, the gloves, the ring, the mitre, the crosier, and the breast-cross. If he has been raised to the dignity of an archbishop, he wears also the pallium.

Hose and Sandals.—The hose are the ceremonial stockings which cover the leg to the knee; the shoes which a bishop wears in pontifical Masses are called sandals. The bishop by his office is a messenger of the Gospel, the successor of those whom Our Lord commanded to go throughout the world "shod with sandals." (St. Mark. vi. 9.) St. Paul explains to us the meaning of this recommendation: "Your feet shod," he says, "with the preparation of the Gospel of peace." (Eph. vi. 15.)

He who bears the good tidings in his apostolic journeys will have to crush the serpent, and bruise his head; let him, then, be shielded against the venomous sting of him that always bites the heel.

The hose and sandals recall also that the bishop has not been raised to the episcopate for ease and leisure, but to be wearied in his journeying to preach.

The Tunic.—Of all the events in the life of Our Lord that which is constantly present in the Church's thoughts is the passion.

Not a detail of that sorrowful drama that is not recalled in the liturgy. In the alb we have seen the white robe with which Our Saviour was clad in the court of Herod; in the chasuble, the royal mantle thrown over His torn shoulders; and now in the tunic of the bishop is placed before our eyes memories not less touching. Its name, its form, recall to us that seamless tunic woven for Jesus by Mary's pure hands, and for which the soldiers drew lots at the foot of the cross. (Inn. III., L. i. c. 39.) The last relic of a condemned one, drawn lots for under the eyes of His Mother—what anguish for such a tender heart!

Why does not the priest take for the sacrifice a vestment so rich in memories? Here we touch upon a mystery. The seamless garment of Jesus Christ which was not divided figured the Church in her unalterable unity, that faithful spouse whom neither heresy nor schism has divided. This is the teaching of the holy doctors: "While the veil of the temple was rent," says St. Athanasius, "the tunic of the Saviour remained whole in the hands of the soldiers. The Gospel has preserved its integrity while the shadows flee." (*Serm. de Cruce.*) The priest is a minister of the Church, but by his sacred office the bishop is her spouse; the closest ties unite him to her. The tunic is a symbol of that mystic alliance.

The Dalmatic.—Above the silken tunic the bishop wears a dalmatic of the same material. The ample folds of this vestment, reserved in the liturgy to the deacons who distribute charity, protectors of the widow and orphan, in a word, ministers and servants of the poor, symbolizes the charity and mercy recommended to the apostles by Our Lord. The bishop, spouse of the Church, should be, as it were, clothed with mercy toward all the suffering members of that Church—the poor, the weak, the afflicted.

The Gloves.—These were originally made of the skin of the kid; the testimony of early writers, as well as the meaning that the Church attaches to them, leaves this point beyond doubt. "Lord," says the bishop, taking the gloves, "set around about my hands the purity of the new man descended from heaven, that, having followed the example of Jacob, Thy well beloved, who covered his hands with the skin of kids, and obtained his father's blessing, having offered him wine and food, I may receive, in consideration of the saving victim offered by my hands, the blessing of Thy grace." From this prayer springs the meaning of the prelate's gloves in the sacred ceremonies.

The Ring.—All nations have looked upon the ring as a sign of dignity: the ring is the crown of the hand. It was given to the bishop because of his pre-eminence among the clergy. But we have seen that he who is raised to the episcopate becomes the spouse of the Church to which God sends him; it is in this title that he receives the ring on the day of his consecration. Says St. Optatus: "As spouse of the Church, and following the example of Christ, he should be ready to sacrifice his life for her, if it were necessary." (Lib. i., *ad Parm.*)

The Mitre—This is the golden crown upon the bishop's brow; it is wonderfully suitable to him who represents Our Lord crowned in the glory of "many diadems." (Apoc. xix. 12.)

This crown does not in the least resemble those of the princes of this world; its form, consecrated by many centuries, has the appearance of two horns. Let them be a reminder of the light which encircled the brow of Moses as he descended from Mount Sinai; many authors so consider it, as do we. For the bishop also is a legislator and guide to the people of God. But it is more: a horn has been always, and everywhere in antiquity, the triple symbol of glory, power, and royalty; a triple character which belongs to Jesus Christ, and with which He wished to clothe His representatives in the supernatural order. The Church has placed two upon the mitres of prelates, and their signification is given to us in the prayers which accompany the imposition of this insignia on the head of the newly consecrated bishop. These two horns are the figure of the wisdom of the two Testaments, the spiritual arms necessary to the bishop to combat the enemies of the Church.

The Crosier.—Our Lord recommended the messengers of the Gospel to take nothing with them; the staff was permitted them, not for defence, still less for attack, but as a badge of their sublime vocation—to be pastors of souls, to guide them, sustain them, raise them up, correct them. These divers duties of the pastoral ministry are recalled to the prelate by the traditional form of his crosier: pointed at the lower end, and curved at its upper one. By the cowardly or idle sheep the spur of reprimand must be felt; but the good pastors goes after those who have wandered far from the sheepfold, over stones, precipices, brambles, and with the hand of a loving friend gives them help. Is it not this tender anxiety for the lost sheep which the Church wishes to indicate by the curved form of the pastoral staff? St. Antoninus and Innocent III. say so expressly.

The Pallium.—This insignia, reserved to archbishops, completes the signification of the shepherd's staff. It consists of a woollen band placed on the shoulders of the prelate, and attached to the chasuble by three golden pins. Its material, borrowed from the fleece of little lambs, reminds the bishop that he should carry on his shoulders the weary sheep, and bring them back to the fold, at the price of his own weariness and sweat. The figure of the Good Shepherd formerly adorned the pallium, the better to imprint this lesson upon the mind of the bishop. The three pins which fasten the pallium to the chasuble are a souvenir of the love of the Good Shepherd; three nails fastened Him to the cross for love of His sheep.

The Cross on the Breast.—Jesus Christ, triumphant and crowned with glory, has kept in His hands, His feet, His side, the wounds of Calvary. In the vestments of the bishop the Church has wished to place under our eyes this double reminder of triumph and suffering. The crown of the pontiff, his throne, his ministers, the gold, the precious stones on his sacred vestments, are the memorials of triumph. The memorial of Calvary and of the wounds we see in the cross which shines upon the gloves, the sandals, and on the bishop's breast.

2. CEREMONIES OF THE PONTIFICAL MASS.

The Throne.—The bishop is the perfect image of Jesus Christ seated at the right hand of His Father; this is why he has a throne, why also he has a place of honor. The various members of the sacerdotal hierarchy surround him, hastening to clothe him in his ornaments, rendering him profound homage, after the example of the celestial hierarchies forming a glorious crown around the throne of Jesus Christ, and happy to serve Him.

The Seven Altar-tapers.—Here is another reminder of heaven; the altar upon which the sacrifice of eternity is offered appeared to St. John adorned with seven candlesticks.

The Kiss on the Hand.—If anything is given to the

bishop, or if he receives something, the minister kisses his hand. This act has been considered from all eternity as an expression of devotion and submission. "Bless God," the Church seems to say to us, "in prosperity and in adversity; His paternal hand is always worthy of love, whether it showers blessings upon us, or whether it takes them away."

This ceremony is the literal translation of the beautiful words of Job in affliction: "The Lord gave, and the Lord hath taken away; blessed be the name of the Lord." (Job i. 21.) And those others of persecuted David: "I will bless the Lord at all times." (Ps. xxxiii. 1.)

The Entrance into the Choir.—This ceremony represents the coming into the world of Our Lord by His incarnation. The cross is borne in advance of the clergy; it has been the beacon of humanity; the world of antiquity saluted it from the beginning with its most earnest vows, its most lively hopes. The incense is here the symbol of the prayers which made the heavens rain the just upon the earth, and the lights recall the prophecies in the midst of the ancient world, the twilight of a divine dawn. The subdeacon and the deacon are the Old and New Testaments, the figure and the reality. The closed book which the subdeacon carries represents the obscurity of the prophecies of the Old Testament. The assistant priest figures the law of Moses under the high priest Aaron; he walks after the subdeacon, for these are the prophecies which led the priesthood of Aaron to the knowledge of the Messias. The two deacons at the side of the prelate represent Abraham and David, who received the most definite promises of the

CIBORIUM.

Formerly above altars was raised a canopy held up by columns. In the middle were hung doves of gold or silver, in which the Host was laid.—See page 21.

incarnation of the Word. Besides which the Gospel puts them at the head of Christ's ancestors: ";The book of the generations of Jesus Christ, son of David, son of Abraham." (Inn. III., l. ii. c. 6.)

The Maniple.—Originally this was a linen intended to wipe away the sweat, and sometimes the tears, of the celebrant. The priest, not being surrounded by ministers as is the bishop, took his maniple before beginning the Mass. But the bishop received it from the hands of the subdeacon at the moment when he mounted to the altar. This ceremonial is preserved, and the prelate does not take the maniple until after the Confiteor.

Opening and Kissing the Missal.—As soon as the bishop goes to the altar the Missal, closed until then, breaking its seals, opens before him; the bishop kisses it and then incenses the altar, while the Introit chants the glories of the redeeming Lamb. The best commentary on this ceremony is the page of the Apocalypse to which it alludes. The resemblances are so striking that they will present themselves unaided to the reader: "And I saw in the right hand of Him Who sat on the throne a book written within and without, sealed with seven seals. And I saw a strong angel, proclaiming with a loud voice: Who is worthy to loose the seals thereof? And no man was able, neither in heaven, nor on earth, nor under the earth, to open the book, nor to look on it. And I wept much, because no man was found worthy to open the book, nor to see it. And one of the ancients said to me: Weep not; behold the lion of the tribe of Juda, the root of David, hath prevailed to open the book, and to loose the seven seals thereof. And I saw: and behold in the midst of the throne, and of the four living creatures, and in the midst of the ancients, a Lamb standing as it were slain, having seven horns and seven eyes: which are the seven spirits of God, sent forth into all the earth. And he came and took the book out of the right hand of Him that sat on the throne. And when he had opened the book, the four living creatures, and the four and twenty ancients fell down before the Lamb, having every one of them harps, and golden vials full of odors, which are the prayers of the saints: and they sang a new canticle." (Apoc. v. 1-9.) We can see in this kiss upon the book the love of the incarnate Word for the will of His Father; He wished to fulfil the Holy Scriptures to the last syllable; and it was not until the consummation of His sacrifice by obedience that He breathed His last sigh.

The Bishop on His Throne.—The bishop, after incensing the altar, goes to his throne and remains there until the Offertory. This was always the custom in the Church from the first centuries; the priest did not return to the altar till the moment of the oblation; during the prayers which preceded it he was seated in the place assigned to the celebrant, away from the altar.

The Pax Vobis of the Gloria.—After the *Gloria* the bishop salutes the people by these words: "*Pax vobis,*" ("Peace be with you.") Herein is revealed anew the pre-eminence of the bishop. "To show that he is the Vicar of Christ," says Innocent III., "the first time that he shows himself to the people he uses this form of salutation: '*Pax vobis,*' because this was the first word of Our Lord to His apostles on the day of His resurrection.

But after this he says: '*Dominus vobiscum*,' with the priests, testifying by this that he is but one among them." (Inn. III., l. ii. c. 24.)

Use of the Calotte.—When, by a special indult, the bishop may wear the calotte in celebrating the public offices, he retains it during Mass to the Preface, except while the Gospel is chanted. He puts it on again as soon as he has drunk the precious blood, and retains it for the rest of the office. These customs revive among us the ancient discipline. The amice formerly was put upon the head in the shape of a veil falling upon the shoulders. At the Preface it was thrown back upon the neck and replaced on the head after the Communion. Useless to say that respect due to the blessed Eucharist has so regulated these customs. During the Gospel the men uncovered the head, to show that the preaching of the Gospel had made the veils of the old law fall away,

The Blessing at the End of Mass.—This goes back to the primitive customs, for during a long time there was no benediction at the end of Mass. When the custom of blessing was established, the privilege was reserved to bishops only. A simple priest was never known to bless the faithful at the end of Mass up to the eleventh century. Later, when the priest had shared the privilege of the bishop, a difference was made between the ceremonial of their benediction. The priest blessed the people with the cross, the paten, or the chalice; the bishop alone blessed with the hand, and his benediction was preceded, as to-day, by the versicles *Sit nomen Domini* and *Adjutorium*. This ceremonial has been preserved for the bishop; as to the priest, he now blesses with the hand, and with the ceremonial already explained.

The Last Gospel.—If the bishop begins it at the altar, and continues it as he goes to the place where he is reclothed with his pontifical ornaments, it is because the recitation of this gospel was not a part of the liturgy. In the thirteenth century it was marked, in rare Missals, as an act of piety for the use of priests while taking off their sacerdotal vestments.

Papal Benediction.—In virtue of an apostolic indult, the bishops may give the papal benediction at Easter and Pentecost, to which a plenary indulgence is attached. This benediction is called *papal* because it is given in the same form as that of the Pope. After the Mass is ended the bishop mounts his throne. A deacon reads in Latin and English the indult by virtue of which the prelate gives the papal benediction. The plenary indulgence given to the faithful who receive the benediction is also published. The prelate gives it standing, and, to add to the solemnity, the joyous sound of the bells mingles with the harmonious tones of the organ.

CHAPTER VI.—MASS FOR THE DEAD.

Omitted Prayers.—Of these is in the first place the psalm *Judica me,* because of these words: "Judge me, O Lord," and the others: "Why art thou sad, O my soul?" The soul for which we pray has already been judged at the secret tribunal of God, and why should we ask the cause of its sadness when perhaps it is exiled from Him Whom it loves?

The *Gloria Patri*, the *Gloria in excelsis*, the *Alleluia*, and the *Ite, Missa est*, are not heard in the Masses for the dead, because the souls in purgatory are not yet allowed to join in the canticles of the angels.

Sign of the Cross at the Introit.—Instead of making it upon himself the priest makes the sign of the cross with his hand turned toward the Missal. Does he bless the altar? No. Or the book? No, again. Why, then, is this benediction? The souls who have been recommended to him are in the mind and heart of the priest. His one desire is to comfort them, and to show this desire earnestly; as soon as he goes up to the altar he applies to them the blessed fruits of the cross; he knows how to despoil himself generously in their favor.

Kissing the Book.—At the end of the Gospel the book does not receive the usual kiss, to show that the souls of the dead have not yet received the ineffable kiss of God, or, again, because having died in the sign of faith there is no need for them to profess their belief in the Gospel. This same reason is the cause of the omission of the Creed from Masses for the dead.

The Offering.—At the Offertory the faithful in former times made an offering which varied in different places; it was usually bread and wine, and a candle. An incident related in the life of St. Peter of Tarantaise will furnish us with an explanation of this offering.

A miner of Pinsot, in the mountains of Allevard, in Dauphiny, was surprised by a landslide, and buried alive. Every Saturday his wife had the holy sacrifice offered for him, and, according to the custom, presented at the Offertory bread, wine, and a candle. One day when the laborers were working in the neighborhood of the scene of the fatal event, what was their surprise to see through the cracks in the rocks a pale light. They wished to discover the cause of the phenomenon; pickaxes soon opened for them a passage to a little habitation. Here a man was enclosed, full of strength and life: it was their unfortunate companion so long mourned as dead. He told them that by a special protection of God the earth in giving way had formed this little retreat, and that each Saturday an angel had brought him bread, with a vase filled with wine, to nourish him, and a taper to give him light; thanks to this aid he awaited the hour of deliverance.

Let us make our offering with faith. An angel will descend to that soul so dear to our heart; it thirsts for God, and a celestial and mysterious nourishment will be given to it; it sighs after the fountain of living water, and a refreshing stream will quench its thirst, and in its profound darkness a ray of eternal light will come to console it.

The Water Poured into the Chalice.—At the Offertory, again, the priest does not bless the water poured into the chalice. Water, a symbol of Christians in the sacrifice of our altars, represents in Masses for the dead more especially the souls in purgatory, and the Church in not blessing the water wishes to show that she has no jurisdiction over these souls.

Omission of the Benediction.—The beginning of the Mass was marked by an act of charity on the part of the priest. In not making upon himself the sign of the cross at the Introit he is, so to speak, despoiled of graces, the divine fruits of the cross, in favor of the souls in purgatory. The end of the Mass shows us the same spirit of charity on the part of the faithful. There is no benediction; those present seem to forget themselves and to only think of those who suffer, of the poor exiles from heaven for whom are all the merits, all the blessings, all the fruits, of the sacrifice. This is truly charity such as the Master taught: devotion and self-sacrifice for others, in a word, forgetfulness of self. Already, under the influence of these charitable sentiments, the priest, in the name of the faithful, has replaced the words: "*Miserere nobis*" ("Have mercy upon us"), at the *Agnus Dei*, by these others: "*Dona eis requiem*" ("Give them rest"). In Masses for the dead it is always *them*, and never *us*. May these words always call forth this spirit.

Absolution.—The Mass ended, absolution is given. An acolyte carries to the head of the coffin a cross, the pledge of our immortal hopes. Did not the divine One Who rose again say: "O death, I will be thy death"? (Osee xiii. 14.) Has not St. Paul called Him "the first-fruits of them that slept"? Thanks to Jesus Christ, dead upon the cross, He will one day raise up him for whom you weep. Through your tears you have seen around the coffin the light of candles; your sorrow, if it be Christian, will find in this light consolation and hope. It is a symbol of the faith of the dead, and did not Our Lord say: "He who believeth in Me shall have eternal life"? (St. John vi. 47.) This light is also a symbol of the glory which the saints enjoy in the bosom of God: "Then shall the just shine as the sun in the kingdom of their Father." (St. Matt. xiii. 48.)

At the Absolution, during the Lord's Prayer, the holy water and the incense are poured forth upon the coffin as a symbol of the effects of prayer for the dead. "**May our prayer**," the Church seems to say, "rise as the perfume of incense even to Thy throne, O Lord, and appease Thy just wrath. May it call down upon this poor soul the blessed dew of Thy mercy."

CHAPTER VII.—HOLY WATER, BLESSED BREAD, AND THE SIGN OF THE CROSS.

1. HOLY WATER.

Its Origin.—In front of the primitive churches, in the midst of an open enclosure, was a fountain for the use of the faithful for washing the face and hands. This was a pious testimony of respect for the Holy Eucharist, which the Christians took in the right hand crossed upon the left, to administer to themselves. The washing of the face was to the same end, for the communicant, before nourishing himself with the consecrated bread, kissed it respectfully, then raised it to his forehead and his eyes. The holiness of the sacrament demanded this preparatory purification. Eusebius, speaking of these fountains, calls them "symbols of the holy expiation"; his language clearly shows that the Church had attached a symbolic thought to the use of these ablutions. The exterior purification could only be an image of the purification of the soul.

Every Sunday before Mass they went solemnly to these fountains to bless the water. The suppression of the custom of receiving the Blessed Sacrament in the hand rendering the ablutions less necessary, the vases diminished in size, and became the holy-water basins

Pyx.
In which the Blessed Sacrament is carried to the sick.

Case for Holding the Luna in the Tabernacle.
(The Luna is the part of the Ostensorium in which the Sacred Host is placed.)

Irons for Making Altar Breads.

Burse for Pyx.

Altar Bread Cutter.

Box in which Altar Breads are kept.

of the present time. The Church continues to bless the water; by her prayers she gives it power to purify souls, but, at the same time, she makes it the memorial of our spiritual regeneration.

The Aspersion.—The blessing given in Baptism might be forgotten; the Church wishes that every Sunday —the day commemorative of the institution of this sacrament—the aspersion of water shall be made upon the faithful before Mass, to recall to them that holy water in which they, Christ's little fishes, found their life.

During this ceremony the thought of our Baptism should be present in our minds; let us regret our lost innocence, lost, perhaps, long ago. And when we come to the holy place, in taking the water which the Church's pious intention has placed at the door, let us not forget that this sacrament has given us admittance to the sheepfold of the Good Shepherd.

Use of the Blessed Water.—Holy water is placed at the entrance of our churches that our souls may be penetrated with a profound respect toward the God Whom we come to adore. To those who will listen holy water speaks thus: "Before presenting yourselves before the Lord purify yourselves of even venial faults; His infinitely pure eyes cannot endure spot neither in the angels nor in His elect. If you would see Him with the eyes of faith through the veil of the sacrament, efface from your soul anything that can lessen its whiteness. If you would receive the caress of your God, wash your heart: 'He that loveth cleanness of heart shall have the King for his friend' (Prov. xxii. 11.) Purify with holy water your hands from their evil works, your mind from its guilty thoughts, your heart from its irregular affections."

But why? To drive away the demon. He is to be found even at the foot of the altar, during prayer, after communion. Holy things are like rich treasures; the latter attract thieves, the former demons.

Why, then, is holy water at the doors of our churches? To prepare us for the eucharistic banquet. In the ages of ancient hospitality, when a stranger was received under the roof, before he was admitted to the intimacy of the hearth, and sat at the table, his feet were washed, to remove the dust of the road. Our Lord consecrated this custom before the last supper. If the stranger was a person of distinction, rich perfumes were mingled with the water of the ablutions.

Strangers and travellers upon the earth: God gives us hospitality in His temple; we come to rest there from the weariness of life; there He breaks with us the bread of friendship.

At the entrance of His palace He receives all as His guests; He purifies us from the stains of the roadside with water in which He has put the strength of His blood.

In ancient times who was honored by his host as the Christian is by his God? If we are to communicate, taking the holy water, let us say with St. Peter: "O my God, wash me wholly: my eyes, which are to see Thee; my tongue, which is to serve as Thy throne; my heart, which in a moment will be Thy tabernacle." If we are not to communicate, let us humble ourselves for not accepting the invitation of Jesus Christ.

God treats all His children as His guests at His

heavenly banquet; His wish would be to see all reunited there each time that they assist at the divine mysteries.

2. BLESSED BREAD.

A Memorial of the Eucharist.—There was a time, in the dawn of Christianity, when the Eucharist was really "the daily bread." The happy witnesses of the holy mysteries all approached the sacred banquet; in the days of persecution they carried the holy species into their houses, to fortify themselves each morning. This blossoming of Christian fervor lasted three centuries. But, jealous of the virtues blooming under the dew of the precious blood, the devil breathed upon souls the icy breath of tepidity. The guests at the sacred banquet grew less numerous day by day. To reanimate Christian fervor a council at Agde, in 506, made communion obligatory at Easter, Pentecost, and Christmas. This state of things lasted until 1215, when the general council of Lateran established the discipline followed in our day.

From the beginning of these guilty desertions the Church, hoping to diminish their number, instituted a symbol which would at the same time express to her children the fervor of the first centuries, and the desires of the Saviour and His chosen ones.

She selected for this even the same material as that of the Eucharist, bread, and she called it *eulogy*, that is to say, *bread of benediction*. The simplicity of the Middle Ages, marvellously interpreting the intention of the Church, called the blessed bread *vicarius*, or that which took the place of the Eucharist. It was really intended to replace the Eucharist in the case of those whom tepidity or indifference withdrew from holy communion.

How many Christians on Sunday in the presence of the Blessed Sacrament ought to reproach themselves with sluggish tepidity? This is not earthly bread, they can say to themselves, which Jesus Christ would like to give me, but the bread of angels; not that bread which changes into the substance of man, but that which changes man even into the same substance as God. In my Father's house celestial dainties abound for those seated at the banquet of the Lamb, and I, like the prodigal, am dying for lack of nourishment. If you languish, O my soul, if you painfully drag your feet through the hard road of duty, search no longer for the reason: you do not receive often enough the bread of the strong.

A Symbol of Christian Charity.—The blessed bread, memorial of the Eucharist, is also the symbol of Christian charity.

The same bread distributed to all, eaten by all, is it not a striking expression of our brotherhood? Nothing is sweeter to the soul than brotherhood. Twice God has willed to make all men brothers: in the cradle of the human race, in Adam, and in the cradle of Christianity, in Jesus Christ. His merciful providence wished to soften by the ties of blood and faith the sorrows of exile.

The spirit of hatred has sown discord in hearts made to love each other, and the Church tries on all occasions to recall to her children the great truth, too easily forgotten, of our common origin and our common destiny

She gathers us all into one house, the rich and the poor, the servant and the master, to teach that we ought to form but one family. She puts upon the lips of all the same prayer: "Our Father, Who art in heaven." Who can forget in saying it that the same Father takes care of all? She distributes the same bread, like a mother sharing with all her children around her hearth. The Master often said: "My commandment is that you love one another, as I have loved you," that is to say, as brothers, and each Sunday the Church repeats this teaching of love by the distribution of blessed bread.

Christians should be one body, the mystical body of which Jesus Christ is the head; now could we find a more expressive figure of the union of several things than in bread made of many grains of wheat united and blended together? "For we being many, are one bread, one body, all that partake of one bread" (I. Cor. x. 17), says St. Paul, because we ought to be all united in Jesus Christ. No more of these distinctions of false pride between the fellow-citizen and the stranger, the master and the servant, the learned and the ignorant, the rich and the poor, but let us only recognize Christians, the sole family of Jesus Christ, fed with one spiritual bread.

Effects of Blessed Bread.—These are enumerated in the formula of benediction: "Grant, O Lord, that all those that eat of this bread may find there health for body and soul, and a preservative against the assaults of enemies." God Himself has often been pleased to manifest the efficacy of this remedy, and St. Gregory Nazianzen speaks of white bread marked with the sign of the cross, which it was customary to bless, and which miraculously gave his mother health. Only by thinking that she had eaten this bread while she slept she was cured. (*Orat.* xix.) These are good reasons for our confidence as well as our respect; we can apply to blessed bread what St. Augustine said of the salt distributed to the faithful: "Although it is not the body of Jesus Christ, it is nevertheless a holy thing, and more sacred than other food, for it is a sacrament, that is to say, the sign of a sacred thing." (*De Peccat. Merit. et Remiss.*) And, again, a council held at Nantes, toward the year 800, went so far as to warn the faithful to "take care not to allow a crumb of the blessed bread to fall to the floor."

3. THE SIGN OF THE CROSS.

Symbol of the Three Principal Mysteries.—The sign of the cross is filled with sacred associations; like a golden vase, it pours over the attentive soul a soothing and vivifying unction. That Christians do not oftener find either perfumes or strength in this sacred sign is because they do not understand enough of its sublime teaching.

In the first place, by its name as well as its form, the sign of the cross recalls the mystery of the redemption. We bring our hand to the forehead, to figure the head of Jesus Christ crowned with thorns, to the breast, in remembrance of His side pierced by a lance, to the left side, and then to the right, and yet can forget those shoulders wounded by the cross, and those hands torn with nails!

The sign of the cross also recalls to Christians the two other great mysteries of the faith, the Blessed

Trinity and the Incarnation. While pronouncing the name of the Father, we raise our hand to the forehead; the forehead, seat of intelligence, principle and source of life, symbolizes God the Father, eternal principle of all life, human and divine, which, by the way of intelligence, begot the divine Word. The Word of God was made flesh, descended, and annihilated Himself; He descended from heaven into the womb of Mary, from the womb of Mary into the humiliations of the manger, from the humiliations of the manger into the labor of the workshop, from the labor of the workshop into the ignominy of the passion, from the ignominy of the passion into the silence of the tomb, from the silence of the tomb into the solitude of the tabernacle, He descended to repair the revolt of the first man and of his posterity, for the madness of wishing to elevate one's self is the foundation of all going astray. The hand which descends from the head to the breast, while the lips pronounce the name of the Son, figures the profound abasement of the Incarnation. The Holy Spirit proceeds from the Father and the Son, and is the love of these divine persons; He is also the spirit of strength which the faithful receive on the day that they are enrolled in the army of Christ. These various attributes are indicated by the transverse line which we make from the forehead to the breast, and which, touching the shoulders, seat of strength, passes over the heart, the throne of love. (Inn. III., ii. 43.)

A Sign of Our Immolation.—Condemned as we are to suffering, as the guilty children of our Father, and the disciples of a crucified God, "we are become as sheep appointed for sacrifice."

The cross formed on us and by us is the sign of our immolation, the solemn profession of our obedience to the grand and universal law of suffering announced by Jesus Christ: "If any man will come after Me, let him deny himself, and take up his cross daily and follow Me." (St. Luke ix. 23.) But to make this sacred sign upon flesh plunged in all the weakness of sensuality; upon a brow which shelters nothing but thoughts of vengeance, pride, and impurity; upon lips soiled by lying or obscene conversation; upon a heart given over to criminal affections, what is this but a tremendous lie? We profess that the sword of immolation has been girded on our entire being, the sword of chastity on our body, the sword of faith in our minds, the sword of restraint on our tongue, the sword of charity on our heart. Let each one answer the question: Is this always true?

Efficacy of the Sign of the Cross.—"The sign of the cross," says St. Augustine, "is to us a pledge of triumph; it reduces to powerlessness all the attacks of hell. That which Our Lord did while on earth by His bodily presence He does to-day by the confident invocation of His name." (*Serm.* xix., *de Sanctis.*)

And whence comes to the sign of the cross such strength? St. Ignatius, martyr, answers: "This sign is like a trophy on the brow of the Christian; a trophy which reminds the demon of his shameful defeat on Calvary, so that at the sight of it alone he trembles, and flies."

The sign of the cross is not only a weapon: it is, above all, an excellent prayer. When we are signed with this sign of redemption, God sees us no longer as sinners, but as brothers of Jesus Christ; it is no longer

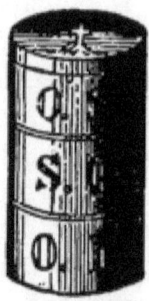

OILSTOCK.
Vessel in which the Holy Oils are kept.

OILSTOCK
for the Sacristy.

ABLUTION CUP.

BAPTISMAL SHELL.

COMMUNION PATEN.
Held under the chin as the communicant receives the Blessed Sacrament.

BAPTISMAL CASE
for the Holy Oils and the Salt.

our crimes which strike His eye, but the wounds of His Son on the cross; He forgets our iniquities, and remembers nothing but the merits of Jesus Christ. The cross, then, prays for us, and the prayer is heard. "The voice is indeed the voice of Jacob," says the Lord, "the voice of the sinner, but the smell is the odor of the garments of Esau. I see only the cross, I see but the blood, I see only the wounds of My beloved Son." He who kneels in the sacred tribunal of penance makes the sign of the cross. Short but sublime prayer! Eloquent cry! Lord, I am deserving of punishment, but oh, remember Calvary!

And, again, what a sublime prayer before receiving communion! He is there before us, the God of heaven; but an instant more and our hearts will possess Him. The purest soul in this solemn moment is seized with fear, the throne of sanctity is necessary for the Holy of holies. The sign of the cross reassures you, calls down upon your soul the blessings which Our Lord has merited by His death.

CHAPTER VIII.—PROCESSIONS.

Image of Life.—Processions are a figure of our life here below. We but pass over the earth, " for we have not here a lasting city, but we seek one that is to come." (Heb. xiii. 14.)

Now is not this religious march a figure of our poor life?

Each procession repeats to those who will hear the language of the liturgy: Life is a passage: it flows away as rapidly as the brook in the valley: it flies like the cloud in the heavens; it vanishes like the breath of a flower, fades like the smile of a child.

In its course the procession advances by roads sometimes stony, sometimes smooth; here the sun's burning rays beat down, a little further great trees throw upon us their refreshing shade.

These are truly like the changes of life: pain is succeeded by joy; joy again by sorrow; both are fleeting, for here everything passes away.

The processions do not return by the same road: does man see again the years that are gone? They have disappeared, the days of childhood, those of youth, and in their turn follows old age, and eternity.

We all have issued forth from the bosom of God, as the brook from its source, the ray from the sun. God is our beginning; He is also our end. Created for Him, our vocation is to go to Him; come forth from His bosom, after our pilgrimage we should re-enter there. The church from which we go out and to which we return will remind us of our divine origin and our divine destiny.

The recollection of our grandeur should not alone present itself to us. Humanity, in the person of Adam and Eve, was driven from the earthly paradise and condemned to exile in this vale of tears; and we ourselves have many times, like other prodigals, left our Father's house. In leaving the church we will be reminded of the punishment of our first parents, and perhaps reproach ourselves for our ingratitude toward God.

The Position of the Cross.—Who will be the guide of humanity in the darkness and dangers of its pilgrimage? Jesus Christ, Whose glorious standard is carried at the head of the procession.

We must follow after it if we would come to His kingdom. He who has always before him Jesus Christ crucified soon feels that in the shadow of the cross pains lose their bitterness and pleasures their seduction. The crucifix precedes us because Jesus Christ Himself has preceded us in the way of trial; His feet have been torn by the stones and the thorns, and He has left His blood on the sharp sides of the stones, on the piercing darts of the thorns; it is a divine balm which will heal all our wounds. What does it matter by what road the Lord wills us to march? Jesus has sanctified its pains in taking them upon Himself. He, the man of all sorrows, has preceded us in all suffering.

Order of the Procession.—Among the virtues there are two above all others recommended to us: humility and charity.

The Church recalls their practice by the order followed in her processions. The most worthy come last, and the least worthy are at the head of the procession, according to the counsel of the Saviour: "And he that will be the first among you, let him be your servant." (St. Matt. xx. 27.) This is the procession's lesson of humility.

The faithful who march two by two by this symbolic number figure the double charity recommended by Our Lord when He sent His disciples two by two to preach the Gospel. (St. Gregory, *Homil.*, xvii.)

The Church invites us to practise this virtue at the moment when the procession is leaving the sanctuary. "Do not forget," she says, "to walk in peace and harmony" ("*Procedamus in pace*").

How maternal, too, is the care of the Church. She

puts her little children close to the cross, by the side of Him Who always kept His tenderest blessings, His sweetest caresses, for them.

The Sound of Bells.—During the procession the ringing of bells repels the assaults of the evil spirits. The bell is the sacred trumpet of the Church militant; its peals remind us that life is the time of combat, and that "the powers of the air" are our chief enemies. But what arms shall we use? Prayer. This is why during the course of the procession the sacred chants arise; we must oppose perpetual resistance to an enemy that never sleeps. "Watch, then, and pray," says the Church with Jesus Christ. "We ought always to pray, and not to faint." (St. Luke xviii. 1.)

Efficacy of Processions.—The common cause of our falls is forgetfulness of our destiny; strangers and travellers here below, we make of this earth a permanent dwelling-place. And when the Church wishes to call down upon her guilty children the pardon of heaven she commands processions, and God allows Himself to be disarmed. St. Anthony cites a memorable example of this. In the fourteenth century Europe, disturbed by the scourge of war, was miraculously restored to peace after solemn processions. The same saint tells us that the blessed Mother of God appeared to a peasant and told him that her Son was very angry with the world because of its crimes. In her merciful compassion for sinners she revealed to him this means as the best manner of appeasing the wrath of God. (III. *Pars. Hist.*, c. iii.)

If we desire that processions may be efficacious with God, let us bring to them the dispositions of which we have spoken. Let us regard ourselves as strangers here below; nothing is ours, all belongs to God. As travellers, we are but passing over the earth; as pilgrims, the end of our journey is heaven. And when, overcome by the heat and fatigue at the end of the procession, we find again the holy place of rest and refreshment, let us think how sweet it will be after the labors of this life are over to rest in eternal peace beneath the shadow of God.

CHAPTER IX.—CHURCHES.

EVERYTHING in the church speaks to the Christian's heart not only the ceremonies, but also the stones, the columns, the plan of the sacred edifice. It is really a catechism in stone, where the mysteries of our faith are carved. Many see but hieroglyphics which they do not understand, there where in olden days the little children learned the elements of religion.

1. THE CATHOLIC TEMPLE A SYMBOL OF THE CHURCH.

Form of a Ship.—In the ark which saved the human race from the deluge, in the bark from which Peter made the miraculous draught of fishes, all the fathers have seen a prophetic figure of the destiny of that new society founded by Jesus Christ. And in their writings nothing is more common than to find the Catholic Church represented under the symbol of a ship. "In the name *ship*," says St. Augustine, "we understand the Church; she sails on the dangerous sea of the world, in the midst of tempests, in the midst of storms, and surrounded by monsters of all kinds. Christ is our pilot, the cross our rudder; the ship has nothing to fear when she considers, not the waves upon which she makes her way, but the pilot Who guides her." (*In Ps.* ciii., *Serm.* iv.)

The first Christians had an especial affection for this symbol, and reproduced it upon the lamps of the catacombs and the Christian burial-places. Nothing, however, better expressed this pious allegory than the churches. In general they had the form of a ship, a form preserved to our own day. The ornamented façade of the edifice represented the prow; the body of the building bore the name of nave, or ship (from Latin *navis*, a ship); the roof, with its sharply joined centre, gives us the form of a reversed ship.

The Main Door.—As it developed, Christian architecture retraced on the doors, the windows, and on the smallest details of ornamentation the history of the spouse of Jesus Christ. The door of the Church is Jesus Christ, as He Himself said. It is to figure His two natures that Christian art has ordinarily divided the main door in two parts, while the single arch that encloses them recalls that the two natures of Our Lord are united in one person. If this symbol is not found in the main door it is reproduced in the window of the façade. The rosewindow above the door shines like a crown on the brow of Jesus Christ, the King of kings.

Windows.—Who has defended the Church against error, which, veiled under a thousand forms, has ceaselessly striven to change the precious deposit confided to her? In the mystical body of Jesus Christ, what is the eye that sees and directs her? Let us look up. "In the shining windows, which shelter us from storms and shed upon us a soft light, we see figured the doctors and aposties who oppose themselves to the storms of heresy, and pour upon the Church the light of true teaching." (Honorius of Autun.)

Grimacing Figures.—Enemies have never been wanting to the Church, enemies within and without; over all has she gloriously triumphed. The figures of men or animals crushed beneath the weight of the edifice proclaim the victory of the Church over the enemies within her bosom. Those outside, who constantly gnaw around her sheepfold, are represented by those other hideous and grimacing figures placed on the walls or the buttresses.

The Blessed Trinity.—In the construction of our churches we find also the mystery of the Holy Trinity. The number three appears in all parts: the nave, the choir, and the sanctuary, in the length of the building; the three naves, in its width; the columns, the gallery, and the windows, in its height. If we take it in detail, here are three arches, here three windows; again, three chapels each one lighted by three openings, or even the altar, with its three steps.

Useless to pause longer over a symbolism which the least attentive observer cannot fail to mark. But why the place of honor given to the mysterious number in our temples? It is the seal of the works of God; the entire creation bears its imprint. The universe appears to us with its three distinct parts, heaven, earth, and sea. Time is divided into past, present, and future. Each day comprises invariably three portions, morning, noon, and night. Matter has its three dimensions, length, breadth, and height. Nature has three kingdoms, animal, vegetable, and mineral. The history of man comprises three acts, to be born, to live, and to die. The human soul has its trinity, which is summed up in three words: mind, understanding, love.

Against this dogma of the Trinity, written in shining characters upon creation, and later revealed by God to His Church, hell has spent its rage. The Church has called forth all her energies to defend it, by the pen of her doctors, the voice of her councils, and even by the architecture of her temples. The ternary, or number three, in ecclesiastical architecture is, then, a chant of love, a hymn of victory; this chant has been sung by man, inert matter, and the whole of creation since its first day. The Church repeats it in her symbolism and in her liturgy; under her inspiration the stones in their turn have spoken to invite the gratitude of man, created in the image of the Blessed Trinity, and in its name regenerated in the waters of Baptism.

The Enclosure of the Sanctuary.—The Church is made up of pastors and the faithful. The divine call, a life more holy than the ordinary, separates the guides of the flock from the sheep themselves. A line of demarcation has always, even in the catacombs, recalled to the clergy their withdrawal from the world, and to the people the respect due the ministers of God. St. Gregory of Nazianzen, speaking of the enclosure which separates the nave from the choir, says that "it stands between two worlds, one immovable, and the other subject to changes; the first that of immortals, the second that of mortals."

2. THE CATHOLIC TEMPLE A SYMBOL OF THE CROSS

Transepts, Apse, and Side Door.—Our fathers added another symbolism to that of which we have just spoken, and, while preserving the form of the ship, the churches took the form of a cross. How was this pious thought realized ? The nave and the transverse prolongations, called transepts, represent the cross of the Saviour, that is to say, His body and extended arms, while the high altar by its position figures the sacred head of Jesus Christ. For this reason that part of the sanctuary where it stands, called the apse in English, is in French styled the *chevet*, or head of the church, the mystical head upon which the Crucified has laid His chief crown. For this head has its crown; it is formed of the chapels which in many churches surround the high altar. To complete this symbolism we love to think of the side door as the wound in Our Lord's side.

Columns.—In some churches the columns are not placed opposite each other. Is this apparent fault in harmony the result of blind ignorance ? This would be a ridiculous supposition. By this apparent disorder the vivid faith of the Middle Ages wished to express that text of Scriptures applied to Our Saviour on the cross "All My bones have been displaced."

The Incline of the Nave.—The Gospel shows us Mary standing beneath the cross, and Jesus Christ inclining His head to breathe His last sigh. These two moving scenes have found their place in Christian architecture. The chapel of Mary was ordinarily placed at the right of the nave, which in many churches was decidedly inclined toward it. When we enter one of these churches, if we direct our steps toward the chapel of the Blessed Virgin, at the sight of the nave leaning toward the side of our mother, let us recall this touching symbolism. It is Mary beneath the cross; she seems to sustain the head of her Son, which leans toward her as if seeking a support when all His friends have abandoned Him; or it is Jesus bending toward His Mother and saying to us: "She is thine too: *Ecce mater tua*."

3. THE BELLS.

The Spire.—Christianity alone shows us in its temples that elevation, that aspiration, which, according to a graceful thought, is impatience of the earth, and ardor for heaven. (*Études Philos.*, t. iii., *Du Culte.*) The ancient religions in their sacred edifices knew but the monotonous ceilings, straight lines and horizontal. This architecture was replaced by Christian architecture; the vault, the semicircle, the spherical and pointed arch, appeared by turns as the richest expression of the destiny of regenerated man; for, to translate them, it was man raising his eyes toward a heaven reconquered by the sufferings of a God. The towers, the arches, the spires of churches force us to detach our eyes from earth and look to a better world. It is the liturgic chant sung in stone: "*Sursum corda*" ("Lift up your hearts").

Lift up your hearts and your hopes, above all the belfry spire repeats to you. "Its silent finger," says a German poet, "shows us heaven."

It shows it to the poor, to the laborers who painfully gain their daily bread, to the numerous victims of persecution, of calumny, to the ill and afflicted, and to all

It seems to say: "Patience, courage, there above is your reward."

Bells.—Tradition is unanimous on their symbolism. St. Hugh of Autun says that "bells, like the silver trumpets of the old law, signify the ministers of the Gospel preaching." And Honorius of Autun adds: "The sound of bells figures the preaching of them whose voices have echoed through all the earth. The towers where they are hung represent the two laws, and in their height between heaven and earth they announce the kingdom of God." (*Gemm.*, i. 142.)

The symbolism of the sound of bells has fixed that of the three peals which announce and precede the public offices. The first, softer than the others, represents the old law, revealed only to the Jews; the second, more solemn, marks the loud preaching of the Gospel; the third, the loudest of all, expresses the confusion of the end of the world.

Cock on the Belfry.—St. Clement (*Epist. to Cor.* xxxix. 2), and several doctors with him, have considered the return of the sun to the horizon as an image of the resurrection of our bodies. By a natural connection of ideas the first Christians loved to find in the crowing of the cock the symbol of that powerful voice which shall give to all the generations plunged in the sleep of death the signal of the great awaking. The poet Prudentius expressly says that the voice of the cock, which calls the other birds from their slumbers, "is the figure of our Judge." (*Cathem.*, i. 16.) The field of rest, placed beside the church, completes the symbol. The cock has been chosen also as the symbol of vigilance. "Placed on the summit of the church," says the *Ra-*

tional, it represents the pastors, for the cock watches during the profoundest night, his crow marks the division of the hours, he wakes those that sleep, and announces the approach of day." (L. i. ch. iv.) Before the use of bells Pope Gregory wrote thus: "The cock is the figure of the preachers, who in the midst of the darkness of this life announce the true dawn of the great day." (*Moral.*, xxxi. 8.)

Part II.—Vespers.

CHAPTER I.—THE DIVINE OFFICE.

1. ORIGIN AND DIVISION.

The Church has placed a feast at each one of the periods of the year consecrated by an important act in the life of Our Saviour.

But this is not enough for her love and gratitude. Each hour of the day or night marked by an event in the life or passion of Jesus Christ sees a public service established to preserve its memory among men.

This prayer bore the name of the Divine Office, or the Canonical Hours, so called because the *Canons* regulated their disposal by hours, and they were divided into seven parts: Matins and Lauds, Prime, Tierce, Sext, None, Vespers, and Compline.

The night, illumined by the stars of Bethlehem, also saw the sorrows of the agony; the first rays of day were the joyous witnesses of the resurrection: Matins, sung in the silence of the night, and Lauds, at the dawn, honor these different mysteries.

Toward the first hour of the day Our Lord appeared to Magdalen at the sepulchre, and to the apostles on the seashore: Prime is the memorial of these apparitions of the risen Saviour.

At the third hour, toward the ninth hour of the morning, took place the scourging, the crowning with thorns, and the condemnation of Our Lord. At this hour, also, on Pentecost, the Holy Spirit descended upon the apostles. All these events occupy the thoughts of the Church at Tierce.

At the sixth hour, toward midday, laden with His cross, Our Lord went up to Calvary. Over His bloody footsteps the Church leads us, and at Sext makes us assist at the sorrowful scene of the crucifixion.

At the ninth hour, three hours after midday, the sun was darkened, the earth trembled, the veil of the temple was rent in twain, the rocks were broken. The office of None calls us to weep at the sight of this awful drama.

In the evening Our Lord received in His side a new wound. Taken down from the cross by Joseph of Arimathea's anxious care, He was laid in His Mother's arms, embalmed, and buried in the sepulchre. The offices of Vespers and Compline honor these last mysteries of the suffering life.

2. ASSISTANCE AT THE DIVINE OFFICE.

For a long time the faithful assisted at the different offices of the day and night. Following the counsels of St. Jerome, the pious Eustachia interrupted her slumber two or three times to chant the hymns and psalms—a devout practice then well known to Christian virgins. (*Epist.* xxii.) The people themselves were not strangers to it.

St. John Chrysostom, raised to the see of Constantinople, felt keen grief that the churches were deserted during the public offices. He earnestly exhorted his flock

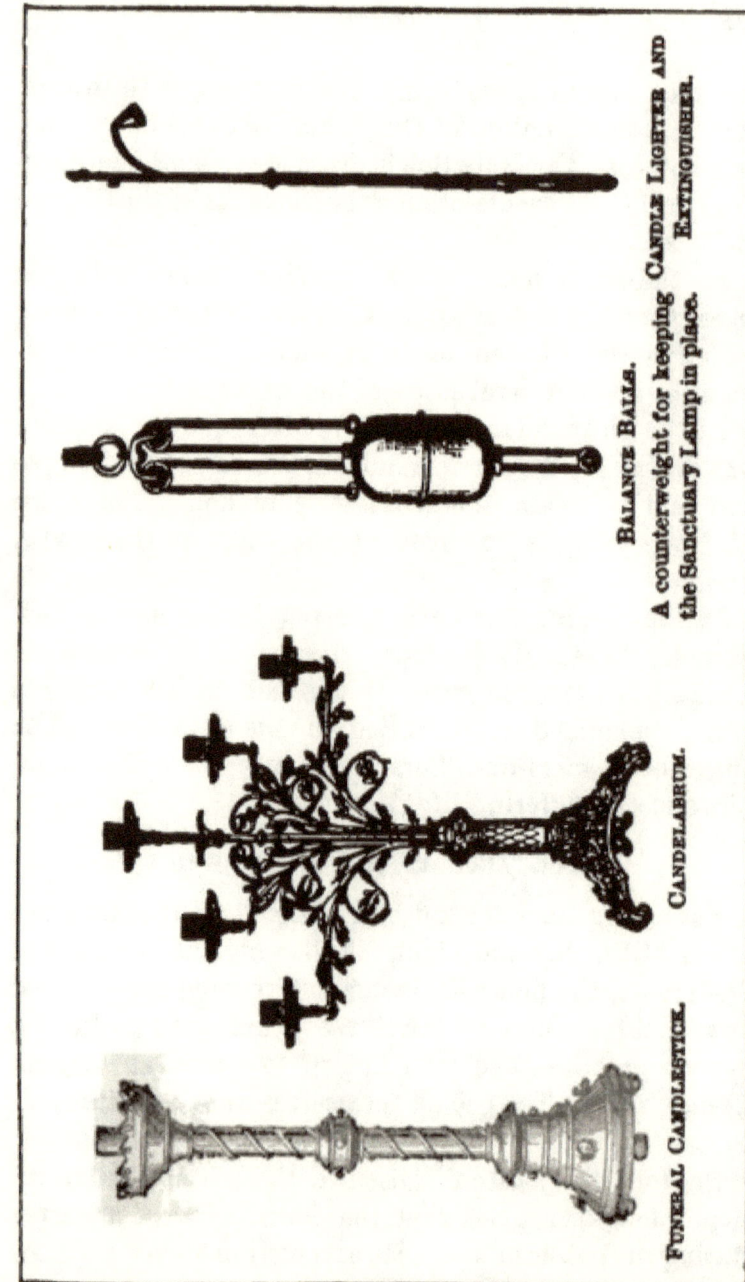

to be assiduous in attending the offices of the night; obedient to the voice of their bishop, the people pressed in crowds to the doors of the churches. (*Sozom.*, l. viii. c. 7.)

These different passages, and the testimony of the ecclesiastical writers, prove to us that men went to the offices of the night, while women prayed in their homes.

Attendance at the divine office was not obligatory except on Sunday. The celebration of the Lord's day began for the Christians of the first centuries Saturday evening, and ended the next day in the evening. (St. Augustine, *Append.* 280.) They united in the psalmody of the first Vespers, and again in that of Sunday night. In the morning they assisted at the holy sacrifice. They went back to the church in the evening, to end the day with sacred psalms. This was the constant practice of the Christians during several centuries.

A great chilling of the primitive fervor led to modifications in the discipline of the Church. Of the divine office which our fathers cared for so much, the majority of the faithful to-day know only Vespers. And even Vespers themselves, are they not often abandoned?

Persons who make pretensions to a certain piety consecrate the holy hour of the evening office to walking or visiting. God will surely have blessed my intentions if the reading of the following pages throws into their souls a ray of that light which enlightens and inflames, makes us know and love.

3. VESTMENTS OF THE CELEBRANT OF THE OFFICE.

The Surplice.—As its name indicates, *superpellicium*, that is to say, the vestment above the fur garments, or pelisses, this white garment formerly was worn over the tunics trimmed with fur in which the priests were clad in winter. The Church consecrated this custom in her liturgy the more readily that she saw in it a pious allusion to the story in Genesis of the lot of our first parents. Innocence and justice had been their first garment; after the fall they were obliged to ask the animals for their fur to cover them. The Holy Book says that "the Lord God made for Adam and his wife garments of skins, and clothed them." (Gen. iii. 21.) Jesus Christ came to give back to guilty man the robe of his first innocence, the white robe represented by the surplice. Old customs are still existing in the Church. Those of her ministers whom she has raised to a certain ecclesiastical dignity wear furs on their camail. What a reminder put before our eyes and theirs !

The vestment of the earthly and the sinner ; the vestment of the heavenly Adam, the liberator; the fault and its punishment; the redemption and its fruits. The white color of the vestment comprises the richest symoolism, and piety can but gain in knowing it. In the first place it is the symbol of innocence. Among the people of antiquity it was a universal custom to blacken the faces of the guilty, and then show them to the multitude. In the Scriptures, on the inspired pen of the prophets, the Ethiopian, burned and blackened by the sun of his deserts, is the image of the sinner plunged in crime (Amos ix. 7), and, on the contrary, the pure soul is compared to the whiteness of the lily or the dove. The whiteness of the surplice represents, then, the innocence of Him Who holds among us the place of the Saint of saints. White is also the symbol of liberation and of liberty. History teaches us that on the day of his liberation the slave was clothed with a white robe. Now the priest also is a freedman. At the last supper, in instituting the Holy Eucharist, Jesus Christ worked this prodigy of mercy in favor of His ministers. He freed them from the slavery of the devil, from the servitude of the flesh and the world, by these solemn words: "I will not now call you servants, for the servant knoweth not what his lord doth. But I have called you friends, because all things whatsoever I have heard of My Father, I have made known to you." (St. John xv. 15.)

The white vestment worn by the priest in the exercise of his sacred functions will recall this glorious emancipation; it will appear to us as the distinctive sign which separates the priest from the faithful. And this is not all. "Has not Jesus Christ," says a great doctor, "also confided to the priest the power to liberate, in his turn, his brethren? Great and sublime privilege given to the priesthood! For he who is invested with this dignity is not only a freedman of God, but more than that, he possesses the right to free others, whether by Baptism or by sacramental absolution." (Tert., *Advers. Marcion*.)

In the priest who comes clothed in white to the holy tribunal, and to the baptismal font, let us recognize him to whom Jesus Christ said: "Amen I say to you, whatsoever you shall bind upon earth, shall be bound also in heaven, and whatsoever you loose upon earth, shall be loosed also in heaven." (St. Matt. xviii. 18.)

White is also a symbol of peace. The ancient authors tell us that peace was asked or announced by hoisting a white flag, or by sending to the enemy a bearer of the flag of truce clad in white.

On the day of the resurrection, the angel at the tomb

of Our Lord wore a white robe, symbol of the peace which Jesus Christ had merited for us by His death, and the happy tidings of which He was soon to carry to His disciples assembled in the chamber of the last supper. When the priest announces the divine word, when he blesses, when he presents himself before God bearing the supplications of his people, he is always clothed in white, like an angel or a messenger of peace. He has the formula of this peace constantly on his lips: *Dominus vobiscum*—" The Lord be with you "; he has it still more in his heart. It is very fitting that he should wear before the eyes of the people this symbolic livery.

For these various reasons white always predominates in the vestments of the priest. If they are black, the cross, the white fringe, the amice, and the alb preserve in the whole of the priestly costume the rich meanings of which we have just spoken.

The material of the surplice is linen. " Woollen and silk," say the liturgists, "can be changed, and receive another shade, but linen loves simplicity, and would not know how to lend itself to the alteration of its color; this is why the doctors of the Church consider it the figure of a simple and candid soul, the enemy of lying. Linen also improves in the tests to which it is subjected, like true sanctity purified by sorrow and perfected by adversity." (*Panopl. Sacerd.* l. ii. c. 7.)

Admirable symbol of the priestly virtue! We should join to the patience of the lamb the simplicity of the dove.

The Rochet.—This is distinguished from the surplice by the narrow sleeves. It is the insignia of episcopal jurisdiction. The bishops-elect receive it from the hands of the Pope, if they are in Rome. Above the rochet they wear the chimere. These two insignia indicate that he who is thus clad exercises the principal jurisdiction in that place. This is why the bishops outside their dioceses cover the rochet either with a surplice or a short, small sleeveless mantle, called mantelet. Only the Pope may wear the rochet everywhere uncovered. By a concession, the members of the chapter, the bishop's senate, wear this badge also.

Cope.—In the first centuries, the clergy wore in the processions of winter, or when it rained, a long mantle called *pluvial*. The hood with which it was ornamented gave it later the name of cope. The custom of wearing it in church during the offices and benediction was introduced by degrees. The cope has not remained without its symbolic meaning. We have seen that the fur on the camail represents the garments of fallen man, while the linen of the surplice is the figure of the white robe of innocence washed in the blood and tears of Jesus Christ. The cope, splendid in gold and precious stones, is the symbol of that other vestment which will be given to the elect in heaven, the mantle of a glorious immortality. Do we desire to receive this one day from the hands of Jesus Christ? Let us clothe ourselves here below in the white robe of the pure in heart.

4. THE CHANT.

If we thoroughly understood the origin of the liturgic chant, the heart, mind, and voice would unite in a concert of harmony to praise the Most High.

The Language of Heaven.—In the vision of Isaias, Jehovah showed Himself to the prophet seated upon a raised and shining throne, around which the seraphim repeated the hymn of eternity: "Holy, holy, holy, Lord God of hosts." (Is. vi. 3.) We see that mention is already made of chants and choruses. St. Paul is ravished to the third heaven; while splendors inconceivable to the eye of man filled his gaze, unspeakable harmony made his heart throb. To express the feelings that filled his soul, he could only say that the ear of man hath not heard anything comparable to the chants of the saints and angels. (I. Corinth. ii. 9.)

Is another witness necessary? St. John saw in heaven, before the throne of the Lamb, twenty-four ancients with musical instruments, while thousands of virgins made ravishing harmony. (Apoc. v. 8; xiv. 3.)

This language of heaven will one day be our own, for the divine art of chanting will never perish. One day the world will see the ruins piled up by the angel of wrath at the end of time; temples and palaces, paintings and statues, as well as the cabin of the herdsman and the forest oak, will be the prey of the flames. The valley of tears will make way for a new world; then there will be no more painting, no more architecture, no more eloquence, but forever there will be music—chanting will last for eternity. Who can say what this harmony will be?

While a monk was at prayer one day, he heard the voice of a bird. Its sweet notes had an unknown charm. The bird hopped from branch to branch, from tree to tree, losing itself in the forest. The monk, drawn by a secret force, rose up to follow it. For a long time he went on after the bird, and one day he stopped. The echoes no longer gave back the beautiful notes;

God's little singer had disappeared. Sadly the monk turned to go back to the monastery, which he reached only after long wandering. All had changed since his departure: it was not the same brother porter who opened the door to him; another superior was at the head of the community; all whom he knew slept under the humble cross in the cemetery. The pious legend adds that a hundred years had sped away since he had gone forth, but, thanks to the beautiful song of the bird, they had seemed as fleeting as a second. For a hundred years one single voice had charmed his ear so that he had never wearied in listening to it. Under the veil of this charming allegory we see what the chants of heaven will be to the blessed.

While the sacred chants fill the temple, let us think of heaven.

It is said that when the soldiers of the French army heard in the mountains of Lebanon the sound of distant bells, they could not restrain their tears. It recalled to them their distant country, their first communion, their parents sleeping in the cemetery; to them it was the voice of their land. For us the chant will always be the voice of heaven.

Chant of the Psalms.—Even in its manner of execution, the liturgic chant recalls heaven. Ecclesiastical history teaches us that formerly the people and the clergy united in singing the psalms together. In some churches one sang alone, while all present listened in silence, uniting themselves interiorly with him. But one day St. Ignatius, the disciple of St. John and bishop of Antioch, like his master, saw in a vision the heavenly Jerusalem. While its glories were unrolled before his wondering eyes, he heard the blessed singing alternately and in chorus the praises of God. Awakening from his ecstasy, he desired to imitate upon earth the melodies of heaven, and the custom of chanting the psalms in chorus spread from the Church at Antioch throughout the entire East.

Chant of the Anthems.—In his beautiful *Treatise on the Celestial Hierarchy*, St. Denis shows us the elect sometimes chanting in choir, sometimes uniting their voices to praise God together.

The Church on earth has rendered the sacred chants on the model of her heavenly sister. After having recited alternately a voice of a psalm, she unites all the voices to sing the anthems. "Yes," let us say with St. John Chrysostom, "there is an admirable harmony between the chant of the Church and that of heaven; it is the same praise, the same joy." Such is the liturgic chant, the language of heaven, which St. Augustine could not hear without shedding tears. His emotion should be less surprising than our insensibility. "The sacred psalmody," says St. Justin, "excites in the heart the holiest and the most ardent desires; it lessens carnal affections; drives away evil thoughts. It is to the soul like a stream which brings to it divine fruits. It clothes the wrestler with virtue, generosity, strength, and constancy. It is a balm for pious souls in all the sorrows of this life." (Quaest. cvii. *Ad Orthod.*)

CHAPTER II.—VESPERS.

1. MYSTERIES OF THIS OFFICE.

IF the night was illumined by the rays of Bethlehem, the dawn by the glories of the empty sepulchre, noon by the splendors of the Ascension, evening, with its sorrows, has also its light, splendors and glories.

It was in the world's evening that Our Lord came to bring us salvation. "The people," say the holy doctors, "were plunged in the darkness of paganism. The shades of evening stretched themselves everywhere; it was the fulness of time and the end of days, the old age of the world, and its last age, as the prophets have sung." (Orig., *Hom. 7. in Exod.;* St. Aug., *Serm.* lxxv. *de Temp.*) At Vespers the object of the Church's praise is "the Word made flesh, and dwelling among us." That beautiful canticle of the Incarnation, the Magnificat, each day carries to God the tribute of her gratitude and love.

It was evening when Our Lord instituted the Eucharist. Not satisfied to clothe Himself with our nature, His love led Him to unite Himself to each one of us in that adorable sacrament, so well named "the extension of the Incarnation." Then was consummated the union of the Spouse with His bride, of Christ with the Church, the soul with God.

The Church, not knowing how to fittingly celebrate this blessing, puts on the lips of her children the canticle *In Exitu Israel*, said by the Jews at the celebration of the Passover, and which Our Lord Himself said after the last supper. It was evening when Jesus Christ received the great wound in His heart, become the fifth of the wounds venerated by the Church; in the evening He was taken down from the cross, and given back to His Mother. Around that afflicted Mother the angels united to console her sorrow. The Church invites us to join their ranks, and to come to weep on Calvary, at the foot of the cross. Go then, O my soul, during that office, to the mountain of myrrh, as the prophet calls it; there is myrrh in abundance; on the cross, around the cross, at the foot of the cross; everywhere sorrow, suffering, and anguish.

With the Spouse of the Canticles, let us make a mystical bouquet of all these bitter flowers; the bad odor of sin will be driven away by its perfume; your wounds will be healed by contact with this blessed balm. Of all these mysteries we will treat most particularly those of Jesus on the cross. The considerations which flow from them always find easy access to our minds, and the heart which loves cannot cease to think of Jesus, and of Jesus crucified.

2. METHOD OF ASSISTING PIOUSLY AT VESPERS.

It is the hour when Our Lord is dead for my salvation, around His blessed cross the Church assembles her children to repeat with them the canticles of gratitude: this thought alone should unite all the Christian family in the holy place for the evening office.

How many men, how many women even, remain deaf to the call of grace and the invitation of the Church! While Jesus Christ, on His new Calvary, sees around Him but a small number of faithful disciples, the public promenades, the pleasure-places are filled with a merry crowd.

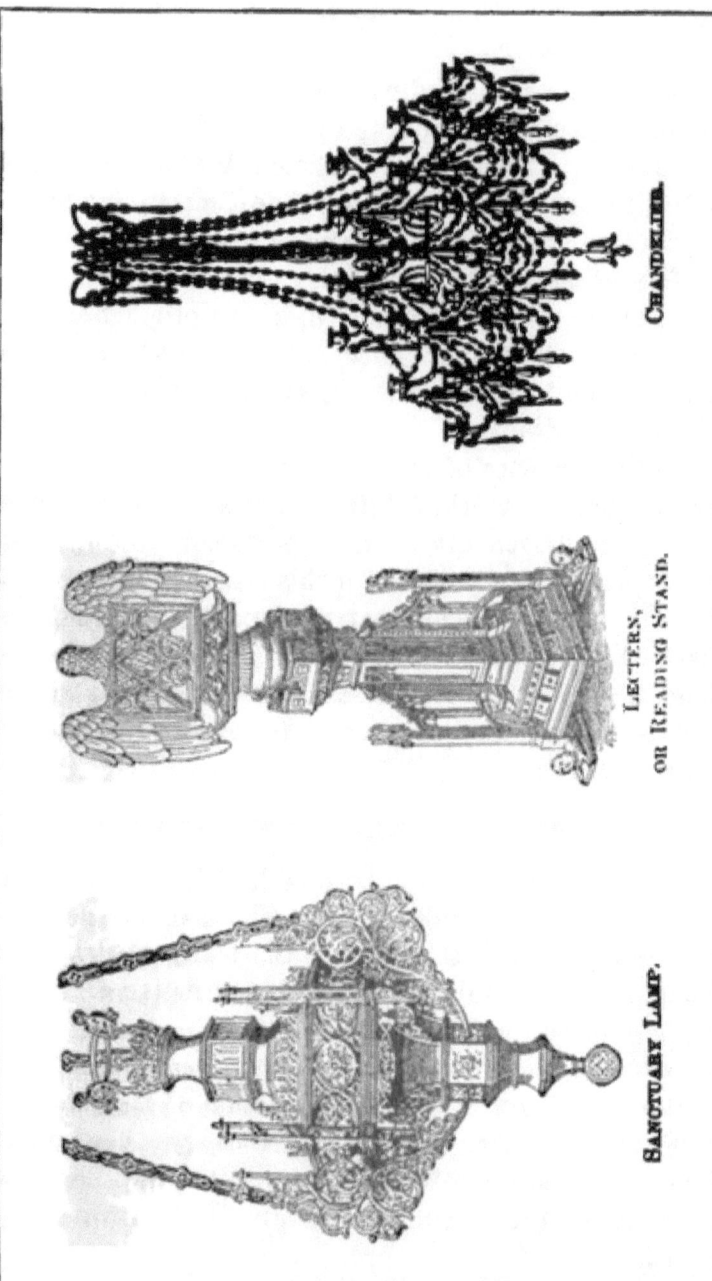

For us, more docile, when the bell announces the office of praise, let us imagine we hear the voices of angels who chant in heaven: "Christ is fastened to the cross, pierced by five wounds; come and adore Him together." Vespers are composed of five psalms, in memory of Our Saviour's wounds. To sing them we should place ourselves in thought at the foot of the cross; our heart will find Mary there, with the beloved disciple, and the holy women.

We will recite the first psalm in the wound of the right foot of Jesus Christ; the second in the wound of the left foot; the third and fourth in the wounds of the right and left hands; the fifth in that of the side. We read in the life of St. Francis Xavier an incident that shows us that we should love this practice. During a frightful tempest the vessel on which he was sailing was about to be submerged. Sailors, soldiers, and passengers, crowding together in confusion, waited but for death. Then St. Francis, mounting the deck, raised his eyes and hands to heaven. "Jesus," he cried, "Jesus, love of my soul, help us. I ask Thee by the five wounds which Thou hast received for us on the cross." And instantly the vessel, which already was sinking, rose up of itself, and gained the top of the waves. Our soul is perhaps like this ship; the tempest roars in heavens black with clouds; the waves of passion threaten to engulf it. Let us fly to the five wounds of Our Saviour; calm will reign at once in our soul.

The presence of angels will also arouse our fervor. "At the signal for the divine office," says St. Bernard, "a multitude of cherubim and archangels descend to our temples. They hasten eagerly to join us; they mingle in our ranks to praise God with us, and animate our chants by inspiring us with their burning fervor." Our angel guardian must not be forgotten. See him at our side; what is he doing?

The chronicles of Citeaux will tell us. During the office, St. Bernard saw beside each religious an angel. As soon as a verse of a psalm was chanted, he wrote in a book with a golden pen. And the saint noticed that the letters sometimes shone like gold, sometimes like silver, sometimes seemed black, and again pale like water. And sometimes even the pen made no mark. St. Bernard, astonished, asked God to explain to him the meaning of this mysterious vision. The Lord told him that this angel was the guardian angel of each religious. The difference in colors indicated the fervor with which each one sung the praises of God. If we would have our good angel write in golden letters in that book where our works are recorded, let us practise the pious method of hearing Vespers of which we have spoken.

The Venerable de Bérulle, founder of the Oratory in France, has written a pious tract on the manner of reciting the office. The following lines which we copy from him will enkindle the fervor of many souls:

"Think that you have to praise God for an infinite number of creatures who are incapable or unworthy to do so. Some are dumb, without voice or soul; they borrow your mind and lips to praise the Creator.

"Others are as if in the state of childhood and in their minority; they look to your height in grace to render homage through you to their sovereign Lord. Others, deprived by their own fault of the grace offered to them, are cursed by God, and unfit to praise Him.

"Double and triple blessing then is given you to praise God for them and for yourself. From this point of view, and with this thought, regard yourself as delegated by all creatures to praise the Lord of all, and pay Him their common tribute. You, then, praise the Lord for all—for the heavens and the earth, the creatures animate and inanimate; for Christians and infidels; for Catholics and heretics; for the blessed and reprobate; for hell itself, though it shudders and resists with its perverse will. You are placed between heaven and hell. Hell is under your feet, and God grant that you have as much fervor to praise the Divine Majesty as the reprobate have obstinacy in cursing it. Heaven is open above your head, and God grant that you have as great elevation of mind and piety as heaven has of rest, of glory, of joy in the possession of its Lord!"

May the Spirit of God, by the unction of His grace, engrave these noble thoughts in our souls, and may they be always present at the beginning of the divine office! Let the empty places around us excite our devotion we will love for those that love not, pray for those who pray not, praise for those who praise not.

CHAPTER III.—THE PSALMS OF VESPERS.

1. PRELIMINARIES OF THE OFFICE.

Pater and Ave Maria.—The Lord's Prayer, recited before Vespers and all the other canonical hours, is the abridgment of all that we shall ask of God during the office. All the intentions which we can have are there recalled: first, the sanctification of God's name, the coming of His reign in our hearts, the accomplishing of His will; then, the granting of all our needs, the pardon of all our faults, victory over temptation, deliverance from all dangers. What graces to ask! What necessities to satisfy! And consequently what motives to pray, and to pray well! The *Ave Maria*, recited before the office, is a souvenir of the fervor of our fathers. The public office was accompanied by the office of the Blessed Virgin; some religious orders still recite it thus. The reason for this is wonderfully beautiful.

The different parts of the office celebrate the mysteries of our redemption; and to Mary, called by the doctors of the Church the coredeemer of the world, for the active part she bore in the work, a testimony of gratitude is due. The recitation of the *Ave Maria* before the canonical hours is the only vestige of this custom remaining to us. The intention of the Church in retaining this prayer has doubtless been to hold Mary up to us as our model, according to the words of St. Ambrose: "May the spirit of Mary reign in each one of us to praise God worthily." (*In Luc.* ii. 26.)

At the *Ave Maria* our thoughts should be borne to Calvary, and we will ask Mary, standing at the foot of the cross, for some of the feelings that filled her heart. These prayers are said in a low voice. It is time to ask ourselves why the *Pater* is said aloud in the Mass, when in the other offices it is otherwise. For the solution of this difficulty we must go back to the first centuries. The Lord's Prayer and the Creed, considered as the watchwords of Christians, were not taught to catechumens until a little while before their baptism. Respect forbade saying these prayers aloud in those assemblies where pagans and catechumens might be present. These being allowed to take part in the offices of the day and night, care was taken to say these prayers secretly. It was not the same case with the Mass. The Church did not admit to the sacrifice those who had not been regenerated in the waters of baptism; there being no fear then of compromising the mysteries by reciting these prayers, they were solemnly chanted.

Deus in Adjutorium.—The priest and the faithful arise, and turn toward the altar. At this solemn moment of the public prayer, the Church cannot forget that the demon, like a lion full of craft and rage, prowls around the faithful band, above all when our heart offers to God the incense of prayer. Do we not know this of our own experience?

In the ordinary occupations of our life our mind is entirely upon that which we do. But when we begin to pray, then a swarm of foreign and importunate thoughts buzz around us; distractions carry us into unknown and fantastic regions; the body is in the holy place, but a mysterious power draws the mind abroad. And what invisible force swells the storm of temptation during prayer? Temptations to idleness, vanity, frivolity, sleep, not to speak of others more humiliating to the Christian who desires to recollect himself before God.

All these things are the work of the demon. Against the attacks of the enemy the Church, before the office, arms us with the cross, and puts on our lips the cry of distress and confidence: "*Deus in adjutorium meum intende*"—"O God, come to my assistance; make haste to help me."

What a holy boldness in these words! What truly filial confidence! He who hopes in God shall not be deceived. "Thou hadst hardly called Me when I had heard thee," says the Lord.

The Church, knowing that her prayer is already heard, that the angels of God come to cover the pious flock with their love and their protection, intones one after another the chants of her gratitude to the adorable Trinity.

Gloria Patri.—We have come into the holy place to glorify God. God is outraged on earth by His own children; at the very hour when we are united at the foot of the altar, what blasphemies are uttered against heaven, what scandals committed in the light of day, what crimes in the darkness! While the sinner raises his voice in insult against God, let us raise ours in praise: Glory be to the Father, the source of all power; glory be to the Son, source of all wisdom; glory be to the Holy Ghost, source of all love. Glory be to the Father Who has created us; glory be to the Son Who has redeemed us; glory be to the Holy Ghost Who has sanctified us. These first words of the *Gloria* go back to the time of the apostles. The Arians having dared to say that there was a time when the Son did not exist with the Father, the Council of Nice, to protest against this blasphemy, decreed that to the *Gloria Patri* these words should be added: *Sicut erat in principio*— "As it was in the beginning, is now, and ever shall be, world without end."

This is the first meaning of the *Sicut erat*. There is

a second which explains in what manner we should glorify God : Glory be to God, *now as it was in the beginning.* Our heart, like a broken harp, cannot give forth melodious sounds ; our lips, whether dumb or soiled, are incapable of praising God as He deserves. We pray then the Blessed Trinity to vouchsafe to receive in the place of our unworthy praise the praises which were offered in the beginning, that is to say, from all eternity, when the Father praised the Son Who is God of God ; the Son praised the Father Whose Word He is ; the Father and the Son praised the Holy Spirit Who lives and reigns with them. Not only do we wish that God may be glorified, now as He was in eternity, but we also ask the Divine Persons that their praises may be always on our lips and in our hearts, and in the world that never ends we may have the happiness to bless and praise them. How sublime is the *Sicut erat!* And to think that it can pass like an icy breath over lips still colder !

But it shall be so no longer. Our hearts shall repeat in ecstasy : "Glory be to the Father, and to the Son, and to the Holy Ghost. As it was in the beginning, is now. and ever shall be, world without end. Amen."

During the *Gloria* the clergy bare their brows, and all heads are bent. These uncovered brows, these bowed heads well express the sentiments of the faithful soul. The best praise to offer God is the practice of Christian humilty, the extinguishing of self.

When pride is enthroned in the heart, how dare we recite the thrice-holy chant ? With lying lips and hypocritical posture pretend to return to God all glory, when the heart has already stolen it from Him ? If our words are always the echo of our true sentiments, and humiliation of body is a symbol of interior humility, we shall escape the reproach of the Master: "These people honor Me with an exterior worship, but their hearts are far from Me."

The Alleluia.—Again a chant of praise, for this Hebrew word signifies *praise the Lord.* The Church wills that all tongues come to render homage to Him Who has redeemed the entire world. The *Alleluia* is ceaselessly chanted around the throne of the Lamb by the celestial choirs; the Church, in placing it on our lips, recalls that He Whose grandeurs we celebrate is the same God glorified by angels. To the same God the same respect, the same love. Alleluia.

The Anthem of the Psalm.—The principal feasts of the saints for a long time had two offices, the office of the *feria,* that is, the day of the week upon which they fell, and that of the feast itself. In this case a double office was recited, as is still done on the second of November. These solemnities took the name of double feasts. Other, less important feasts had two half-offices, one of the *feria,* the other of the saint. These were called semi-doubles.

Later the Church, to render the divine office less onerous, suppressed on the feasts the office of the *feria.* As a remembrance of the older custom on *doubles,* the anthems were doubled, being said before and after the psalms; on the *semi-doubles,* half of the anthem, or the first words, was placed at the beginning of the psalm, and the whole was recited at the end. This custom exists still in the Church.

2. THE FIRST PSALM.

The first psalm of Vespers on Sunday celebrates all the glories of Jesus Christ: His eternal generation; His eternal priesthood; His eternal empire over all people become His footstool.

But, some one may say, Vespers especially honor the sorrows of Jesus Christ and His blessed Mother, and here is the Church, kneeling at the foot of the cross, singing nothing but hymns of joy and chants of triumph. Beyond the humiliations of Calvary and the silence of the sepulchre, the glories of the resurrection show themselves to her. And in her joy she cannot cease repeating to her children: Jesus Christ, humiliated on the cross, humiliated in the world, will soon triumph. The Holy Spirit announced it many centuries ago by the mouth of the Royal Prophet.

"The Lord said to my Lord: Sit Thou at My right hand."

Crucified between two thieves, trodden under the feet of the populace like a worm of the earth, Jesus Christ will take His place, even on the throne of God, on the day of His glorious ascension.

"Until I make Thy enemies Thy footstool."

Jesus Christ has not only children in the world; He has also enemies. Those who attack the Church, the Pope, the pastors; those who live obstinately in sin,- these are the Saviour's enemies. They refuse to fall to-day at the feet of the mercy which raises and pardons; one day an irresistible force will throw them at the feet of that justice which crushes and punishes. The enemies of Jesus Christ will be the footsool of His tribunal on the last day when He comes to judge.

"The Lord shall send forth the rod of Thy power from out of Sion: rule Thou in the midst of Thine enemies."

On the clouds of heaven shall shine the cross so often insulted. With this sceptre of power in His hand Jesus Christ will judge us. Too late all will recognize in Him the King of kings and Lord of lords. It is the hour of that reign so often invoked: *Adveniat regnum tuum*.

"Thine shall be the dominion in the day of Thy power, amid the brightness of the saints: from the womb before the day-star have I begotten Thee."

The power of princes and kings is in Thee, as in its source. It flows from Thee upon the elect on Thy right hand; it is by Thee that kings reign. The world has not perceived it through the ages; it shall see it in the day of Thy might. The saints, despised here below, will stand in their splendor, like a rich diadem around the King of glory; they are the princes of the eternal kingdom. May the strength of the great King, may the majesty of His elect, not find us unprepared! It is He of Whom the Father has said: "Before the day-star I have begotten Thee."

"The Lord hath sworn, and will not repent: Thou art a priest forever according to the order of Melchisedech."

This is the true Priest-King, Whose Vicar Rome has the glory of sheltering. The sacrifice of Calvary He has continued to offer on all the Catholic altars, where He is at the same time high-priest and victim. He will be priest until the end, and eternity will have its ineffable sacrifice, its divine banquet.

"The Lord upon thy right hand hath overthrown kings in the day of His wrath."

The pride of kings has conspired against the religion of Jesus Christ, above all against His divine priesthood. The watchword, Destruction to the altar, has passed over many lips. Vain efforts! The Lord protects His Church; He has broken all the crowned conspirators in the day of His wrath.

"He shall judge among the nations, He shall fulfil destructions; He shall smite in sunder the heads in the land of many."

The nations will have their turn. The stroke of vengeance will pour curses on those " who have met together against the Lord and against His Christ, and who have said: Let us cast their yoke from us." (Ps. ii. 1–3.) They will fill up the vast abysses of hell. As to the multitude who cry: "There is no salvation for him in his God" (Ps. iii. 2), Jehovah will break them against the earth. A comparison naturally presents itself to the mind. The prophet says: "He shall smite in sunder the heads of a great number," and later Our Lord repeats sadly: "Many are called, but few are chosen." Let us not follow the multitude; they hasten to their loss.

"He shall drink of the brook in the way: therefore shall he lift up his head."

The brook in the way is sorrow. Jesus Christ has drunk there in long draughts. He has humiliated Himself even to taking the form of a slave; He has eaten the bread of a laborer by the sweat of His brow; He has known the privations of exile. This is the way marked out for each Christian: suffering, humiliations, tears; but the reward follows. The true seed of glory is suffering.

8. THE SECOND PSALM.

The second psalm of Vespers sings the blessings which Jesus Christ has merited for us by His death. This is also the canticle of thanksgiving for the institution of the Eucharist.

"I will praise Thee, O Lord, with my whole heart in the assembly of the just, and in the congregation."

At the recollection of all that Thou hast done for me during the course of my life, more particularly in the week that has just passed, I feel that I must praise Thee, O Lord, in the fulness of my heart. The solitary and private praise which the Christian gives to God in the sanctuary of his heart is not enough. To those who say that a prayer said at home is as good as one made in the church, the Holy Spirit has taken care to answer that it is necessary to praise God in the heart, but also in the assemblies and congregations of the people.

"Great are the works of the Lord : sought out are they unto all His pleasures."

All the works of the Lord bear the triple seal of power, wisdom, and goodness. There is nothing useless in creation ; all there is great, all responds wonderfully to the designs of God. "To move the heart of man by the grandeur, the harmony, the beauty of the spectacle which creation offers him ; to raise his mind to God, the architect of all these marvels. So that the vast universe is a book always open before our eyes." (St John Chrys., *In Psal.* cx.)

"His work is His praise and His honor : and His justice endureth for ever and ever."

"God does everything for love," says St. Chrysostom.

When He strikes or when He blesses; when He pours upon the fields the dew of heaven or the treasures of His wrath; whether He sends sickness or health, poverty or abundance, honor or humiliation, above all shines His goodness as well as His glory. Even when crime seems to triumph over innocence, be far from us the least murmur: there is a justice which endureth for ever and ever. And the victim and murderer will fall into its hands. If this divine justice is patient and slow, as has been said, it is because it is eternal.

"The merciful and gracious Lord hath left a memorial of His marvellous works: He hath given meat to them that fear Him."

A memorial of the creation, the Incarnation, the Passion, the Resurrection, the Ascension, the Eucharist is truly the abridgment of the marvellous works of God; the greatest work, wherein mercy and goodness have, in a sense, exhausted their divine inventiveness. I see nothing greater than communion but the incarnation, and after the holy Table there is but heaven. Jesus Christ has not instituted this sacrament only to be adored. He immolates Himself as victim that He may give Himself as food to them that fear Him. Let us not put asunder that which God has joined; let us assist at the sacrifice, but also take our place at the holy Table. The essential condition for participating in this heavenly food is the fear of the Lord; a tender and filial fear of God makes us bring to the divine banquet a pure conscience and all necessary dispositions.

"He shall ever be mindful of His covenant: He shall show forth unto His people the power of His works."

In communion man contracts a close alliance with

God, an alliance sealed in the blood of the august Victim. Oh, how fragile are our pledges and our promises! For many the very day of communion passes in forgetfulness of such a grace. But God remembers; He will demand a rigorous account of His eucharistic visits. Above all, God will remember to reward and bless the earthly angels of the Eucharist. On the last day He will raise them up; He will clothe their bodies, so often nourished with the celestial bread, with a mantle of glorious immortality; the virtue of the Sacrament of the Altar, a virtue concealed to-day, will then be divinely manifested.

"That He may give to them the heritage of the gentiles: the works of His hands are judgment and truth."

"He who eats My flesh and drinks My blood," says Our Lord, "hath everlasting life, and I will raise him up on the last day." (St. John vi. 50–57.) Jesus Christ will remember this; His promises are founded on justice and truth. Heaven, the true inheritance of all nations, is thus assured to the soul nourished by the sacred bread, for the Saviour said: "He hath eternal life."

"Faithful are all His commandments; they stand fast for ever and ever: they are done in truth and equity."

To attain to this glory we have received certain precepts. Let us keep the laws of the Lord, for they are faithful, they can never deceive. All that they promise they fulfil: the assured recompense of the good, as well as the punishment reserved for the wicked. The second character of the laws of God is that they do not change. The Gospel is to-day what it has been for eighteen hundred years. As in the past, heresy and philosophy would like to change it; philosophers and heretics pass, and the law of God remains. Such stability will perhaps seem surprising to this generation, accustomed to see human laws fly before the breath of political storms. All surprise will disappear at the last words of the verse: "They are done in truth and justice." Here is no deception, no prejudice, no error; a gold without alloy: *in veritate*. All mankind, without exception, are equally under the law; it includes nothing arbitrary, nothing superfluous, nothing impossible: *et æquitate*.

"He hath sent redemption unto His people: He hath commanded His covenant for ever."

The Eucharist applies to us the merits of the redemption. The sacrifice of Calvary is renewed on the altar every day. The covenant of God with man must be eternal; nothing can break it except sin.

"Holy and terrible is His name: the fear of the Lord is the beginning of wisdom."

Let us approach tremblingly to this august banquet; He Who gives Himself there to us, however poor and humble He may appear, is the same God Whose name is holy and terrible. If we do not feel this pious fear in our soul, let us ask it of the Holy Ghost; it is one of His gifts and the beginning of wisdom. "Fear," says St. Bernard, "contains a true savor; now savor makes a man wise, as science makes a learned man, and riches a wealthy man, for the word sage, or wise, comes from savor." "Fear," St. Francis de Sales says, "precedes love ordinarily and serves as its harbinger; it is St. John the Baptist going before the Lord; it is the steel needle piercing the material to draw through and leave after it the golden or silken thread which will embellish."

"A good understanding have they all that do there after: His praise endureth for ever and ever."

Following the order of the gifts of the Holy Ghost, understanding comes after wisdom; it is like its mystical blossom, the divine flower. In the Eucharist all is mystery; our faith needs a ray of that divine light to come and enlighten it. The priest asks this before the sacrifice. "Send forth Thy light and Thy truth; by the light of this celestial torch I will go unto Thy holy mountain and into Thy tabernacle." God enlightens the humble and fearing soul, and for all eternity it will chant the praise of Him Whom it has loved with fear and feared with love.

4. THE THIRD PSALM.

The flower needs dew, fruit the sunshine, and man craves happiness. He asks for it of all that presents itself to him. Riches, power, glory, beauty, offer to him but a bitter and impoisoned fruit. Where then is this happiness to be found which all so desire? The Holy Spirit has revealed it to us in the third psalm of Vespers. "Fear is the beginning of wisdom," the prophet-king had sung. He will now show to us that it is also the road to true happiness, even in this life.

"Blessed is the man that feareth the Lord: in His commandments he shall have great delight." How many are there who see in the precepts of God but a yoke and a burden! A few find therein the unction and sweetness that God has concealed for His faithful servants. The first steps in the law of the Lord are nearly always diffi-

AMBRY.
In which the Holy Oils are kept.

POOR BOX.

ALTAR CARD.

STANDING LAMP.

ALTAR VASE.

CRUETS.
In which the Water and Wine are presented to the Priest at Mass.

cult. Courage ; after the labors you will taste delights unknown to the crowd.

"His seed shall be mighty upon the earth : the generation of the righteous shall be blessed."

Would coming generations be feeble and weak if the fear of the Lord and the love of His commandments were held in honor ? Would youth be cut down in its flower and springtime if all fathers and mothers had fulfilled the duties laid upon them ? The Holy Spirit answers : *Potens in terra erit semen ejus.* The countries where faith still reigns show us a vigorous race. Place these noble branches of a powerful root beside that other generation which has for its cradle a country where Jesus Christ is a God forgotten or unknown, and you will understand the profundity of these words: The fear of the Lord will give power and strength to the generations.

"Glory and riches shall be in His house : and His justice endureth for ever and ever."

The avowed esteem of the good, the secret esteem of the wicked form a crown around His brow. His acts may be criticised publicly : what chatter, what jests we hear everywhere on the conduct of those who practise their religion ! This is but on the surface ; in reality they are approved, praised, esteemed. God also recompenses the just man in this world. The fear of the Lord has made him sanctify Sundays and the feasts ; the richest blessings will bring abundance into his storehouses and increase his riches. Glory and fortune, that rock of shipwreck to the majority, will not change him ; his virtue, his simplicity remain unalterable : everywhere and always he is the just man.

"Unto the righteous there hath arisen light in the darkness: He is merciful, compassionate, and just."

Life is full of darkness. Doubts, sorrow, and trials shed upon our soul the blackness of night. For the unhappy sinner there is no torch to guide. But the righteous, on the contrary, is surrounded with light; the light of consolation, the light of counsel. This light is God Himself, God compassionate, merciful, and just. Before this triple manifestation of compassion, mercy, and justice, the darkness disappears, like the clouds of night before the rising sun.

"Acceptable is the man who is merciful and lendeth; he will guide his words with judgment: he shall not be moved for ever."

An immense indulgence for all the frailties of poor human nature fills the heart of the righteous. Has a fault been committed, he does not criticise, he does not blame, but he pities his brother. "*He lends*" in so doing, says the prophet-king, for he who judges not shall not be judged; he who condemneth not shall not be condemned; to him who has shown mercy will mercy be shown in large measure.

Wisdom also guides all his words; affable with inferiors, charitable with equals, respectful to superiors, and always, with all, the perfume of kindliness in his speech. Wisdom excludes from his conversation calumny, evil-speaking, and lying. It teaches him to speak and to be silent at the right time. That is why, adds the psalm, he will never be moved and vanquished by the demon. Has not St. James said that "if any man offend not in word, the same is a perfect man"?

"The just man shall be in everlasting remembrance: he shall not be afraid for evil report."

Time effaces everything from the memory of man, everything except virtue. St. John Chrysostom says: "Hear what is necessary to raise a monument which shall perpetuate your name. Is it heaped-up marbles? No. High walls or towers? No. But the examples of good works." (*In Psal.* cxi.) The greatest conquerors are forgotten or unknown to the masses, yet all the Christian family knows the humble virgin of Nanterre or the shepherd of Pibrac. The name of the just man engraved in the memory of mankind is also written in the book of life. At the last day, when the terrible sentence: "Depart from Me, ye cursed," shall throw the reprobate into hell, he will not fear. To him will be said: "Come, thou blessed of My Father, possess the kingdom prepared for thee."

"His heart is prepared to hope in the Lord; his heart is fixed: he shall not be moved until he look down on his enemies."

There are those who, in trial, are always ready to complain, murmur, to despair, to accuse Providence. Christians, these, without faith and without love. Very differently does the just man act. His first glance then is toward heaven, his first thought for God, his first feeling hope. He throws himself entirely into the paternal arms of the divine mercy. This confidence clothes his heart with such strength that he despises his enemies, the devil and his infernal legions.

"He hath dispersed abroad, he hath given to the poor; His justice endureth for ever and ever: His horn shall be exalted in glory."

The confidence of which we have just spoken is not rash; it is the recompense of charity. Priests often see it at the dying bed. The hand which has sown alms clasps the crucifix in ecstasy. In that last hour God pours immense consolations into the charitable heart. Death does not cause it to fear. It knows that the penny given in alms returns a hundred for one; that the sowing of good works, *justice*, to use the language of the prophet, will bring forth eternal fruit. Let us give if we would be enriched, because God assures a double recompense, beginning in this world, to him who relieves the poverty of his brothers: glory, that is to say, the blessings of the unfortunate, then abundance and prosperity in his earthly possessions.

"The sinner shall see it and be wroth; he shall gnash his teeth, and consume away: the desire of the wicked shall perish."

The man who now laughs at your faith and your love will one day be the witness of your triumph. When the Sovereign Judge says: "I was hungry, and you gave Me to eat" (St. Matt. xxv. 35), he will understand too late the worth of charity. Despair will seize his heart; he will tremble and gnash his teeth, as he sees all his vain hopes vanishing. And you in the midst of celestial choirs, you will repeat for the first time in heaven the canticle of eternal praise: Glory be to the Father, and to the Son, and to the Holy Ghost. As it was in the beginning, is now, and ever shall be, world without end. Amen.

5. THE FOURTH PSALM.

This psalm, as well as the following one, was chanted by the newly baptized as they came out of the sacred fonts.

The remembrance of Baptism should have its place in the office of Vespers beside the Eucharist, because the blood and the water which sprang forth under the iron of the soldier's lance figured these two sacraments, according to the unanimous opinion of the doctors of the Church. At the urgent invitation of the Church let us thank God for the grace of Baptism, so ill appreciated; let us also renew our resolution to serve better a God so powerful.

"Praise the Lord, ye children: praise ye the name of the Lord."

All you who, by such a touching favor, have in holy Baptism become the children of God, praise the Lord. The greatness of such a blessing, refused to so many others, calls for all your gratitude. Praise His holy name, which is nothing else than power, wisdom, His bounty shown in this sacrament.

"Blessed be the name of the Lord: from this time forth for evermore."

When the brow is still wet with the waters of Baptism, when the heart still beats with the unspeakable emotions of holy communion, the lips of the child can only bless. Soon he will hear blasphemies against God, murmurs against Providence. "Take care," the Church anxiously warns him. "In youth, in middle age, in old age, in prosperity, as in trial, bless always the name of the Lord. Never insult the God of your Baptism and of your first communion." At this verse the heads are bowed. By this humble position, and still more by the ardor of your love, repair all the blasphemies which earth vomits forth against heaven.

"From the rising of the sun unto the going down of the same: the name of the Lord is worthy to be praised."

Respect this divine name, whose grandeur everything proclaims. Look around you: from the dawn to the sunset, from the east to the west, from springtime to winter, everything chants the praises of God. Deaf and thrice deaf he who does not hear this great concert of nature; blind and thrice blind he who does not see the name of God written on all the works of creation. The star or the insect, the oak or the blade of grass, the drop of dew or the immensity of the ocean, the grain of wheat or the bunch of grapes, as well as the angels and mankind, chant the power, the wisdom, the goodness of the Creator: "*A solis ortu usque ad occasum laudabile nomen Domini.*"

"The Lord is high above all nations: and His glory above the heavens."

The greatest enemy of the Christian, that which causes most desertion from the army of the soldiers of Jesus Christ, is human respect. Would the promises of Baptism be so soon forgotten if we were penetrated with the grandeur of God and the nothingness of man? Let us take for our device and war-cry this verse of the psalm: "The Lord is high above the nations, and His glory above the heavens." The nations and the princes who command them, the thrones and the armies that sustain them, the opportunities and honors which they afford, all the most ambitious grandeurs of the earth, before the Lord are as a grain of dust raised by the wind, or the drop of water which falls from an over-full vase. These expressions are those of the Holy Scriptures. The prophet, to make them stronger, adds: "that all nations are as nothing before the Lord." (Is. xl. 15-17.) Who then to please man would dare despise the Lord? That we may have an idea of His glory we are told that it is above the heavens. To proclaim that the Lord has made His tent of the pavilion of the heavens, His throne of the sun, His mantle of the light; to say that the lightning is a ray of His glory, the thunder the accents of His voice, the empurpled clouds His triumphal chariot, are so many rude images by means of which the Christian loves to represent to himself the glory of God. The Lord is infinitely above the splendors which fall within the cognizance of our senses or which our imagination can invent. "*Et super cœlos gloria ejus.*"

"Who is like to the Lord our God, Who dwelleth on high: and regardeth the things that are lowly in heaven and earth?"

This was the cry which rallied the angels under the banner of Saint Michael: Who is like unto God? This thought alone should preserve us always faithful. Who is good like God? Who is beautiful as God? Who is great as God? Who is powerful as God? Who is wise like God? Who is faithful like God? In the moment of temptation let us ask our heart this question; it will assuredly turn to the side of the Sovereign Good.

The prophet-king, in this same verse, speaks of the

divine Providence. Nothing escapes the direct action of God; He provides for all. Neither a bird of the air nor a hair of our head can fall to the ground without His permission. Incredulous philosophy repeats unceasingly: We are too little for God to occupy Himself with us. If these philosophers would come to Vespers, they would hear the Word of the Holy Ghost: "The Lord Who dwelleth on high regardeth the things that are lowly in heaven and on earth."

"Who raiseth up the needy from the earth: and lifteth the poor from off the dunghill."

Behold, all that God has done for humanity in the Incarnation He continues for each one of us in holy Baptism. We have been this needy one in the dust, this sinner in the mire: figurative expressions which depict to what degree of humiliation and degradation original sin has reduced man. God takes him by the hand and raises him up.

"That He may set him with the princes: even with the princes of the people."

The Christian is called to reign with the angels, the princes of the heavenly court. His throne is ready; each good work is a new diamond added to his crown. But the conquest of this eternal kingdom suffers violence; the renunciation of ourselves and of creatures is the victorious sword which will open to us the gates. The sign of our royalty has been imprinted on our brow by the Church; holy Baptism is only the consecration of the Christian.

"Who maketh the barren woman to dwell in her house: the joyful mother of children."

The Church is this barren woman. Everything seemed to condemn her never to know the joys of maternity.

MISSIONARY'S COMPANION.

Containing all that is necessary for Baptisms and Sick Calls.

SACRISTY BELL.

ALTAR BELL.

CHIMES.

GONG.

Her divine Founder has established her in virginity and martyrdom. And behold the world has seen, astonished, "this infant republic multiply herself by chastity and death, though these are sterile means and contrary to the design of increase." (Balzac, *Socrate Chrétien.*)

6. THE FIFTH PSALM.

The grandeur of its images, the richness of its poetry, the depth of its prophecies make this psalm the most beautiful chant of the old law. David therein celebrates the deliverance of the Hebrew people on the day after the Passover, the passage of the Red Sea, the tremblings of Sinai, the miracles of the desert. The lips that celebrated the miracles worked in favor of the ancient people prophesied at the same time, says St. Augustine, the marvels which should shine on the steps of the new nations. We will look at this sublime psalm on its prophetic side. It will appear to us as really a history of the Church, her combats, her triumphs, and the blessings showered upon her.

The Hebrew ritual prescribed that this psalm should be recited during the celebration of the Pasch, and several authors have thought that this was the psalm which Our Lord said after the last supper. (Baronius, *Ann.* 34.) This consideration can but increase our fervor.

"When Israel came out of Egypt: the house of Jacob from among a strange people."

Israel and the house of Jacob figure the Church and the Christian people ; Egypt, the servitude of the demon from which Baptism has freed us, and also the world fallen into the power of the infernal despot. The unfortunate people over which he reigns speak a language of which we should be ignorant. Lying, evil-speaking, olasphemy, and impurity are its principal elements. May the language of the world be to us always foreign and unknown !

"Juda was made His sanctuary: and Israel His dominion."

Under these two names, of which the first means the *praise of God*, and the second *strength of God*, the prophet designates the children of the true Juda, the family of the divine Israel. The Church has become the only sanctuary where God is worthily praised, as well as the scene where He manifests His power. The expression which the Royal Prophet uses says much more. The Church has been chosen as the instrument of sanctification upon the earth. It is the divine salt which preserves from corruption, according to the words of Jesus Christ; without her the abominations of Sodom and Ninive would have been surpassed long ago. The impetuous torrent of vice, in its lamentable overflow, has always encountered a breakwater against which its waves have dashed in vain: the sanctity preached and practised by the Church. If the body social, all covered with leprosy and infected with contagion as it is, subsists still, thanks are due to the spouse of Christ; her divine life repels death. Those who will not see this miracle, so evident and constantly renewed, cannot help recognizing the fact that God has wrought by the Church and in favor of the Church His greatest marvels; the power He has chosen "for His dominion," says the sacred text. Without pretending to enumerate all that the Lord has done for His spouse, let us recall briefly that she has felt all the swords of persecution crossed on her breast; that she has been the butt of the hatred of princes and of nations, that twenty times events seemed to have dug her grave. Constantly attacked, she has always been victorious. Thrones have crumbled, dynasties have disappeared, crowns have fallen, nations have been wiped out, and the Church is always standing, because she is the throne of the power of the Lord : " *Israel potestas ejus.*"

"The sea beheld, and fled : Jordan was turned back."

The world is often compared to the sea, because of its depths and its storms. It has wished to oppose the mission of the Church, raising against her the waves of evil passions. During four centuries the blood of martyrs reddened its waters. The spectacle presented to it bore so unmistakably the seal of sanctity and of might that it has opened a passage to the holy one it persecuted. Its waves were, so to speak, turned back by admiration and awe. "*Mare vidit et fugit.*" This is not all. Mankind, relinquishing itself to the course of its passions, descended toward the abyss, like the river whose waves throw themselves into the ocean. The Church has renewed for it the miracle of the holy ark on the shore of the Jordan. They have returned to their source, that is to say, to God. This beautiful thought is St. Augustine's. (*In Psal.* cxiii.)

"The mountains skipped like rams : and the little hills like lambs of the flock."

The conversion of the pagan world has filled the entire Church with joy. To express it David uses a figure as bold as sublime. " The mountains skipped like rams, and the little hills like lambs of the flock." But what are these mountains ?. What are the little hills ? By the former St. Augustine understands the apostles and all the preachers of the Gospel, raised by their ministry to sanctity and to heights which the eye could not measure; by the latter, the faithful whom the word of the Gospel has begotten to the Church ; the name of Christian demands that they should raise themselves above the majority by a higher life. (*In Ps.* cxiii.)

"What aileth thee, O thou sea, that thou fleest, and thou Jordan, that thou wast turned back ? Ye mountains, that ye skipped like rams : and ye little hills like the lambs of the flock ?"

The prophet, as the witness of all these prodigies, demands their cause : sea, Jordan, mountains, hills, answer me.

"At the presence of the Lord the earth was moved, at the presence of the God of Jacob."

The Lord has shown Himself to the earth : He has perpetuated His presence in the midst of His children by the institution of the adorable Sacrament of the Eucharist. Alone and forgotten in His tabernacle, He governs from it the earth ; He *moves* it. The explanation of the sanctity and power of the Church is found in this promise : " I am with you always, even to the consummation of the world." (St. Matt. xxviii. 20.)

"Who turned the rock into a standing water : and the stony hill into a flowing stream."

The rock was the figure of Jesus Christ, says St. Paul ; the rod of Moses is the lance of the soldier, and the water bursting abundantly from the opening represents the torrents of grace flowing from the pierced side of Jesus Christ. Our Lord calls us to these divine springs: "If any man thirst, let him come to Me, and drink." (St. John vii. 37.) Let us hasten; each one of His wounds has become a life-giving fountain. St. Bernard says that "the earthly paradise had four rivers whose waters flowed in all directions, bringing freshness and fruitfulness. And in Jesus Christ, our paradise of delights, we find four springs: the first is the source of truth; the second, the source of wisdom; the third, the source of virtue; the fourth, the source of charity. Let us add to these another, the fifth, the source of life, promised to man after the trials of exile, and toward which the prophet sighed when he said: My soul thirsts for God, fountain of living water. It was, perhaps, to open these first four sources that Our Lord was wounded in four places before breathing His last sigh; to figure the fifth, after His death His side was opened by a lance." (*Serm. i. de Nativ., Serm.* lxvi.) May he who thirsts for truth, wisdom, virtue, charity, and life, come to quench his longing at the divine spring, at the feet of Jesus crucified!

"Not unto us, O Lord, not unto us: but unto Thy name give the glory."

Our deliverance from slavery, the wonders of sanctity and power wrought by the Church, the conversion of infidels, all the testimonies to the divine goodness should not puff us up with pride. To God, to God only, be the honor and glory; to us humiliation, for how many would serve the Lord better than we if they had been called to the faith! Bowing our heads, let us pay homage to God for all our works, all our goods, all our honors, all our talents. The glory which they have procured for us goes back to God as to its source **and** end.

"For Thy mercy and Thy truth's sake : lest the **gen**tiles should say : Where is their God ?"

It would seem that the nations, enlightened by the events of history, should recognize the divine intervention in the government of the Church. But this is not so. Whenever a tempest assails her, if the arm of God is slow to be displayed, the Christian hears repeated the old blasphemy of impiety : Where then is your God Who has promised to be the pilot of this worm-eaten ship which you call the Church? He is deaf to your prayers, or powerless to help you. Let them rave ; our hope is unalterably fixed upon a God *full of mercy and faithful to His promises*. He would interfere sooner did not mercy claim her right ; His patience gives the persecutors time to repent. Justice will have its hour ; then the world once more will see the accomplishment of the promise that never fails : "The gates of hell shall not prevail against the Church."

"But our God is in heaven : He hath done whatsoever He would."

What man can say to himself that nothing resists his will, that he has done whatsoever he would? Some can, but will not ; others would, but cannot. God alone has an infinite power at the service of a will entirely merciful. Why do you fear, ye men of little faith ? Our God is the God of heaven ; all that He willed has been faithfully performed ; it will be so for ever.

"The idols of the gentiles are silver and gold : the work of the hands of men. They have mouths, and they shall not speak ; they have eyes, and they shall not see. They have ears, and they shall not hear; they have noses, and they shall not smell. They have hands, and they shall not feel; they have feet, and they shall not walk; neither shall they speak through their throat. Let all who make them become like unto them: and all such as put their trust in them."

In these verses the prophet shows to Christians the folly of the pagan worship of idols made by man of gold or silver. They have ears, and do not hear the prayers addressed to them. Why then the incense burned on their altars, the flowers and the garlands? They cannot smell their perfumes. Their hands are never extended in blessing. You never see them come to your help, for, though they have feet, they rest immovable on their pedestals. Dumb gods, they never give you a word of consolation or hope. These are the gods which the world worshipped for centuries, and we should still offer them incense if God had not taken us away from idolatry: "*In exitu Israel de Egypto.*"

"The house of Israel hath hoped in the Lord: He is their helper and protector.

"The house of Aaron hath hoped in the Lord: He is their helper and protector. Those who fear the Lord have hoped in the Lord: He is their helper and protector."

The house of Israel, as we already know, is the Christian people; the house of Aaron, the high-priest of the old law, represents the Catholic priesthood. Ask of history, and it will tell you that the divine protection has never failed it.

By those who fear the Lord, and who have put their confidence in Him, we may understand all mankind who, outside of the Church, serve God with filial fear. Their confidence will never be deceived ; the way of the Lord will never fail them. One day or another, the light of truth will shine forth to enlighten them.

"The Lord hath been mindful of us: and hath blessed us.

"He hath blessed the house of Israel: He hath blessed the house of Aaron.

"He hath blessed all those that fear the Lord: the least together with the greatest."

The Lord remembers all. There is but one thing which He forgets, according to the Holy Book, and this is pardoned sin. He remembers our confidence, to bless us. Age, dignity, power, cleverness count as nothing; great and small are equal before Him. If His heart feel a preference, it is for those whom the prophet mentions first.

"May the Lord add blessings upon you: upon you and upon your children."

And as for you, the Church seems to say, who have come into the holy place to praise and bless, be you blessed. May the Lord add new blessings to those which He has already given you; may He fill your measure and that of your children.

"Blessed be ye of the Lord: Who hath made heaven and earth."

St. John Chrysostom says that "man blesses when he praises and exalts those who distinguish themselves by riches, glory, and power. These are ephemeral blessings which add nothing to what we possess. It is not so with the blessings of the Lord." (*In Ps.* cxiii.) His power has made heaven and earth ; may His goodness pour upon your fields the dew of one and the fatness of

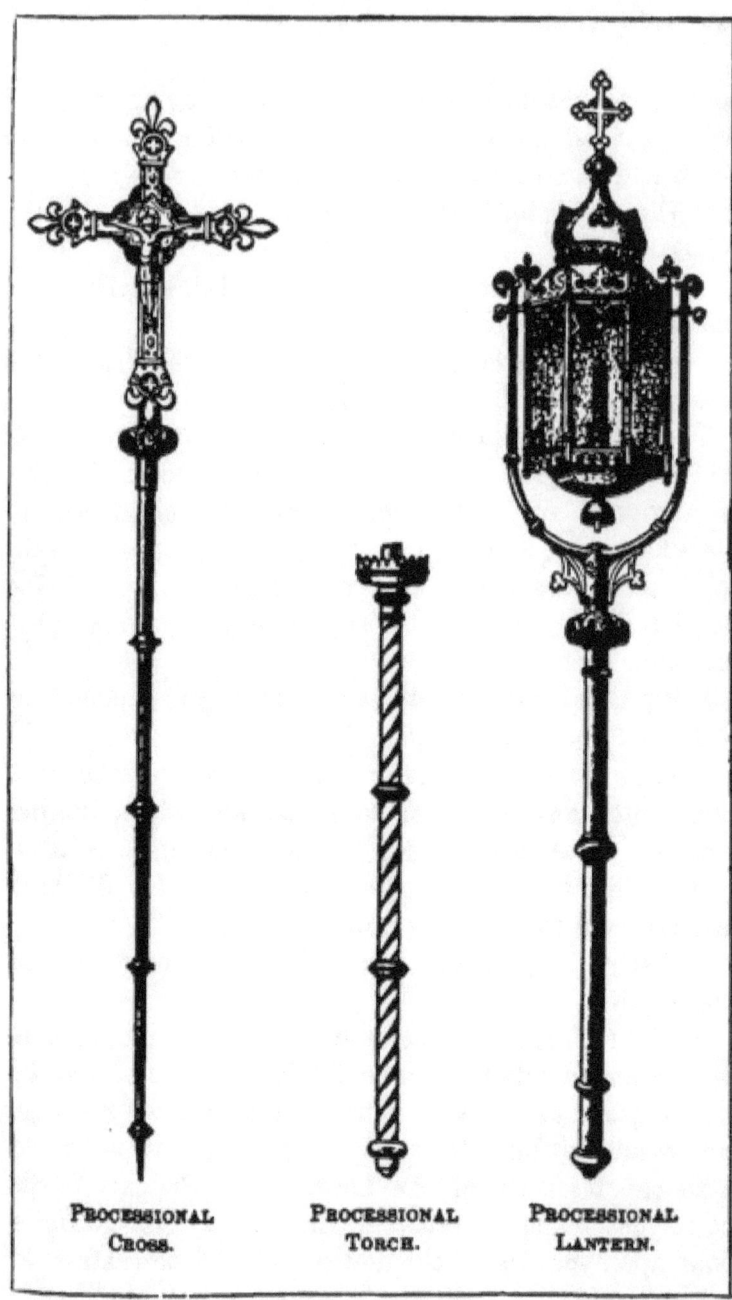

Processional Cross. Processional Torch. Processional Lantern.

the other; may He give you the blessings of time and of eternity!

"The heaven of heavens is the Lord's: but the earth hath He given to the children of men."

Infinity is the dwelling-place of the Lord. When we say that He dwells in the highest heaven, it is only to make it understood that He there manifests His glory to His elect. He has given over to man the earth and all the riches which it holds.

"The dead shall not praise Thee, O Lord: neither all they that go down into hell."

At the thought of Thy love, Thy greatness, O Lord, we make the resolution to remain always Thy children, for those that are dead to grace can no longer love Thee nor praise Thee. They are like those unhappy souls who are plunged into the eternal abyss.

"But we who live bless the Lord: from this time forth for evermore."

Let us always live in the love of God, in His holy grace, and we shall delight to sing His praises. The divine office will bring us regularly each Sunday to the foot of the altar, to thank the Lord for His numberless blessings, while we await the happy day which shall open to us the gates of the eternal temple, where the light is without night, happiness without alloy, and praise shall never end.

7. THE LITTLE CHAPTER.

The chanting of the psalms is followed by the recitation of the Little Chapter. This short extract from the Holy Book is thus named from the Latin word *caput*, head, because, on the feasts, it is usually taken from the beginning of the epistle of the day, and is read by the celebrant. We see that among the Jews and the early Christians each reunion was accompanied by the reading of the sacred books. The assembly listens in silence and standing, out of respect for him who presides; if the leader, our head, rises to read the Holy Scriptures, should not the faithful rise also to listen to it?

The Chapter ended, all respond, *Deo Gratias*, as we say grace after our repasts.

CHAPTER IV.—HYMN, MAGNIFICAT, AND ANTHEMS OF THE BLESSED VIRGIN.

1. THE HYMN.

DURING the night the followers of the impious Arius ran through the streets of Constantinople singing hymns which breathed forth their pernicious doctrines. The Christians were exposed to meeting them and hearing them. To fortify their faith by orthodox chants, St. John Chrysostom, who then occupied the see of that illustrious Church, added to the divine office certain hymns. Their origin in the West goes back to the pontificate of St. Ambrose. During the persecution stirred up by the Empress Justina, mother of Valerian and a furious Arian, the great prelate was in a sense besieged in his church with all his people.

To conquer sleep and weariness, Ambrose composed hymns which were sung with the psalms. This singing, which delighted the faithful, remained in the divine office. Other churches, filled with holy jealousy, imitated that of Milan, and, in remembrance of Ambrose, the hymns were called Ambrosian. The doxology—for so the last strophe which ends the hymns is called—is the chant of victory over the ruins of Arianism; it is also an honorable reparation offered by the Church to the Blessed Trinity, and to Our Lord Jesus Christ above all, so infamously outraged by the Arians.

We cannot enter into an explanation of the hymns of Vespers; they vary according to the feasts. We will content ourselves with saying a word of that of Sunday. The light was created on the first day, which is Sunday. On the same day there burst from the tomb that divine Light which enlightens the spiritual world of intelligences, and has become the sun of the heavenly Jerusalem. The hymn celebrates these two great memories. As we thank God for this double blessing, let us sigh for the day when it will be given to us to contemplate the radiant clearness of the eternal light.

2. THE MAGNIFICAT.

The hymn finished, the voice of a child makes itself heard, and all the assembly turns toward the altar. This chant, short and piercing like a cry, bears the name of versicle, that is to say, *return*. The Church has placed it before the canticles and the prayers of the office, to bring us back to meditation so that if our mind has up to this time been wandering in outside affairs, now at least it may return to God to praise Him with Mary and by Mary.

Magnificat Sung Each Day.—The Incarnation is the gift of God above all others; St. Paul calls it "the great mystery of godliness." (I. Tim. iii. 16.) Gratitude without limit should respond to infinite mercy. But how shall we praise worthily the humiliations and tenderness of a God made flesh? Even the language of angels would be but stammering. What has the Church done? She repeats each day the canticle of the Blessed Virgin, that sublime chant in which the august Mother of God offers, in the name of humanity, the homage of her adoration and gratitude. The *Magnificat*, the canticle of the Incarnation, recalls to us each day that God has stripped Himself of His glory to clothe Himself in the livery of poor and suffering humanity.

God is made flesh: this thought alone ravished into ecstasy the holy Magdalen and many saints. Let it at least arouse in our hearts some feeling of love for a God " Who has so loved the world that He has delivered His only-begotten Son."

Why is this canticle said in the evening? Why at Vespers rather than at Compline? We have already seen that it was the evening of the world when Jesus Christ came among us, that then paganism had spread everywhere, in minds and hearts, the shadows of its darkness. It was also the sixth age of the world. For this reason the *Magnificat* is sung at Vespers, the sixth canonical hour of the divine office.

Ceremonies of the Magnificat.—During this canticle, taken from the Gospel, the clergy and people stand, out of respect for the sacred word. As at Mass before the reading of the Gospel, the sign of the cross is made at the first words of Mary's canticle. Then the celebrant, leaving his place, goes to the altar, kisses and incenses it. The Introit of the Mass has already given us occasion to study the meaning of these two ceremonies. At the *Magnificat* they have the same signification. " Let Him kiss me with a kiss of His mouth " (Cant. i. 1) was the cry of humanity while it awaited the coming of the Messias. The priest, representing Jesus Christ, by the kiss which he gives the altar, on the spot where the bones of the saints are laid, announces to the world that its prayers have been heard; the Word Incarnate has given us the kiss of love and reconciliation. (*Spicil. de Solesmes*, t. iii. ch. 29.) The earth, thrice blessed at this hour, has sent up, even to the throne of God, the perfume of an acceptable prayer. God was praised and glorified by a God. The odor of the incense poured out upon the altar and in all the holy place, again can recall to us the graces given to the holy humanity of Jesus Christ, and from Him, as from their source, shed upon the world. We should not forget the august Mother of God. This incensing is a symbol of the perfumes with which her virtues filled Elizabeth's house at Hebron. And the priest, leaving his place and mounting the steps of the altar, should remind us of Mary, who, says the Gospel, "rising up in those days, went into the hill country with haste, into a city of Juda" (St. Luke i. 39).

Explanation of the Magnificat.—"My soul doth magnify the Lord." Never has purer praise mounted to God. All creatures praise the Lord; none can do so as Mary did. What soul is like to hers?—full of grace, immaculate, more shining than the sun by the splendor of her virtues. She alone could say: My soul doth magnify the Lord. She alone is without sin and without the least stain. Since the pure soul is a harmonious canticle, celestial praise, let us live in such a manner as to be able to say each Sunday: "*Magnificat anima mea Dominum.*"

"And my spirit hath rejoiced in God my Saviour."

Mary well understood the grandeur of the mystery wrought in her. Her soul was so filled with God that it longed to break the bonds of its earthly tabernacle to be united more closely with Him. The blissful emotion that Mary felt when the Word descended into her breast would have killed her a thousand times over had not a miracle preserved her life. What a cause of humiliation for us! The same God comes into our heart, and it hardly beats more rapidly. We know nothing of those joys which inundate the souls of the saints. Tepidity, distaste, weariness, these are most frequently our feelings while Jesus Christ dwells in us. O Mary, give us a little of thy love for Jesus, that our souls may always rejoice in God our Saviour.

"For He hath regarded the humility of His handmaid: for behold from henceforth all generations shall call me blessed."

God seems to regard and take pleasure only in humility, a virtue so powerful as to call down the Son of the Eternal God into the bosom of a virgin. How profound it was in Mary! Let us admire the terms in which she speaks of the sublime dignity to which she was elevated. "The Lord hath regarded the humility of His handmaid." What a beautiful model, unhappily little followed! "Without speaking of worldly persons, we often hear those that are pious talking complacently of the graces which they have received." When they are exposed to the breath of flattery and praise, these graces are scattered like the dust. "He who humbleth himself shall be exalted." The humble Virgin, who calls herself the Lord's handmaid, shall hear all generations proclaim her grandeur. The first name lisped by the child shall be thine, O Mary; later it will console the agony of the dying. Everywhere temples will arise in thy honor, associations under thy patronage. All ages, all conditions will crowd around thy altars. Each generation bending the knee will proclaim thee blessed.

"For He that is mighty hath done great things unto me: and holy is His name."

The dignity to which the title of Mother of God has raised Mary merits the praises and gratitude of all the centuries.

St. Thomas says that "God could, if He would, have made more perfect works except the Incarnation, the divine maternity, and the beatitude of man, which consists in the vision of God. His power could make nothing better, nothing greater, because there could be nothing better and greater than God Himself." (P. i. quæst. 25, art. 6.)

In the harmony of praise which the generations send toward Mary's throne heresy mingled its blasphemies against the adorable mystery of a Virgin-Mother. Nothing shall shake our faith. He Who has wrought these marvels is almighty and thrice holy: "*Qui potens est et sanctum nomen ejus.*"

"And His mercy is from generation to generation unto them that fear Him."

Mary has just said, "the Lord has done great things unto me"; but the divine mercy, which has deigned to stoop even to me, will overflow, throughout the ages, upon those who fear God. Humanity is the Lord's great family; all its members will have part in His mercy.

The earth henceforth will be His kingdom. "Let him not despair, then," says St. Bernard, "he who fears the judgment of God because of his sins; mercy is for those who fear the Lord."

"He hath shown strength with His arm: He hath scattered the proud in the imagination of their hearts."

The greatest work of God, that in which He put forth, so to speak, all His power, is, as we have said, the Incarnation. When the mystery of the Word made flesh was revealed to the love of the angels, and the proud spirits refused it their homage, God dispersed their rebel hosts, and hurled them into the abyss. His chosen people, the Jews, being vain and haughty, did not recognize in Jesus Christ, poor and humiliated, the redeeming Messias promised to their fathers; the breath of God dispersed them to the four points of the compass. No longer do they form a people, a race, or a nation. This is the dispersion of the Jews prophesied by Mary: "*Dispersit.*"

"He hath put down the mighty from their seat, and hath exalted the humble."

The demons, fallen angels, were the princes of this world before the coming of Jesus Christ; on the altars of the false divinities they had really their throne. Before the Child in the crib their temples crumbled, and the power of Satan was destroyed.

The Jews are also dethroned princes. Sons of the kingdom, elect of God, they merited, by their treachery, seeing the gentiles substituted for them. The latter, in the person of the centurion and the woman of Chanaan, threw themselves humbly at the feet of Our Lord, and Jesus Christ, filled with admiration, cried out: "Amen I say to you, I have not found so great faith in Israel. And I say to you that many shall come from the east

PAX.
Small plate in some countries carried round at Mass to communicate the Kiss of Peace.

MISSAL.

MISSAL MARKS.

MISSAL STAND.

MISSAL STAND COVER.

and the west, and shall sit down with Abraham, Isaac, and Jacob in the kingdom of heaven. But the children of the kingdom shall be cast out into the exterior darkness." (St. Matt. viii. 10, 11.) Thus is accomplished the prophecy: "He hath put down the mighty from their seat, and hath exalted the humble."

"He hath filled the hungry with good things: and the rich He hath sent empty away."

This verse is the continuation of the preceding one; it still alludes to the Jews and gentiles. "The whelps," said the woman of Chanaan, "also eat of the crumbs that fall from their master's table." She represented the gentile people, hungry and supplicating for the good things of heaven. The favors of God were showered upon them in abundance, while the Jews, until then filled with the gifts of heaven, were banished from before the face of the Lord.

"He hath upholden His servant Israel: being mindful of His mercy."

How was it that a people so unfaithful were chosen by the Lord? Why had the Messias willed to be born of this race which He was about to curse? Because He remembered His merciful promises.

"As He spake unto our fathers: to Abraham and his seed for ever."

God had promised a saviour to Adam, to Abraham, to Jacob, and to David.

God is faithful to His word; the malice of man could not prevent Him from fulfilling it. The second part of the verse assures us that the mercy which the Lord remembered in His Incarnation should always rest with the posterity of Abraham. the father of the believing.

The true race of Abraham is the Christian people. God has chosen it for the child of His love. How have we responded to the goodness of the Lord in our own case? By ingratitude when it was not by revolt.

Listen and see what passes on the earth; you will feel a thrill of horror. Why does not Heaven send upon so many crimes a new deluge or another rain of fire? It is the reign of mercy, which pardons always: *Abraham et semini ejus in sæcula.*

The Prayer.—The anthem of the *Magnificat* ended, the priest says, "Let us pray," and the assembly turns toward the altar, that is, toward the east, and prays, still standing. These two circumstances it is important to explain. From the beginning of Christianity the churches have been so constructed that the priest and people turn toward the altar, looking to the east, for prayer; a liturgical arrangement to which Christian art has always conformed when circumstances permitted, and which is called *orientation.* The east was the cradle of the human race; the terrestrial paradise was placed on that side, according to the testimony of Genesis. (Cornel. *in Gen.* ii. 8.)

Man was expelled thence after his disobedience. On this distant shore what can the poor exile do? He loves to turn his eyes toward that point where lay all that was dearest to his heart: his land, his family. Under the influence of this sentiment so natural to man, the Church has caused us to look in the direction of that earthly home whence all the children of Adam were banished.

But this gaze, while it wakens our regrets, ought also to call forth hope. By the side of the gate of Eden, guarded by the flaming sword of the seraph, Jesus Christ has opened another door which leads to heaven: "Sing to God, ye kingdoms of the earth," cries the Prophet. "Sing ye to God, Who mounteth above the heaven of heavens to the east." (Ps. lxvi.)

As we turn toward this point of the horizon we sigh after our future home. (St. Thom., II. 2. quæst. 84, art. 3.) We seem to say with David: "As the hart panteth after the fountains of waters, so doth my soul pant after Thee, O God." The east, the witness of the happy days of man's innocence and the glories of the Ascension of the Saviour, will see the same Jesus descend on the clouds of heaven, surrounded by angels, and become the Judge of the living and the dead.

"His feet," says the prophet Zacharias, "shall stand in that day upon the mount of Olives, which is over against Jerusalem toward the east." (Zach. xli. 2.) By this practice of her liturgy the Church warns us to be like the faithful and vigilant servant, who, never to be surprised, waits each hour the return of his master. The earthly paradise, the inheritance of heaven, the last judgment: what tremendous memories for the pious and recollected heart!

The Christian congregation, turned toward the east, remains standing during the prayer. This custom is very ancient in the Church.

From the beginning she prescribed that the prayers of Sundays and during Paschal time should be said standing, in token of joy, and kneeling for all the rest of the year as a sign of mourning. A passage of St. Jerome's shows the antiquity of this practice. "St. Paul," he says, "remained at Ephesus till Pentecost, the time of joy and victory, when we bend not the knee, neither bow ourselves toward the earth, but when, arisen with Our Lord, we raise ourselves toward heaven." (*Comment. Epist. ad. Eph.*) For the same reason the *Angelus* or, during the Paschal time, the *Regina Cœli*, is on Sundays said standing.

The *Dominus Vobiscum*, contrary to the custom in the Mass, not only precedes but follows the prayer. Here is another reminder of the resurrection of Our Lord. When He appeared on Easter Sunday evening to His apostles, He saluted them with these words : *Pax vobis*; and the gospels tell us that He repeated the words on leaving them. (Hugh of St. Victor ; *Rational.*)

Benedicamus Domino.—Many graces have been given us during the office which is just ending, and, especially in the prayer made by the minister of God in the name of all. "Let us bless the Lord," the Church sings by the voice of a child; for from children, the Prophet says, God receives the most perfect praise. To praise the Lord worthily, let us become like children in innocence and simplicity. Some writers believe that these words are sung by a child in remembrance of the canticle of the three children in the fiery furnace, to whom they have been attributed. May our hearts, more than our lips, repeat the chant of gratitude : *Deo gratias !* Yes, let us thank God, Who has permitted us to speak in His temple the language of angels !

Thanks be to a God dead for us upon the cross, that adorable mystery the memory of which we have just been celebrating ! Thanks be to God, Who has given us what His minister has asked for us in his last prayer ! Yes, let us repeat : For ever, thanks be to God ! *Deo gratias!*

The Commemoration of the Dead.—As members of the Church militant, we have just associated ourselves with the canticles and the joy of the Church in heaven; before we separate, let us unite ourselves to the sorrows of our brethren of the Church suffering. At this moment let the thought of the violence of their anguish and the sweetness of the ties which unite us to them be present in our minds. There are a father, a mother, children, brothers, sisters, and friends. Let us offer to God for them all the merits which we may have gained during the office of Vespers. This last prayer will then fall on these poor souls like a merciful dew: "*Fidelium animæ, misericordiam Dei requiescant in pace*"—"May the souls of the faithful departed, through the mercy of God, rest in peace."

3. THE ANTHEMS OF THE BLESSED VIRGIN.

These are four in number: the *Alma Redemptoris Mater*, the *Ave Regina Cœlorum*, the *Regina Cœli*, and the *Salve Regina*.

The Alma Redemptoris.—This anthem is commonly attributed to Herman Contractus, a Benedictine monk, in the monastery of St. Gall. He was always remarkable for a tender piety toward the Blessed Virgin. His death occurred toward the year 1054. The *Alma Redemptoris* is sung from Advent to the Purification.

The Ave Regina Cœlorum.—Tradition says that the apostles reunited around the dying bed of the Blessed Virgin, singing the praises of her who was so soon to become their glorious queen: "Hail, Queen of heaven," they said. "Hail, mistress of angels; hail, thou who hast borne the Light of the world. Rejoice, glorious

Virgin, most glorious of all God's creatures. Farewell, and pray for us."

This was, according to certain authors, the origin of the *Ave Regina Cœlorum*. It is sung from the Purification to Holy Thursday.

The Regina Cœli.—Under the pontificate of Saint Gregory the Great, the city of Rome was decimated by a frightful plague. In order to appease the anger of God, the holy Pontiff ordered a solemn procession on Easter Day, in which the picture of the Blessed Virgin, said to have been painted by St. Luke, was carried with pomp and ceremony.

His confidence was not deceived. Heavenly voices were heard in the air which sang: "Joy to thee, O Queen of heaven, alleluia; for He Whom thou wast meet to bear, alleluia; as He promised hath arisen, alleluia." And the Pope, joining with the angels, cried out: "Pour for us to Him thy prayer, alleluia."

At that instant was seen, on the castle of Adrian, an angel who dried a sword wet with blood, and sheathed it. The plague had not another victim. This anthem is sung from Holy Saturday to Trinity Sunday.

The Salve Regina.—Nothing certain is known of the author of this anthem. It is commonly attributed to Adhemar of Monteil, bishop of Puy and member of the Council of Clermont, where the first crusade was resolved upon. Subsequently he took the cross, and composed for the crusaders the *Salve Regina*. This chant ended with the words: "And after this our exile show unto us the blessed fruit of thy womb, Jesus." The last words were added by St. Bernard. Sent as legate to Germany, he assisted one day in the divine office at Spire. Suddenly, under an inspiration, he added, genuflecting three times: "O clement, O pious, O sweet Virgin Mary"—words which were carved in the marble of the basilica, on the site where St. Bernard had uttered them.

According to several historians, the holy abbot of Clairvaux had learned these three invocations of the *Salve Regina* from the angels themselves. We will let them tell the story.

"One night the saint was awakened by the sound of celestial voices, which sang in the church of the monastery the praises of God and of the Virgin Mary. He arose quickly, and hastened secretly into the church to see more closely the marvellous things which were happening there. He beheld the Blessed Virgin between two angels, who held in their hands a golded censer and incense. One of them, taking St. Bernard by the hand, led him to the altar, at the right of the Blessed Virgin. There he heard the angels singing the *Salve Regina* complete, as we have it now."

During the chanting of these anthems let us represent to ourselves Mary on the night of the crucifixion, consoled by angels and the apostles. May our praises and prayers also rejoice her maternal heart!

CHAPTER V.—COMPLINE, AND THE BENEDICTION OF THE BLESSED SACRAMENT.

1. COMPLINE.

IT sometimes happens that the faithful assist at Compline. To satisfy their piety, we will here give an explanation of it.

Compline honors the burial of Our Saviour. We recite

this office close to the sacred tomb. Our heart will find there the Blessed Virgin, St. John, Magdalen, and the holy women.

The Lesson.—The religious of St. Benedict gathered after Vespers to hear reading from the Holy Scriptures and to recite certain psalms; then they went to their rest. This was the origin of Compline. The Church soon introduced these prayers into her liturgy. The lesson which begins this office recalls the ancient reading of the Scriptures by the monks.

The Confiteor.—Compline, the last office of the day, said at the sepulchre of Jesus Christ, naturally brings to the mind the wholesome thought of death. In a few moments slumber will close our eyes, an image of that other sleep which soon also will close them and for ever. It seems very wise in the Church to precede this office by the recitation of the *Confiteor*, and to end it with the *Credo*, so that if it should be that we should pass from the arms of sleep into those of death, we might die in faith and repentance. It is good to say the *Confiteor* then with sentiments of the keenest sorrow, as if about to appear before the Sovereign Judge.

The Psalms.—By their number the psalms of Compline recall the four last things. The words of the first psalm are perfectly suitable to the burial of Jesus Christ; the Church says them on Holy Saturday. Already we see in them the light of the resurrection.

"When I called upon Him, the God of my justice heard me: when I was in distress, Thou didst enlarge me."

The second psalm is composed of the first six verses of the thirtieth psalm, said on the cross by the dying

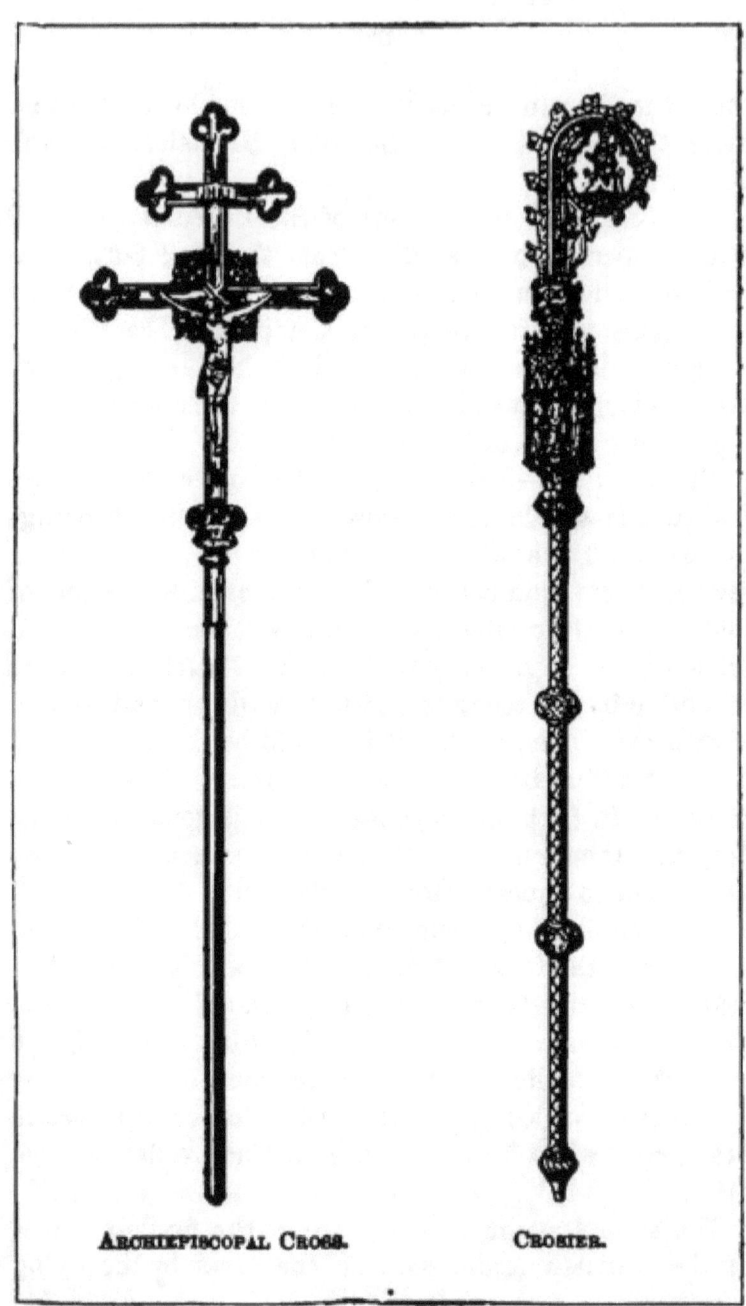

ARCHIEPISCOPAL CROSS. CROSIER.

Christ. The Church has made it the prayer of the Saviour in the tomb.

At the end of the day, the last it may be of our life, from the tomb in which sin has laid us, let us unite ourselves to Our Lord, and say with Him: "In Thee, O Lord, have I hoped, let me never be confounded: deliver me in Thy justice."

The third psalm shows the reason for this confidence of the Just One in the midst of the darkness of the tomb, and for that of the just man in the darkness of the night: "He that dwelleth in the help of the Most High, shall abide in the protection of the God of heaven. He shall say unto the Lord: Thou art my upholder and my refuge: my God, in Him will I trust."

We have not forgotten that in olden times, to honor the mysteries of the birth and agony of the Saviour, the faithful came to pass several hours of the night at the foot of the altar. The last psalm of Compline was an invitation to the night prayer, like a formula of this pious appointment. These holy habits have disappeared.

But on the mountain, in the desert, in solitude, there are still angels of the nocturnal prayer; they are our ambassadors before Jesus Christ. To this concert of praise which rises from the earth, the angels add theirs; when all is silent they praise their God and ours.

Let us say with the Church:

"Behold now, bless ye the Lord: all ye servants of the Lord.

"Who stand in the house of the Lord: in the courts of the house of our God.

"Lift up your hands by night to the holy places, and bless the Lord.

"May the Lord of Sion bless thee: Who hath made heaven and earth."

The anthem sums up in a cry of distress all the prayers of the psalms of Compline: "Have mercy upon me, O Lord, and graciously hear my prayer."

The Chant of In Manus Tuas.—After the Little Chapter there takes place between the faithful a tender colloquy, which it suffices to know to taste all its sweetness and touching simplicity. It is the prayer of a child to its father; a voice pure and young thus begins it: "Into thy hands, O Lord, I commend my spirit."

The faithful answer: "Into Thy hands, O Lord, I commend my spirit."

The choir: "Thou hast redeemed us, O Lord, the God of truth."

The faithful: "I commend my spirit."

The choir: "Glory be to the Father, and to the Son, and to the Holy Ghost."

This doxology is the chant of joy; but the coming of night, the dangers which it brings with it, cast upon the Christian's soul a certain melancholy, and instead of finishing the *Gloria Patri,* he pauses to confide himself to the mercy of God: "Into Thy hands, O Lord, I commend my spirit."

The choir: "Keep us, O Lord, as the apple of an eye."

The faithful: "Protect us under the shadow of Thy wings."

What could be more touching than this prayer? The Christian, alarmed by the deceits of the devil, is he not like a little child who seeks in the arms of his father an assured refuge? This Father so good, Whom he loves, leaves him but one desire: to see Him face to face in the fatherland of heaven. The chant of the *Nunc Dimittis* translates the burning ardor of the Christian soul.

The Last Chant to Mary.—The anthems of which we have spoken, and which ordinarily end Vespers, are said at the close of Compline.

To Mary is sung the last chant of the office, Mary the refuge of Christians in their last hour. The Blessed Virgin is called the Star of the morning; it is she who has guided our uncertain steps in the dawn of our life; she has warmed our young hearts by the pious practices of her worship; she has pointed out the rocks under the feet of her child. For all these blessings receive our gratitude, O tender Mother. But thou wilt be to thy children still more the star of the morning in that great day of eternity which will shine after the darkness of the tomb. We come to ask thee to be favorable to us then; in the midst of the fears of our last hour, in the passage from time to eternity, appear to our dying eyes like the morning star, harbinger of a beautiful day; like the star of the sea, messenger of a happy voyage.

2. THE BENEDICTION OF THE BLESSED SACRAMENT.

Following the sorrows of Calvary and the humiliation of the tomb, Jesus Christ received the adoration of the angels and the saints.

For the Christian, a traveller here below, after the weariness of the way, will come the sweetness of home; after the labors of the day, the reward of his Father. At the close of the day, the faithful image of our short existence, Benediction repeats all these things to us by an exquisite symbolism.

In the Isle of Patmos, whither persecution had sent him, St. John had a vision. Before his wondering eyes were unfolded all the splendors of the heavenly Jerusalem. In the midst of a dazzling light he saw "a great multitude which no man could number, of all nations and tribes. And they all bore on their foreheads a mysterious sign; they were clothed in white robes, and carried palms in their hands. In the sight of the throne and the Lamb that was slain, they fell upon their faces, and adored God. And another angel came and stood before the altar, having a golden censer, and there was given him much incense, and it ascended up before God." At the same time celestial chants fell upon the ear of the apostle. The multitude of the saints repeated: "Amen. Benediction, and glory, and wisdom, and thanksgiving, and honor, and power, and strength to our God for ever and ever. Amen."

St. John saw also an altar of gold, and under the altar the souls of those who had shed their blood for Jesus Christ. "On the altar were candlesticks, and in the midst one like to the Son of man; clothed in a garment down to His feet, girt around with a golden girdle. His head and hair were white as snow, and His face was as the sun shineth in his power. His feet were like unto fine brass as in a burning furnace; His voice was like the sound of many waters; His eyes like flames of fire. In His hand were seven stars, and from His mouth came out a sharp two-edged sword." (Apoc. i.-viii.)

After this marvellous account, we ask if this was a

vision stolen from heaven or borrowed from the earth. What happens in our churches that has not received from the earliest times the impress of the glories of heaven ? Are these not the same wonders, above all at the hour of Benediction ? A few candles sufficed for the celebration of Vespers and Compline, but now behold they sparkle everywhere, and their light plunges us in waves of a mysterious and heavenly brilliancy. The mosaics and the marbles of the sanctuary recall the gold and white stones which form the walls of the city of God. (Tob. xii. 22.) Already we are on the point of crying out with the apostle: "I saw the holy city, the new Jerusalem coming down out of heaven from God, prepared as a bride adorned for her spouse." (Apoc. xxi. 2.)

Before the altar, as in heaven, a great multitude is prostrated; all are overwhelmed: they are truly of all ranks and all nations; the rich is beside the poor, the learned elbow the ignorant. All adore the Lamb that was slain. In this crowd the majority wear the white robe which is worn at the celestial wedding-feast; the purest wool, the spotless snow, the most brilliant sun could not give us an idea of the white splendor of a soul adorned with grace. These faithful disciples also hold a palm in their hands, the palm of martyrdom of which the fathers of the Church speak : concupiscence is its fire, our passions are the executioners, mortification is the sword.

In the temple, as in heaven, sacred chants arise, chants of glory also, of gratitude and of love. The organ recalls to us that "voice like the sound of many waters." (Apoc. xiv. 12.) And to fill the office of the angels, we see children clothed in white; the smoke of their censers envelops in a mysterious veil the throne of the God of the Eucharist.

The candlesticks meet our eyes, and in the midst of the candlesticks, upon His throne of love, the Son of man, as He was seen by the beloved apostle. Rend yourselves, O eucharistic veils; let us see the God of our altars clothed in the splendors of His glory ! Let us kiss His sacred feet from which pour torrents of light ! Let us contemplate His divine face, more splendid than thousands of suns; that hand so merciful and always open, where are shining seven stars, that is to say, the seven sacraments which He gives to relieve our miseries! Let us hear that penetrating voice which called the world out of nothing. Let us bathe in that stream of living water which rises at the altar in the Heart of Jesus, and gives life to souls.

At the sight of the marvels of which he was the witness in heaven, the beloved apostle, he who had leaned his head familiarly on the breast of Jesus Christ, and received the last legacy of His tenderness, fell prostrate, filled with holy fear. The priest, who, like St. John, has received more especially Mary for his mother; the priest, within whose breast in the morning Jesus has lain, see him also filled with saintly fear, falling on his knees as soon as he approaches his Master, and, after the example of the adoring angels, veiling his face.

This veil is called a scarf. The scarf is a reminder of that drapery which the first Christians took, at the hour of prayer, to cover their hands and shoulders, in token of supplication. The ancients in the Apocalypse wore these draperies, and they were white in color.

Having incensed the Blessed Sacrament three times, in honor of the adorable Trinity, the priest raises his voice in prayer.

In the midst of this crowd humbly kneeling, what should be his position? He is standing. This must not surprise us: we are in heaven; the priest visibly represents Jesus Christ, and the first martyr saw Jesus Christ in heaven "standing praying to His Father." (Acts vii. 55.)

Let us say with St. Nilus: "Henceforth let us enter into the church with as much respect as if we were entering into heaven, and there let our thoughts and our words have nothing in them of earth."

Let us take for our model St. Vincent of Paul. Seeing the humble and modest posture which he assumed at the altar, one would have said that, transported into heaven, he saw with his bodily eyes the adorable person of Jesus Christ. Or indeed St. Alphonsus Liguori, whose faith was so vividly penetrated at the foot of the altar with the presence of the King of angels, that more than once he suddenly arose, held out his arms to the tabernacle, and cried out: "Behold, how beautiful He is! Love Him with all your hearts."

The Ostensorium, in which the sacred host is placed, has the form of a sun, because Jesus Christ is a sun; His divine rays enlighten minds and warm hearts. If we are blind to the faith, let us cry to Him with confidence: "Master, grant that I may see." If the cold of indifference has frozen our heart, let us beg Him to give us love.

Part III.—The Liturgical Year.

CHAPTER I.—DIVISION OF TIME IN THE CHURCH.

THE liturgical year is divided into different periods: Advent, Christmas, Septuagesima, Lent, Easter, and Pentecost. Before explaining these divisions of the liturgical year, it will be well to speak of the division of time in the Catholic Church, and under that head we will say what is necessary on the months, weeks, days, vigils, feasts, octaves, and ember-days.

The Months.—The year was originally composed of ten months; and as this is the time that elapses between one inundation of the Nile and the next, it was supposed that this division was borrowed from the Egyptians. (Sepp, *Vie de Jésus-Christ*, t. i. p. i. ch. 8.)

Begun on the 25th of March, at the vernal equinox, the year ended on December 25th, at the winter solstice. Following their order, the months were called first, second, third, and so on. This primitive way of designating them remains to the months of September, October, November, and December, the seventh, eighth, ninth, and tenth months of the Egyptian year. Later, the course of the sun having been taken as the base of

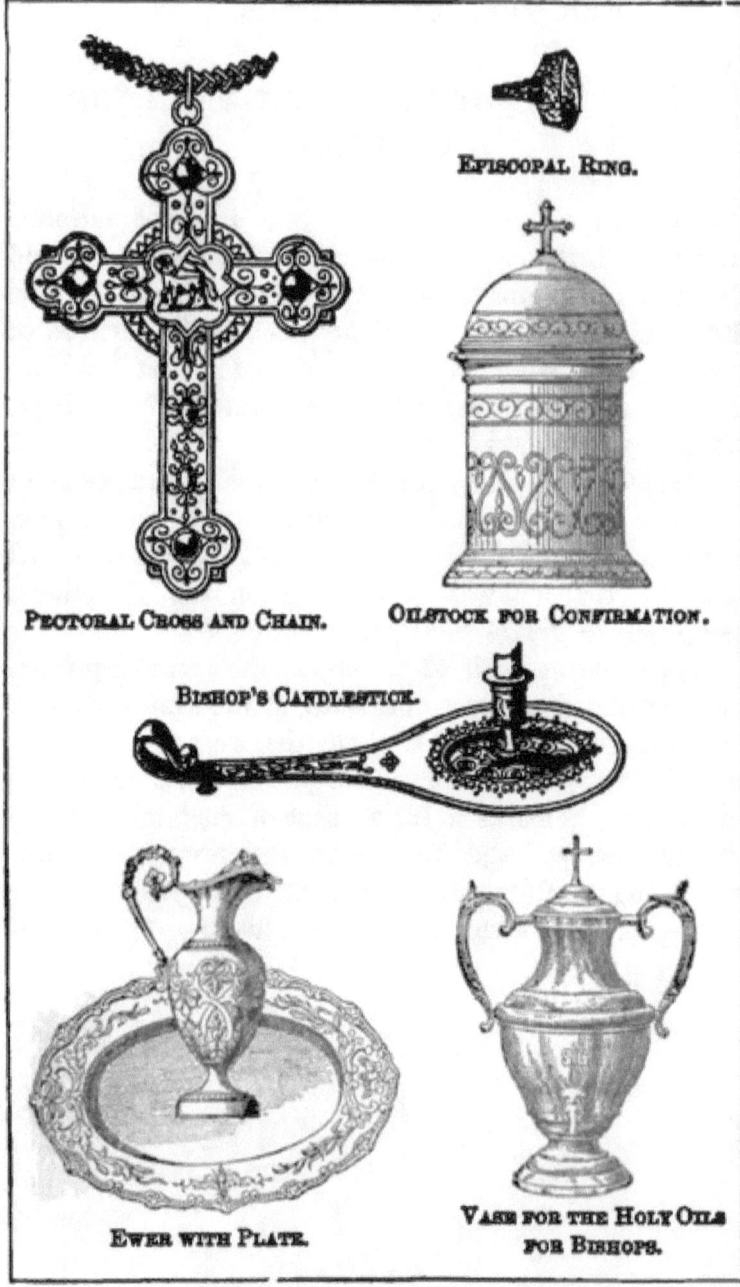

the division of the year, and this orb making its annual revolution in 365 days and some hours, there were added to the ancient year two new months, January and February. The former opened the year, and its name came from Janus, adored among the Romans as the principle and the end of all things, and for this reason represented with two faces. This month seemed to make a salutation of farewell to the year just closing, and to look a welcome to the new.

The second month, February, took its name from Februa, one of the titles of Pluto, god of the lower regions. This was in memory of the sad feasts celebrated at that time in honor of the dead and their king. (In France this month was long called the month of purgatory.)

As to the other months, they lost their original appellations and received others. Mars, the god of war, gave his name to the third month, because at this time the troops left their winter quarters to enter upon the campaign. Venus, or Aphrodite, whose feasts were celebrated in the first three nights of the fourth month, gave to it her name, April. May, which brings to nature her pure skies and perfumed flowers, was thus called from Maia, the mother of the earth and all the forces which animate it. June owes its name to Junius Brutus, who made this month illustrious by the expulsion of the Tarquins.

July saw the birth of Julius Cæsar, hence its name.

Augustus, his successor, for the same reason left his name to the following month. The four last, why it is unknown, preserved their original names of the order of their coming, although they are no longer the seventh, eighth, ninth, and tenth months, but the ninth, tenth, eleventh, and twelfth months of the year.

Each one of these twelve months had thirty days, which made a year of three hundred and sixty days. But as it was really a year of three hundred and sixty-five days, the five days that remained were divided between January, March, May, July, and October, which then counted thirty-one days. But Augustus could not endure that his month should be shorter than that of his predecessor, and a day was taken from February, the sad month of the dead, to be given to August. Example is contagious. The Roman astronomers thought that the last month of the year should not be shorter than the first; they took then a second day from February to give to December, and this unlucky month, doubly shortened by these foolish pretensions, counts now ordinarily but twenty-eight days.

Weeks.—Neither the Greeks nor the Romans knew the division of months into weeks. The former divided them into three decades, or periods of ten days; the latter into three terms, which were: the Calends, the Nones, and the Ides. The first of the month was called Calends, from an old Latin word which signifies to call, because the people called together were told on that day of the feasts which were to be celebrated in that month. The second day of the reunion of the people was called Nones, or the ninth, because it preceded the Ides by nine days. Then the Ides, from the old verb *iduo*, to divide, fell on about the fifteenth of the month, and divided it nearly equally.

The Church, which in her liturgy speaks the language of the Romans, has preserved also the division of the months as it existed among this people. To-day certain acts of the Roman court are still dated the Calends, Nones, and Ides.

It is truer, however, to say that the division of months and weeks was generally known to antiquity. "The week," says the celebrated Laplace, "since the highest antiquity, in which its origin is lost, comes down without interruption throughout the centuries, and mingles with the successive calendars of different peoples. It is very remarkable that it is found the same over all the earth. Perhaps it is the oldest and most indisputable monument of human knowledge. It seems to indicate a common source from which it has spread." (*Système du Monde.*)

What can this source be unless it is the commemoration of the creation of the world in six days, and of the rest of the Creator upon the seventh?

Days.—The Orientals were the first who gave to the days of the week the names of the planets; they called each day by the name of the planet which presided over its first hour. Thus, according to their astronomical tables, the sun presided at the first hour of the first day of the week; the moon at the first hour of the second day; Mars at that of the third day; Mercury over the fourth; Jupiter over the fifth; Venus over the sixth, and Saturn over the seventh. Hence it followed that the first day was consecrated to the sun, the second took the name of the moon, and so on with the others.

However, from the time of the apostles, the week-days had names exclusively Christian. St. John already calls the first day "the Lord's day" (Apoc. i. 10). The others were designated under the name of *ferias:*

second, third, fourth feria, beginning with Sunday. The seventh feria kept its name of *Sabbatum*, day of the Sabbath.

The word feria comes from the Latin *feriare*, to immolate, or *feriari*, to rest one's self, and designated among the Romans those days of sacrifice when business was suspended. The Christians, for whom all days without distinction should be consecrated to the worship of God and be *ferias* by the cessation of sin, called all the days of the week ferias. "The Christians," says Origen, "consider all days like days of the Lord, and even like the day of the Pasch, because every day the heavenly Lamb immolates Himself for them and is eaten by them." (*Hom.* x. *in Gen.*) Each day of the week recalls to Christians some pious mystery. Sunday was the witness of the glories of the resurrection of Jesus Christ, and the miracles of the descent of the Holy Ghost upon the apostles. It was on Sunday that God created light; "in Christianity," says Bellarmin, "this day honors the double birth of Jesus Christ,* that of the Church, and the creation of the world." The Holy Trinity then has a just title to receive on that day the homage of man which the ancient Church has consecrated to it. Has not the first day of the week been illumined by the splendors of creation, the resurrection of the Son, and the descent of the Holy Ghost?

Monday was consecrated to the consolation of the dead, as All Souls' follows All Saints' day; Tuesday to the honor of the angels, and especially to the angel guardians; Wednesday was for a long time dedicated to

---

* His birth at Bethlehem, which occurred on Sunday; His birth into the glorious life on Easter Sunday.

the holy apostles Peter and Paul, as the day, following tradition, commemorative of their arrival in Rome and their glorious martyrdom. St. Joseph has replaced the holy apostles. To Thursday is attached the remembrance of the Blessed Eucharist. Especially since the institution of the feast of Corpus Christi, this day seems destined to be a continual octave of the mystery of our altars, as Sunday is the unceasingly renewed octave of the feast of Easter.

Friday is consecrated to the Passion of Our Lord, and Saturday to the Blessed Virgin. If the Church honors the day of the martyrdom of her children, could she forget the sorrows of Mary on the day after the passion? At the foot of the cross, feeling in her mother's heart the steel-clad points of the nails and lance, the bitterness of the blasphemies, and of the gall offered to drink, she was more than martyr: this is the expression of the holy doctors. The solitude of the following day, the absence of her Jesus, the memory always before her eyes of His passion, His death and burial, pierced her torn heart with a new sword. (Alexander de Halès, q. iii., *Sum. Theol. quæst. ult.*)

Vigils.—The Christians formerly passed the night preceding a solemn feast in prayer in the church; this holy practice bore the name of vigil, or watch. Several motives recommended it to the piety of the faithful. During the night the Word of God was made flesh; during the night He came into the world; during the night He will come again to judge mankind. Grave abuses led to the suppression of these holy meetings for nocturnal prayer, the vigil of feasts. That of Christmas, by a privilege easily understood, was alone excepted.

But the name of vigil was always retained for the day that preceded a feast, and most frequently the primitive fast was preserved.

The vigils of primitive institution, and which for this reason enjoy the privilege of never being omitted, are: Christmas, Epiphany, Easter, and Pentecost. Others have been instituted later for certain feasts of the Blessed Virgin and the saints. These are: the Assumption, All Saints, the Nativity of St. John the Baptist, the feasts of the apostles, and the feast of St. Lawrence. All vigils supposed a fast and abstinence.

Ecclesiastical discipline has varied on this question, yielding to the needs of people and time; in America to-day fast and abstinence are practised on the vigils of Christmas, Easter, Pentecost, the Assumption, and All Saints. All other vigils are observed without fast or abstinence, and they are confined to the office which is assigned to them.

According to the way we keep them the vigils render the feasts more solemn. By mortification they make us compassionate the trials of the saints during their earthly pilgrimage; they say to us that to be glorified with them it is necessary to share their suffering, and that penitence is the gate of heaven. (Alcuin, *De Parasceve*.)

Feasts.—The word feast comes from the Greek *festia*, the domestic hearth, family reunion, from whence the name of festival given to the repast which accompanies these reunions. Among the Christian feasts some are movable, that is to say, that the day upon which they fall varies; of these are Easter, Pentecost, Corpus Christi, Trinity. All the others are celebrated each year on the same date; for this reason they are called immovable.

Cardinal feasts are those which are followed by a certain number of Sundays, such as Epiphany, Easter, and Pentecost; it is upon these that all the plan of the divine office of these Sundays turns. Feasts were primitively celebrated upon the days on which they fell. We have now in America but six holy-days of obligation; these are: the Circumcision, Ascension of Our Lord, the Assumption of the Blessed Virgin Mary, All Saints, the Immaculate Conception, and Christmas day. Three others, under the name of transferred feasts, are celebrated on the following Sunday: Epiphany, Corpus Christi, Sts. Peter and Paul; the others are suppressed. The Church nevertheless, as in those happier days when the faithful united in the temples to keep the feasts, still offers the sacrifice especially for them.

The feasts are not all celebrated with the same solemnity. Their variety is compared by St. Denis to the celestial hierarchy. For the saints who reign in heaven are not the same in merit and in glory. "One," says St. Paul, speaking of the glory of the elect, "is the glory of the sun, another the glory of the moon, and another the glory of the stars. For star differeth from star in glory." (I. Cor. xv. 41.)

Thus, according to the renown of the saints, the Church on earth has established a rite more or less solemn to honor their memory each year. Feasts are *doubles*, *semi-doubles*, or *simples*. The first are so called because they had originally a double office, that of the feria and that of the feast. The second have a demi-office, half of the feast and half of the feria. The third have a simple memento in the office of the day, by the prayer and the lesson of Matins.

Octaves.—The eighth day which follows certain feasts is celebrated as solemnly as the feast itself, under the name of Octave, and the intervening days are called "days of the octave."

The octaves, intended to solemnize the greatest feasts, originated with the Jews. Solomon willed that the dedication of the temple should last eight days; the same thing occurred at its re-establishment under Zorobabel. Following the steps of the old law, the Church celebrated the most solemn feasts with octaves. In the first place Easter was prolonged for an entire week. Following came the octave of Pentecost, then that of Christmas, and the Epiphany. The feasts of saints had none until the eighth century.

The octave was in the beginning but a repetition of the feast, and only on the eighth day. The intermediate days made no memorial of the feast; later they had an office, and the solemn feasts, even of saints, lasted eight days. As to its meaning, *octave* is simply the *eighth.*

The number eight, in the language of the fathers, represented the eternal day of judgment and the resurrection of the flesh; in other words, the eternity which follows the seventh period of the world. The intention of the Church is to carry our thoughts to the unending feasts of heaven. The vigil, with its severe penitence, has associated us with the laborious life of Our Lord and His saints; the octave leads us to assist at their triumphs.

Five octaves are established to honor Our Lord; they

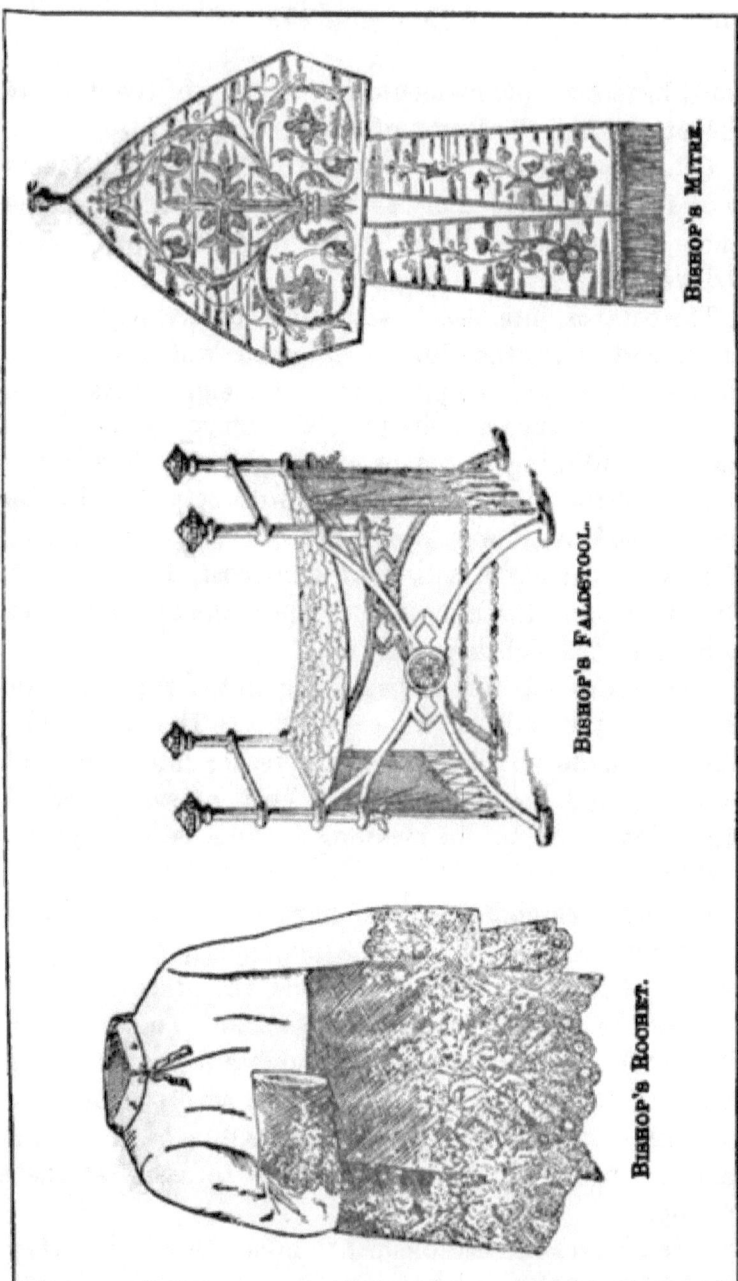

are: Christmas, the Epiphany, Easter, Ascension, and Corpus Christi. Three feasts of the Blessed Virgin have octaves: the Nativity, Assumption, Immaculate Conception. The Nativity of St. John the Baptist, the martyrdom of Sts. Peter and Paul, All Saints, the feasts of St. Stephen, St. John the Evangelist, the Holy Innocents, St. Lawrence, have their particular octave. It is the same with the dedication of a church and the feast of a patron.

Ember-days.—This name is given to the fast which the Church observes at the beginning of each one of the four seasons of the year. In instituting them the Church wished in the first place to oppose the practice of penitence to the follies and disorders of the Bacchanalia, which the pagans renewed four times a year. Besides this, God has always shown a holy jealousy for the first-fruits of everything: to Him belongs the Sunday, the first day of the week; to Him then should be consecrated the first week of each season, as well as the first day of the year. The days of the week chosen for ember-days are Wednesday, Friday, and Saturday. From the beginning of Christianity these days were sanctified by fasting and assistance at the holy sacrifice, because of the memories which they recall: Wednesday saw the infamous sale of Judas; Friday was the day of Jesus Christ's death; Saturday that of His rest in the sepulchre. If we consider the number of days consecrated to the fast of the four seasons, twelve a year, it is impossible to doubt that the Church had another end in view than the expiation by penitence of the sins of which we are guilty—one day of expiation for each month of the year. (St. Leonard, Sermon on the fast of the tenth month.) To mortification the Church joins prayer, to call down the dew of heaven upon the fruits of the earth, and to ask of God priests according to her heart. The ordinations take place on the Saturdays of the ember-days, and the Church has thought it suitable to beg, after the example of the apostles, by prayer and fasting, the light of the Holy Spirit in such an important action. Among these levites whom the hand of the bishop is to consecrate for eternity, there is one, perhaps, who will one day have the guidance of our soul; let us invoke for him all the apostolic graces.

CHAPTER II.—THE TIME OF ADVENT AND OF CHRISTMAS.

1. ADVENT TIME.

The Four Weeks of Advent.—The time of preparation for the sweet mysteries of the birth of Our Lord is called Advent, that is to say, the coming. Its four weeks recall to Christians the four thousand years of prayers and sighs which preceded the coming of the Messias.

The O Anthems of Advent.—Seven days before Christmas is sung at Vespers an anthem called "*O* of Advent," because it begins with this exclamation; it is a cry sent out to the Messias. It is sung at Vespers; for was it not in the evening of the world that the Messias came? It is sung at the *Magnificat* to show that the Saviour for Whom we wait will come to us through Mary. (Guéranger, *The Liturgical Year.*) Again, the repetition of the anthem expresses well the ardent sighs, constantly renewed, of the patriarchs; the Introit has already offered us the same figure.

Practices of Advent.—There remain among us to-day few traces of Advent as it was observed by our fathers. They sanctified it by prayer, fasting, and abstinence. The old-time penitence is always practised in monasteries, but among the faithful the Church has preserved but its symbols. During Advent she clothes herself in purple, and this sign of mourning shows us how the Church unites herself to the desire of Israel, who waited in sackcloth and ashes the coming of the Messias. As a sign of widowhood it expresses the sorrow of the Church, who awaits that Spouse Whose absence costs her heart so dear.

Marriages are not celebrated in Advent, their worldly joy being little in agreement with the holy tears and chaste pangs of penitence. Moreover it is toward other nuptial feasts that the Church turns the eyes of her children : these are those of the eternal marriage, begun here below in the eucharistic banquet. The *Alleluia*, which continues its tender harmony in these days of penitence, should make us sigh for the joys of the festival of the Lamb.

Except on feast-days, the two angelical hymns, the *Gloria in excelsis* and the *Te Deum*, are not sung till the great day when they are chanted at the crib of the infant God. The *Ite, Missa est*, is replaced by the call to prayer : "*Benedicamus Domino*"—"Let us bless the Lord"; for we cannot pray too much in these holy days of waiting.

Feast of the Immaculate Conception, December 8th.—The deluge of iniquities which has inundated the world for four thousand years is about to end; Mary, the heavenly dove, brings the good tidings to the world. The dark night which has weighed upon humanity will soon see its shadows scattered; she whom the Holy Spirit compared to the dawn will appear in this holy season, like a forerunner of the Sun of justice. The star which precedes the morning shines upon the horizon. A thousand times blessed be the day which brings us so much joy! May all Christians hail with gratitude the solemnity of the Immaculate Conception of Mary!

Faith teaches us that at the moment when God united the soul of Mary, which He had just created, to the body which it was to animate, not only had that soul not contracted in the least the stain which till then had disfigured every human soul, but it was filled with grace tremendous in extent and ineffable in beauty. A feast in honor of this glorious mystery existed in the East in the sixth century. The Church of Lyons introduced this solemnity into France. The definition of the Immaculate Conception as a dogma was made under the pontificate of Pope Pius IX., December 8, 1854.

The Blue Scapular of the Immaculate Conception.— The venerable Ursula Benincasa, on the day of the purification, saw Mary, who appeared to her clad in a white robe and a blue mantle. She held the infant Jesus pressed against her heart, and a multitude of virgins, clothed like their glorious queen, formed her train. Our Lord showed her the wish that He had of seeing a congregation of virgins arise, who, placing themselves under the invocation of Mary Immaculate, should take the habit in which His Mother was then clad. He promised the greatest graces to those who should be faithful in following the rules of this new Congregation. Ursula begged Our Lord to shower His favors upon those who, living in the world and devoted to the Blessed Virgin, should live chastely according to their state and wear a blue scapular. To prove to her that her prayer was heard, God showed her, while this blissful vision lasted, angels clothing a great number of Christians with this holy habit.

The indulgences attached to the blue scapular of the Immaculate Conception are innumerable. "As for me," says St. Alphonsus Liguori, "I would take all scapulars. But above all you must know that the scapular of the Immaculate Conception, which is blessed by the Theatine Fathers, besides all its partial indulgences, has all the indulgences granted to whatever religious order, whatever devotion, whatever person there can be. And particularly that by reciting six times *Pater*, *Ave*, and *Gloria*, in honor of the Most Holy Trinity and Mary Immaculate, can be gained each time all the indulgences of Rome, of Portiuncula, of Jerusalem, and of Galicia, which amounts to 533 plenary indulgences, without speaking of partial indulgences, which are innumerable." (*Glories of Mary*. These indulgences have been confirmed by Gregory XVI. in a decree dated July 12, 1845.)

Translation of the Holy House of Loretto, December 10th.—This feast up to this time is not of obligation in the universal Church, but it is celebrated in many countries, and has for its object thanksgiving to God for the blessing with which He has enriched the West, when, in order to compensate it for the loss of the holy sepulchre, He miraculously transported to Catholic ground the house in which the Blessed Virgin received the message of the angel, and where the Word was made flesh.

Many of our readers may be ignorant of this marvellous event, which we will repeat here. It was under the pontificate of Celestine V., and when the Christians had entirely lost the holy places in Palestine, that the little house wherein was wrought the mystery of the Incarnation in the womb of Mary was transported by angels from Nazareth into Dalmatia, or Sclavonia, to a little mountain called Tersato.

The miracles which were wrought every day in this holy house, the legal investigation which the deputies of the country went to Nazareth to make, to prove the translation into Dalmatia, as well as the universal conviction of the people who came to venerate it from all parts of the world, seemed to be incontestable proofs of the truth of the miracle. Nevertheless, God wished to give another, which should have, in a sense, Dalmatia and Italy for witnesses. After three years and seven months the holy house was transported across the Adriatic Sea to the territory of Recanati, into a forest belonging to a lady called Loretta; and this event threw the people of Dalmatia into such desolation that it seemed that they would not survive it, and to console themselves they built upon the same spot a church consecrated to the Mother of God, over the door of which they put this inscription: "*Hic est locus in quo fuit sacra Domus Nazarena quæ nunc Recineti partibus colitur.*" At the same time there were many inhabitants of Dalmatia who came to Italy to fix their residence near to the holy house.

This new translation made such stirring of Christian hearts that a multitude of pilgrims came from nearly every part of Europe to Recanati, in order to honor the house now called "of Loretto." To prove more and more fully the truth of this event, the inhabitants of the province sent first to Dalmatia, and then to Nazareth, sixteen persons who were the best qualified for the service, who made in these places new investigations; but God deigned to demonstrate the certainty Himself by renewing twice in succession the miracle of the translation even in the territory of Recanati. For at the end of eight months, the forest of Loretto being infested with highwaymen who stopped the pilgrims, the house was transported to a point a mile further, and placed on a little height which belonged to two brothers of the family of Antici; and when these brothers had taken arms against one another in dispute over the division of the offerings of the pilgrims, the house was transferred to an enclosure a little further removed, and in the midst of the public way, where it has remained and where has since grown up the village called Loretto.

2. CHRISTMAS TIME.

The Expectation of the Blessed Virgin, December 18th.—The origin of this feast goes back to the tenth council of Toledo, in 656. The bishops who composed this holy assembly having found the ancient custom of celebrating the Annunciation on the 25th of March somewhat inconvenient, seeing that most frequently this joyous solemnity, coming in passion time, was transferred to the paschal season, and that these two liturgic periods offered too great contrasts with the mystery of the Word made flesh, they decreed that henceforth the Spanish Church should celebrate a feast in memory of the Annunciation eight days before Christmas, a solemn feast which should serve as a preparation for the birth of Our Lord. Later the Spanish Church wished to celebrate the feast of the Annunciation on the 25th of March with the universal Church, but nevertheless preserved a vestige of the custom which she had observed for several centuries. She ceased to celebrate the Annunciation of Mary on the 18th of December, but turned the piety of the faithful to the consideration of the divine Mother during the days which immediately preceded her delivery. A new feast was established under the title of the Expectation of the Blessed Virgin.

"This feast," says Dom Guéranger, "which is called Our Lady of the O, because of the great anthems chanted on these days, is celebrated in Spain with great devotion. During the eight days which it lasts a solemn Mass is sung early in the morning, to which all women with child, of whatever rank they may be, make it a duty to assist, to honor Mary in her waiting, and to beg her help for themselves." (*Liturgical Year*, "Advent.")

History of the Feast of Christmas, December 25th.— The birth of Jesus Christ in the stable of Bethlehem, His adoration by the poor shepherds, are the objects of this feast.

Its French name of Noel, often used also in English, especially in old English hymns and carols, is the abridgment of the word *Emmanuel, God with us*. The prophet had given this name to the Messias, and this great solemnity of the Church saw its accomplishment. In the popular language the word Emmanuel did not remain unaltered; the feast of Emmanuel soon became the feast of *Nouel*, then *Noel*. It was at first celebrated with the feast of the Epiphany, January 6, for it was

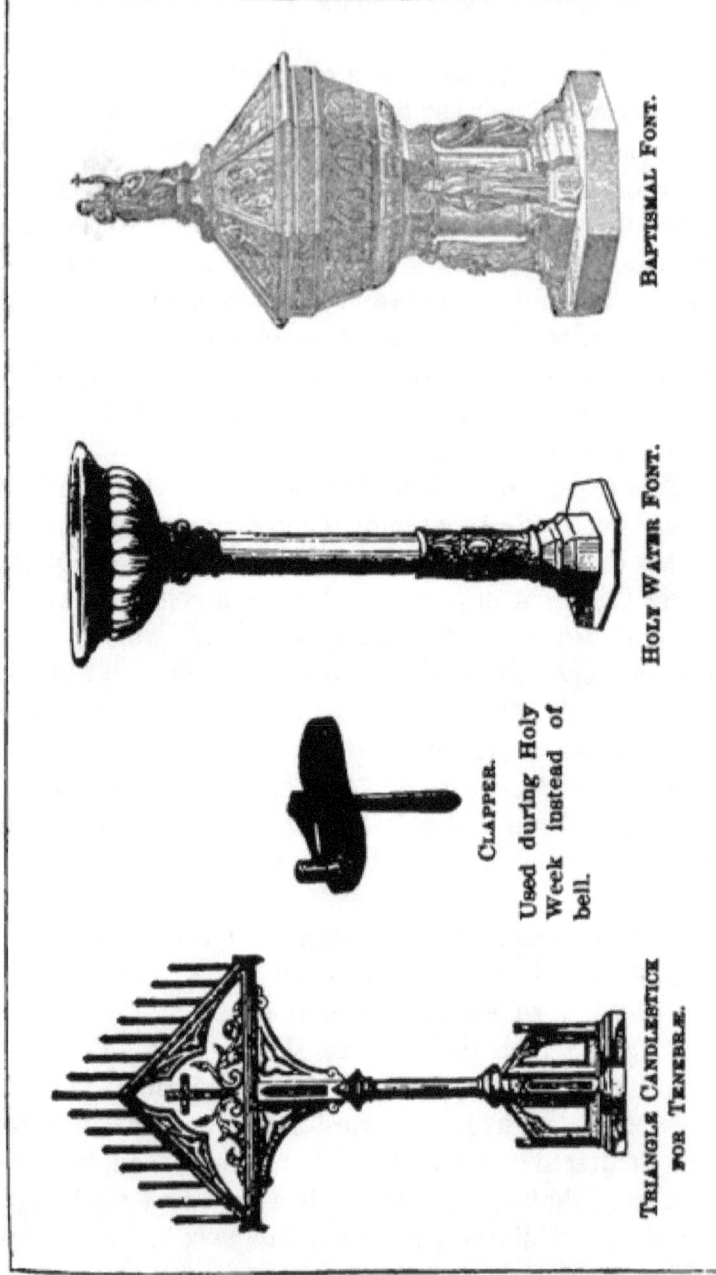

believed that Jesus Christ was born then. Pope Julius I. having instituted the most exact researches, it was discovered that this great event took place on December 25th, and from that time the feast was transferred to that date; the Epiphany continued to be solemnized on January 6th. This change goes back to the beginning of the fourth century.

This explains a peculiarity of the octave of Christmas, as old as the feast itself; although it is an octave of the first order, it admits solemnities which are excluded from the octaves of Easter and Pentecost. The reason for this goes back to what has just been said. When the birth of the Saviour was celebrated on January 6th, the 26th of December honored St. Stephen, the 27th St. John, and the 28th the Holy Innocents. When the Nativity was finally fixed as the 25th of December, it was thought best not to remove these feasts. It is then in the octave of the Epiphany that the original octave of the Nativity of Our Lord is to be seen; hence it enjoys the same privileges as the other two great feasts of the year, because we count the Sundays after Epiphany, instead of those following Christmas, as those after Easter and Pentecost are counted. (Guéranger, *The Liturgical Year*, "Christmas.")

Communion was for a long time obligatory at Christmas and Pentecost as at Easter. As a sign of the great joy brought to the earth by the birth of Emmanuel, abstinence is done away with on Friday when the feast falls upon that day.

The Feast of Christmas at Rome.—On this day the Pope blesses the sword and ducal hat which he sends to the Christian princes who have best served the cause of the Church. At Santa Maria Maggiore, which has the honor of possessing the holy manger, this relic is exposed all day. At St. Anastasia is offered to the veneration of the faithful the veil of the Blessed Virgin and St. Joseph's chlamys, or cloak, in which the infant Jesus was wrapped at the moment of His birth.

In the Church of the Agonizing is exposed a piece of the swaddling-bands of Our Lord; at Santa Maria *in Trastevere* is shown near the high altar the place from which a fountain of oil miraculously burst forth at the birth of the Saviour. Let us add that at St. Lorenzo, beyond the walls, on the feast of St. Stephen, two rocks of his stoning are exposed. On the feast of St. John, at St. John Lateran, is shown the cup from which, at the order of Domitian, the apostle drank poison which did him no harm; the tunic with which he raised from the dead the emperor's ministers who had tasted the same poison; and the chains with which he was bound when he was brought from Ephesus to Rome.

The Three Masses of Christmas.—"The Catholic faith recognizes three substances in Jesus Christ," says Innocent III.: "the divinity, the flesh, and the soul. The Scriptures speak of the three births of the Son of God: His divine birth in the bosom of His Father; His birth according to the flesh of the Virgin Mary; His spiritual birth in our souls. The mystery of these three births is represented to us by the three Masses which the Church says. The eternal birth of the Word is completely concealed from us; the prophet says of it: 'Who could speak it?' To express these impenetrable mysteries, the first Mass is said during the darkness of the night. The temporal birth of the Saviour is partly concealed and partly known; hidden as to the manner, known as to the fact. The hour of dawn, consecrated to the second Mass, well recalls this mixture of light and darkness. His spiritual birth is fully light; it is shown by the actions of him who has become the tabernacle of Jesus Christ. These mysteries are expressed in the third Mass, celebrated during the day." (Inn. III., *Serm.* iii., *in Nativ. Domini.*)

Since this is the meaning of the Christmas liturgy, at the first Mass let us adore with the angels the eternal birth of the Word; at the Mass at dawn let us prostrate ourselves with Mary and Joseph before the divine infant in the crib; at the Mass of the day let us join with the shepherds, and make Jesus the offering of a heart in which He may be born.

Christmas Cribs.—The origin of this devotion, practised in the bosom of many Christian families, and in the churches, goes back to St. Francis of Assisi. Three years before his death the saint wished to celebrate at Grecio the feast of the Nativity of Our Lord with all possible solemnity, in order to excite men to the most lively devotion for this mystery. But, to avoid all adverse criticism, he asked the permission of the Sovereign Pontiff, and having obtained it, he had a crib prepared, in which he placed hay and an ox and an ass.

Then the brothers were called together; the people on their part crowded there; the forest re-echoed with cries of joy; the numerous and shining candles lent their light to the holy night, which passed in chants of praise and sweetest hymns. The man of God remained close to the crib, penetrated with the tenderest piety, his face bathed with tears and his soul inundated with happiness. Solemn Mass was celebrated on the crib itself. A worthy soldier, deserving of credence, declared that he saw sleeping in the crib an infant of wonderful beauty, and Francis clasping him in his arms, trying to awaken him from his slumber. This sweet story is from St. Bonaventure, author of the life of St. Francis. (*Légende de St. François*, ch. x.)

Feast of the Circumcision, January 1st.—This is celebrated on the octave of Christmas. On this day Our Lord received on His innocent flesh the mark of sinful man and the seal of the children of Abraham. At the same time He received the thousandfold blessed name of Jesus. "Why is it," asks St. Bernard, "that He is circumcised and still called Jesus, that is to say, Saviour? For circumcision is much more for him who needs salvation than for him who saves others. But this connection of the holy name of Jesus with the circumcision is not without its great mystery. It was in the first place to show that this child had not come to save except by blood; then to efface, by the glories of this august name, the apparent ignominy of the circumcision, as the opprobrium of the cross was in some sort effaced by the magnificent inscription over it: 'Jesus of Nazareth, King of the Jews.' In fact, if we reflect upon this we shall find that the divine wisdom has nearly always joined in the mysteries of our redemption great abasement with grandeur, and humiliation with exaltation. If the Son of God takes an earthly mother, it is a virgin-mother, incomparably purer than the cherubim and seraphim. If He is born in a stable, He is there announced by angels, recognized by the shepherds, adored by the Magi, and feared by the proudest of kings. If He is forced to fly into Egypt, miracles make Him respected there, while the blood of the innocents renders His birth celebrated in all Judea. Even His death, wholly infamous as it appears, is made glorious by an eclipse of the sun and by the convulsion of all nature. It is then for the same reason that He is called Jesus in His circumcision. This name makes us consider Him, not as a sinner, but as He who taketh away the sins of the world." (Serm. on the Circumcision.)

We will speak at greater length of this blessed name when we consider the feast established to honor it.

New Year's Day.—The feast of the Circumcision opens the civil year. This has not always been the case. In Europe generally, in the fifth century the year began on the 1st of March; in the eighth century the year opened on Christmas day; in the tenth century on Easter. Christian ideas were then dominant in the world. Charles IX., by an edict dated from the château of Roussillon, in Dauphiny, in the year 1564, ordered that it should begin on January 1st. There is something touching in the union of the first day of the year with the holy name of Jesus. That the days that follow may be blessed to us, the Church has marked the first hour with the name of salvation and redemption.

A tradition carries back to Tatius, one of the first kings of Rome, the custom of gifts made upon this day. The courtiers offered to this prince branches of vervain, gathered in the woods sacred to Strenia, the goddess of health, with the intention of calling down upon him her protection in the course of the year just beginning.

The offering having brought happiness, the custom became general. Each year the people went into the woods of Strenia to gather vervain, considered by the ancients as a symbol of happiness, health, and affection, and it was offered to those whom they loved. To these gifts of good augury others were soon added of meal, figs, a little piece of money, or a date covered with a light layer of gold-leaf—an expressive wish to the person who received the offering, for by it was shown the desire to call down upon him in the course of the coming year sweetness and abundance in the things necessary to life. These primitive presents were replaced by provisions of all sorts, by clothing, furniture, and pieces of gold or silver. The name of Strenæ was none the less left to the more delicate offerings.

Feast of the Epiphany, January 6th.—This glorious date recalls Our Lord adored by the kings of the East. The feast instituted in honor of this mystery was for a long time blended with that of Christmas, under the name of *Theophany, manifestation of God*. It took that of *Epiphany*, or *manifestation on manifestation*, when the two solemnities were separated. This was really the second manifestation of the Saviour. The first had been to the Jewish people, represented by the shepherds; the second was for the Gentiles, the first-fruits of whom were brought to Jesus in the persons of the Magi. Following a venerable tradition, to which the painters of the catacombs gave an important authority, the Magi were three in number. "These," says Dom Guéranger, "are the veritable ancestors of the gentile Church. One was from Chaldea, the second from Arabia, the third from Ethiopia. They represented at the crib the three races of

humanity offering their homage to the new-born King."
(*The Liturgical Year*, "Christmas.")

The Gospel speaks of their presents: gold, frankincense, and myrrh. This mysterious number honored in the first place the Blessed Trinity in the Person of the Word Incarnate, but it also prophesied the triple character of the divine infant. He had come into the world to reign, and gold witnessed to His supreme power; He was to exercise a sovereign priesthood — frankincense, which should smoke in the priest's hand, was a present worthy of Him; His death would open heaven — myrrh, a perfume reserved in ancient times to embalming, was there for the burial of the divine victim. " Where," asks St. Leo. "had they discovered the inspired nature of these gifts, these men who had not yet seen Jesus? While the star shone on the eyes of their bodies, more penetrating still did the ray of God's light illumine their hearts." (Serm. on the Epiph.)

As to their names of Melchior, Caspar, and Balthazar, their use is too recent for us to adopt them. It would be as difficult to sustain the responsibility of doing so as it would seem to us bold to attack them directly. Their bodies, transported from Persia to Constantinople, and later from Milan to Cologne, rest to-day in the cathedral of that great metropolis, in a magnificent shrine, the most beautiful monument of the goldsmith's skill of the Middle Ages. (Guéranger.)

The date of the 6th of January recalls to the love of the Church still other memories. On this day Our Lord, baptized by John, heard the voice of the Father proclaiming His divinity; on this same day He worked His first miracle in Cana, and St. Augustine tells us that the 6th of January was also the day of the miraculous multiplication of the five loaves in the desert. (*Serm.* i., *de Epiph.*)

All these events make this feast the great manifestation of the Divinity of Jesus Christ, and fully justify its name of Epiphany. However, the preference of the Roman Church is for the mystery of the calling of the gentiles. Nothing is more natural, since that mystery is supremely glorious for her. For has not Rome, the capital of paganism, become the head of Christianity by the vocation which on that day called all the nations to the light of the true faith?

The two other mysteries, the baptism of Our Lord and the wedding at Cana, have nevertheless a memorial in the office. Besides this the Church has consecrated a particular day to their celebration: the octave of the Epiphany to the baptism of Our Lord, and the second Sunday after Epiphany to the wedding at Cana.

The miracle of the multiplication of the loaves is not mentioned in the liturgy except in Lent.

In spite of the solemnity of this feast, its vigil is not a fast. We have not forgotten that formerly it made one feast with Christmas. Since their separation, the memory of their union has been preserved by a vigil and fast in common.

It would seem that the celebration of marriages, forbidden during the Advent period of mourning and penitence, would be resumed after the joyous feast of the Nativity. Why is the prohibition prolonged until after the octave of the Epiphany? Again, it is a trace of the ancient discipline. Christmas being celebrated on the 6th of January, the solemnizing of marriages was

Memorial Tablet.

Bishop's Throne.

Pulpit.

banished from the liturgy to the end of the octave, January 13th.

The kings of France, up to the fourteenth century, presented as the offering of this day gold, incense, and myrrh. In the Middle Ages the faithful offered them also, to have them blessed, and they then preserved them as a pledge of heavenly favors. This pious custom still exists in Germany.

Some authors have thought that they saw in the popular family festival of Epiphany a relic of paganism. It would seem to us more natural that our fathers wished to symbolize in the festival the wedding at Cana, and in the old custom of the king of the Twelfth-Night cake, the kings at the crib. A custom preserved in the mountains of Scotland comes to the support of this opinion. Instead of the bean in the Twelfth-Night cake, these people use a bit of myrrh, a grain of incense, and a piece of gold.

Feast of the Holy Name of Jesus.—Pope Clement VII. instituted this feast in the year 1530, at the request of the Friars Minor.

Our Lord was announced under many names by the prophets; He is called Admirable, the Counsellor, the strong God, Emmanuel, Prince of peace; and only the name of Jesus sees all heads bow and a feast established in its honor. Why this privilege? The name of Jesus, and that alone, comprises all that the others say; at the name of Jesus is presented to the mind all the mysteries of the redemption; the thirty-three years of Our Lord's life are unrolled then before our eyes, with their labor, their anguish, their sufferings. This name shows us all, from the crib to the cross. Let us take care not to think that it is to the name itself that the Church has consecrated a feast. The object of this solemnity will be explained to us by the following passage from an ancient breviary : "And now comes, beloved brothers, the great solemnity in which our holy mother the Church honors at the same time all the mysteries of the universal redemption which are kept on the different dates of the Christian year. The word Jesus means Saviour. Let us apply ourselves, then, in the solemnity of this divine name, to the reparation of all the faults of negligence or weakness committed on each one of the feasts of Our Saviour, that at least once a year we may venerate by the solemnities of our hymns and our canticles a name so salutary. And that which we begin on earth may we continue eternally in heaven!"

The object of the feast being known, let us say something of the indulgences attached to the name of Jesus. For a long time the Angelical Salutation ended at the words: "*Et benedictus fructus ventris tui*" ("And blessed is the fruit of thy womb"). By the authority of Urban IV. was added the name of Jesus, and an indulgence of thirty days was granted to all those who pronounce it in saying the *Ave Maria*. To increase the piety of the faithful, John XXII. accorded thirty days more indulgence. (Mich. de Insulis, *In quodlibeto de Rosario*, c. 5.) Later Sixtus V. opened the treasury of the Church to all those who invoked the name of Jesus. This indulgence was of twenty-five days. At the hour of death those who, having been faithful during life to invoke this name, pronouncing it then with the lips or the heart, may gain a plenary indulgence. (Decree of June 12, 1587.)

The piety of the faithful is not satisfied to have unceasingly on the lips the name of Jesus; it delights in engraving it upon stone and cutting it in the sacred ornaments. It has invented a monogram, that is to say, a sort of figure which contains the letters of this name interlaced into one character. It was composed of its first three letters: IHS. This monogram comes to us from the Greeks, as the first two letters attest. The Latin form of the last letter is explained when we know that the Greeks of the Lower Empire used it frequently. The Latins placed a cross over the second letter, as if to say that Jesus has saved us by the cross. St. Bernardine of Sienna made this monogram popular. He constantly wore it on his chest, surrounded by shining rays of gold. This relic, religiously preserved in Rome in the Church of Santa Maria in Ara Cœli, is exposed every year, on the feast of the saint, to the veneration of the faithful.

Purification of the Blessed Virgin and Presentation of Our Lord in the Temple, February 2d.—The name alone shows the object of this feast: Mary submitting to the purification prescribed by Moses, and making the offering to God of her divine Son.

The Church, by a solemn procession, honors the journey of the Holy Family to Jerusalem, and by the blessing of candles the manifestation of that Divine Light which Simeon sung. This last ceremony gave to the feast its popular name of Candlemas. In the hand of the Christian, the blessed candle symbolizes Jesus Christ, Whom the holy old man Simeon had the happiness to hold in his arms. (See what has been previously said of candles, page 11.)

Purple, the color of mourning, worn in the blessing of candles and the procession, and saddening the joys of this feast, well expresses the sadness of Mary's heart when Simeon announced to her " that a sword of sorrow should pierce her heart." For the Mass the Church wears white, the color of joy, in remembrance of the joys of that day when, for the first time, the Messias received solemn homage. The manger had seen the shepherds and Magi prostrate at His feet, but to-day the Temple hears Him proclaimed the Light of nations and the glory of Israel.

CHAPTER III.—SEPTUAGESIMA AND LENT.

1. SEPTUAGESIMA.

History of this Time.—To the forty days of Lent Pope Telesphorus added a week of penitence for clerks. This week bore the name of Quinquagesima, or the Fiftieth. Following this, some of the popes having authorized two repasts on Saturday to sustain the body weakened by the rigors of the fast of the preceding day, more severe than that of the other days, to make up for these seven Saturdays taken from Lent, an eighth week was added, and it bore the name of Sexagesima. Then, as, out of respect for the ascension of Our Lord, Thursday was solemnized as Sunday, a ninth week was established, called Septuagesima, to complete the forty days of fast. These different names of Septuagesima, Sexagesima, Quinquagesima, have been preserved in the three Sundays which precede Lent, and the liturgic period which these embrace was called the time of

Septuagesima. If we take the exact signification of the word Septuagesima it indicates an interval of seventy days from the Sunday which bears this name to Easter. Although there are in reality but sixty-three days, the Church has adopted this expression, taking, according to the custom of the Scriptures, the number outlined for the actual number.

In spite of the changes wrought in the ecclesiastical discipline, Septuagesima has remained a time of half penitence and prayer. The Greek Church always begins her Lenten period from the week of Septuagesima; holy considerations of charity make her Western sister associate herself with her mourning. The spouse of Jesus Christ had another motive which reveals to us her profound knowledge of the human heart; a mother full of solicitude, she knows all its weaknesses.

After the sweet joys of Christmas, after the beautiful feasts of the Epiphany season and the more tumultuous ones of the carnival, could we at once enter into the penitential life without transition? Assuredly not. The evening twilight precedes the night; it is necessary to let the last echo of the feasts fade away little by little, before intoning the sad chant of mourning: Septuagesima becomes the preparation for Lent.

Symbolism of Septuagesima.—"There are two periods," says St. Augustine; "one passing now in the temptations and trials of this life, the other that which will pass in the security and joys of eternity. These two periods we celebrate, the former before Easter, the latter after Easter. The time before Easter expresses the anguish of this present life; that which we celebrate after Easter signifies the beatitude which we shall one day taste. This is why we pass the former in fasting and prayer, while the second is consecrated to canticles of joy." (*In Ps.* cxlviii.)

The two places which correspond to these two periods are Babylon and Jerusalem. Babylon is this world; Jerusalem is heaven. Now, the Jewish people, figure of the Christian people, was enslaved in Babylon seventy years, whence the number seventy for the days of expiation. "The Church," say the liturgists, "has fixed this number of days to put us in mind of the captivity of Babylon and our own." (Alcuin, *Cap. de Septuag.*—Gavant., p. iv. tit. 5.)

The Church, in these days, thinks but of the sorrows of her exile; clad in mourning, like the Hebrew captives, like them she weeps when she remembers Sion. In the strange land she can but repeat the sweet chants of her country, though her silent harps no longer voice the canticles of the heavenly Jerusalem. Neither the *Alleluia* nor the *Gloria in excelsis*, the *Te Deum* nor the *Ite, Missa est*, rise in the saddened arches of her temples till the day of the resurrection.

Devotion of the Forty Hours.—The worldly rejoicings which precede Lent demanding reparation, the Church established the prayers called the Forty Hours, in honor of the forty hours which elapsed between Our Lord's condemnation and His resurrection. This devotion was inspired by the Spirit of God in the pious Cardinal Gabriel Paleotti, Archbishop of Bologna, in the sixteenth century. It owes its propagation above all to Pope Benedict XIV.

2. THE TIME OF LENT.

Instituted by the apostles in memory of the forty days of Our Lord's fasting, Lent extends from Ash Wednesday to Easter Sunday. St. Jerome observes that the number forty is always that of pain and affliction. (*In Ezech.*, c. xxix.) The Scripture furnishes us proofs of this in great numbers. We will mention: the forty days and forty nights of rain in the deluge; the forty years of exile in the desert; the forty days of siege which preceded the destruction of Jerusalem; the forty days' fasting of Moses and Elias.

Three great thoughts fill all the Lenten liturgy. The Church in the first place proposes to her children's meditation the drama of the Passion of Jesus Christ: each week she follows step by step the development of the deicidal conspiracy. And then Lent was to those who were aspirants for baptism the last preparation, and the Old as well as the New Testament furnished lessons intended to make the catechumens understand the grandeur of the blessing which they were to receive. Besides this the public penitents became also during the holy season the object of the maternal solicitude of the Church, and the numerous instances of mercy with which the Epistles and Gospels are especially filled opened their hearts to confidence, the inseparable accompaniment of pardon. These three considerations are the key to the Epistles and Gospels of this holy time.

Ash Wednesday.—Ashes were not in the beginning laid upon the heads of any but sinners submitted to public penance.

Before the Mass of this day the guilty presented themselves at the church to avow their faults and to receive the ashes on their heads. They were covered at the same time with the haircloth of penance, and driven solemnly from the church doors, which did not open again to them till Holy Thursday. Through humility pious Christians mingled with the penitents. After the abolition of public penance, the Church, not wishing to deprive her children of the great teachings contained in the pious ceremony of the ashes, preserved the custom of laying them on the brows of the faithful at the beginning of Lent. Let us respond to her holy intentions, and bring to this ceremony the sentiments of Adam and Eve after their sin. The sentence pronounced against them will fall upon us: "Remember, man, that dust thou art, and unto dust thou shalt return."

But beside this sadness the Church has placed hope. The sign of the cross made on our foreheads with the ashes reminds us that death has been conquered by the divine Crucified One, and that, thanks to Calvary, the dust has become for redeemed man the cradle of a life glorious and immortal.

First Sunday of Lent.—In France this is called *Dimanche des Brandons*, or Sunday of the Torches. The reason for this is that the young people who had given themselves over too much to the license of the carnival presented themselves at the church on the first Sunday of Lent, a torch in the hand, to make a public reparation of their excess.

The reparation has fallen into disuse, but the custom of fires has survived, and the popular name of *Sunday*

PRIEDIEU.

STATION OF THE CROSS.

STATUE.

CONFESSIONAL.

of the Torches, or the brands, remains to the first Sunday of Lent.

Fourth Sunday in Lent, called Lætare Sunday.—This name is derived from the first word of the Introit of this day. Everything speaks of joy in the liturgy of the fourth Sunday of Lent, because on this day were enrolled those who were to receive baptism at Easter, and the Church saw approaching the time for the restoration of the public penitents. In Rome on this day is blessed the golden rose, and the explanation of this ceremony will make us understand the cause of the Church's joy. We will translate Cardinal Peter of Capua. "We read," he says, "that the Lord Jesus, at the approach of His passion, wishing to strengthen His disciples against the scandals and humiliations to come, foretold to them often the glory of His resurrection, and even showed His glory to three of them in His transfiguration on Thabor. It is to follow the steps of the divine Master that, on the fourth Sunday of Lent—that is to say, that which immediately precedes Passion Sunday, which opens the way of sorrow—the Sovereign Pontiff, to soften the sadness of the days which are to come, announces to the faithful the glory of the resurrection, bearing a golden rose in his hand. This glory is, in fact, figured by the flower. Our Lord said that 'His flesh should flourish like it.' (Ps. xxvii. 7.) Among all the perishable beauty, nothing is equal to that of the flower; we have the testimony of the Saviour for this, Who said that: 'Not Solomon in all his glory was clothed like one of these.' (Matt. vi. 29.) Now, among the flowers, the rose is the most beautiful. It is then by a just title that it has been chosen to figure that glory 'which eye hath not seen, nor ear heard, nor hath it entered into the heart of man to conceive.' (1. Cor. ii. 9.) Why is it a *golden rose* which is anointed with musk and balm ? Gold, the most precious metal, is very proper to represent the glory of Jesus Christ in His resurrection. Balm preserves the body from corruption, and expresses here the immortality of the risen Saviour. Musk is the most odoriferous of the aromatics; it is thus a symbol of the fame of Christ which His resurrection has spread everywhere, like a sweet odor, by the ministry of His apostles." (*Spicil. Solesm.*, t. iii. p. 495.)

This rose is carried by a clerk who precedes His Holiness, then is laid in the middle of the altar on a rich silken veil embroidered with gold. The Sovereign Pontiff usually sends it to some prince or important personage, to honor him, or as a testimony of gratitude for service rendered to the Church.

Passion Sunday.—In the Mass of the preceding Friday has been read the gospel of the raising of Lazarus. We learn from St. John that many of those who were witnesses of this miracle went, under the influence of jealousy, to the Pharisees, to inform them of what had happened. The next day, which was the Sabbath, the death of the Saviour was decided upon. From that moment Our Lord had to flee and hide Himself. To express this unheard-of humiliation, the Church veils the cross. She veils at the same time the images of the saints, for it is right that the glory of the servant should efface itself when his Master is humiliated; and the fifth Sunday of Lent was called Passion Sunday, because, in fact, the way of sorrow began for Jesus

Christ in the council-hall where the black plots against His life were woven.

Feast of the Annunciation, March 25th.—The time of Septuagesima and Lent represents the militant life of man driven from the earthly paradise, and winning heaven by labor and sorrow. Fallen man had received a promise, and his tears were become less bitter. The Annunciation of Mary and the Incarnation of the Word are the accomplishment of this divine promise. In these days of penitence may man draw from this mystery proposed to his love new courage in the combat which he must sustain! No more cowardice nor murmurs in the midst of trials; the Word made flesh has foreseen them, and submitted to them Himself. One feast a year is not enough for gratitude. A voice was needed to repeat unceasingly to man the love of God in giving Himself to the world: the prayer of the Angelus received from the Church this sweet mission. Thrice a day the beloved voice of the bell repeats the message of the angel, the humility of Mary, and the abasement of the Word. The thrice-repeated Angelus will be the expression of man's gratitude toward the adorable Trinity, Who has so mercifully intervened in this mystery. Who does not know it? The voice of the bell struck nine times brings us the musical invitation of the nine choirs of angels; let us unite ourselves with them to adore the Incarnate Word, and salute Mary. The custom of reciting a prayer in honor of Mary at the sound of the bell goes back to Urban II. This Pope ordered that all the faithful should pray morning and night to call down the blessing of Heaven on the crusades. And, since prayer said in common is more powerful, the bell gave the signal for this great manifestation of Catholic faith. We know that Jerusalem fell into the hands of the Christians. Till that time the prayer had not been said at noon. It was Calixtus III. who, following the steps of his predecessor, completed the pious practice, hoping that God, once more disarmed by prayer, would grant victory to the Catholic army then fighting in Hungary against the Turks. These various struggles ended, the Angelus remained as a chant of triumph. Some authors see in the evening Angelus a commemoration of the joyous mysteries wrought in the silence of the night; in the morning Angelus the glorious mysteries; and in that of noon, the sorrowful mysteries. These pious reflections can but make us say this prayer, which has been enriched by numerous indulgences, with greater devotion. In the first place, there is an indulgence of a hundred days each time that the Angelus is said kneeling at the sound of the bell. The Christian faithful to this daily practice may gain each month, on whatever day he chooses, a plenary indulgence. The Angelus is said standing on Sunday in honor of the Resurrection, as is the *Regina Cœli* during the Paschal time.

This feast goes back to the highest antiquity. We read in the Bollandists that each year Mary celebrated the anniversary of that great day when the Word, assuming our flesh, raised her to the ineffable dignity of the Mother of God. As witnesses of these feelings of gratitude, the apostles associated themselves with her, and established the feast of the Annunciation in the entire world.

Feast of the Seven Dolors. — Tradition says that Mary, meeting her Son bearing His cross, fell under the weight of her anguish. Upon the place of this awful meeting a chapel was raised which took the name of St. Mary of the Spasm, and a feast was celebrated under the same name for several centuries. At the provincial Council of Cologne, in 1413, to rebuke the audacity of new heretics called Hussites, who had laid sacrilegious hands upon the images of Jesus Christ crucified and His holy Mother, was instituted the feast of the Commemoration of the Seven Dolors of the Blessed Virgin Mary, and its celebration was fixed for the Friday of Passion Week. This feast, substituted for that of the Spasm, or rather blended with it, was eagerly accepted by the faithful. To represent the anguish of Mary, painters have shown her with her heart pierced with seven swords. According to Benedict XIV., this was the origin of the custom: Seven merchants of Florence withdrew to a mountain near that city, and there laid the foundation of the Order of Servites, or Servants of the Blessed Virgin. These pious founders, in meditating on the sorrows of their august patron, discovered seven, of which some are found in the Gospel, and others are based on other pious reasons. These sorrows are: 1st, the prophecy made in the temple by the holy old man Simeon; 2d, the flight into Egypt; 3d, the loss of Jesus in Jerusalem; 4th, the meeting of Jesus and Mary on the way to Calvary, 5th, the crucifixion; 6th, the descent from the cross; 7th, the burial. In these seven swords we may believe that Christian art has wished to represent the abyss of sorrow into which the soul of Mary was plunged; the number seven being taken for universality. This is the translation of the words of Holy Scripture applied to Mary: "Thy sorrow is great as the sea" (Lament. ii. 13).

CHAPTER IV.—HOLY WEEK.

1. PALM SUNDAY.

The Procession.—The verdant palms in the hands of the faithful, the crowd of children, of men and women walking in procession, the sacred chants full of joy, vividly present the scene which Jerusalem saw five days before the passion. But the triumphal entry of the Saviour into Jerusalem was but a prophetic figure of that other triumph which He would receive in the midst of angelic harmonies in the heavenly Jerusalem. The gates of the celestial city, closed since the sin of Adam, could not open but to the bloody trophy of Calvary. It is this new triumph which the gates of the church indicate at the return of the procession, closed as they were until then, and yielding to the power of the cross, which seems thrice to open a breech in them as it knocks, while the voices of children, angels of the earth, rise in the sweetest melody of the sacred chants.

The Mass.—The Mass of Palm Sunday is a striking contrast to the procession; sadness succeeds the joyous canticles; after the gospel of triumph comes the sorrowful story of the passion, an image of the too-prompt change worked in the Jewish people; its inconstancy made it pass quickly from adoration to outrage, from the chants of Hosanna to the cries of "Crucify Him, crucify Him!"

2. OFFICE OF TENEBRÆ.

In the middle of the choir stands a triangular candlestick, surmounted by fifteen candles, in memory of the twelve apostles, and the disciples represented by the three

Marys. These candles, except the one at the top of the candlestick, are successively put out after each antiphon. During the chanting of the *Benedictus* those on the altar are extinguished. Then, in the midst of this profound night, whence the name of *Tenebræ*, or darkness, given to the office, a clerk carries behind the altar the candle which remains lighted at the top of the candlestick, hides it for some moments, and then its light returns to shine in the sanctuary. By this candle the Church represents to us the abandonment of Jesus Christ, His burial and resurrection. In the midst of the darkness of the sanctuary, an image of that which threw a veil of mourning over the world, a confused noise is heard; let us throw ourselves, then, at the foot of the cross where our God has just expired, and let this sound bring to our heart the echo of the upheaval of nature, the trembling of the earth, the opening of the tombs, the breaking of the rocks and the rending of the veil of the temple.

When, during the chant of the *Miserere*, the candle is carried behind the altar, our saddened heart should accompany the Saviour to the tomb. But that our sorrow be not without hope, this candle is not extinguished, and its flame says to us that Jesus Christ in the tomb lives still in His soul and in His divinity. Hope will give place to joy when the candle concealed behind the altar comes to shine anew in the sanctuary; we will then salute in it the Conqueror of death bursting gloriously from His tomb.

3. HOLY THURSDAY.

Mass of Holy Thursday.—The solemnity of the Mass of Holy Thursday makes a truce for a moment in the sorrows of the Church.

How can she contain the transports of her joy in this memorable anniversary of the institution of the Eucharist and the Catholic priesthood? The single Mass celebrated on this day in each church, the communion distributed to the clergy and the faithful, present to us the gospel scene when Jesus Christ, the only consecrator of the last supper, and the apostles were seated at the eucharistic table.

In honor of this solemnity the bells ring out during Mass their joyous peals; then, till Holy Saturday, they remain silent. This silence alone is a sign of great mourning, but it recalls to us also the silence of the apostles, not daring to raise their voices to defend their Master. Contrary to the usual practice of feast days, the kiss of peace is not given before the communion. By the suppression of this touching symbol of friendship the Church has intended to rebuke the perfidious treason consummated on the evening of this day.

The Repository.—The various names of tomb, repository, paradise, that is to say, *garden*, given by the people's piety to the chapel which each one hastens to ornament with his richest hangings and his first flowers, alone show the mysteries to which the Church desires to turn our thoughts. The procession to the repository, by the light of candles and torches, already expresses funeral pomps. The incense poured out upon the way of the Blessed Sacrament recalls to us the aromatic herbs of the embalming; the silence of the priest, the mute sorrow of Mary and the disciples; the chants of triumph, the joyous canticles of the angels of heaven; the return without pomp, the sad descent from Calvary. In this *paradise* the chalice will be the tomb of the Saviour; the pall with which it

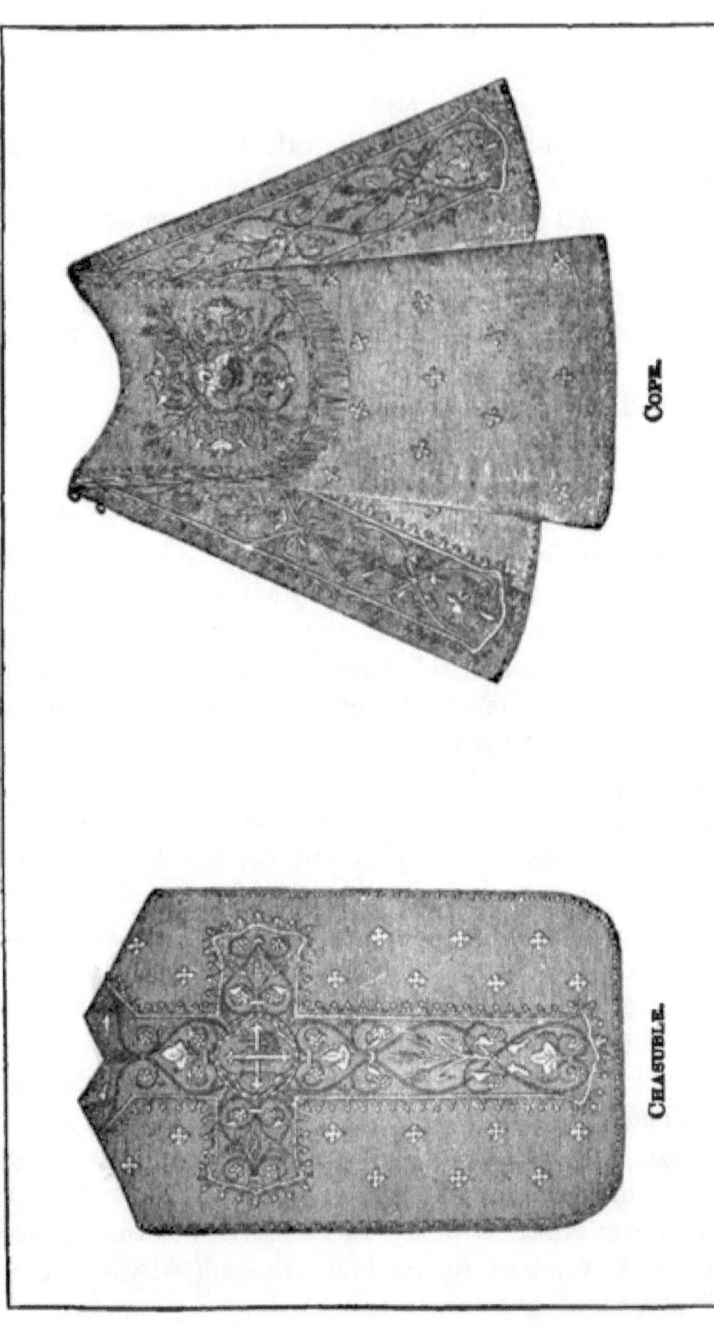

is covered replaces the stone rolled before the sepulchre, and the paten laid above it represents the seal of the Pharisees. (Gavantus, p. iv. tit. 8.) A white veil envelops this mystic tomb, in memory of the winding-sheet which was used in the burial.

Blessing of the Holy Oils.—In this consecration everything is full of mystery: the day, the moment, the ceremonies. The day, Holy Thursday, feast of the Eucharist, seemed marvellously suitable to the consecration of the matter of the sacraments, which all, in some sort, bear upon that of our altars. The moment: the oil of the sick is blessed before the *Pater* in that part of the Mass which represents Our Lord on the cross, making Himself infirm in order to cure us, and dying for us. What abundant graces spring then from all the wounds of the Saviour upon that matter henceforth sanctified! This, become the channel of these precious graces, applied to the members of the sick man will give him health, often of body, always of soul. It is after the communion that the oil of catechumens and the holy chrism are consecrated, because the two sacraments of which they are especially the matter were instituted after the Resurrection, and the ceremonies which follow the communion symbolize that part of the life of Our Saviour. (See the Mass, page 24.)

We have said there was mystery in these ceremonies. The breathing of the bishop and the twelve priests who assist him upon the holy oils signifies the intervention of the Holy Spirit, of Whose breath it is the symbol, be it because of its name or because of the manner in which He was communicated to the apostles on the evening of the Resurrection. When the prayers of the liturgy have raised the matter of oil to that degree of power intended for it by God, the Church sees in it but the Spirit of love and peace which is there present by His virtue. This is why the bishop and the twelve priests come in turn to salute with a triple genuflection the holy chrism and the oil of the sick; this is why they respectfully kiss the vase which contains them.

The Washing of Feet.—The Pope washes the feet of thirteen priests of different nations. The Church ordains that, after the example of what is done in Rome, the bishop washes the feet of thirteen poor men.

Why thirteen? Some see here the intention of representing the perfected number of the Apostolic College, the traitor Judas having been replaced by St. Matthias, and God having added St. Paul to the apostles previously chosen. Others, with Benedict XIV., find the reason for this number in a fact of the life of St. Gregory the Great. This holy pontiff each day washed the feet of twelve beggars. One day he remarked a thirteenth, whom no one had seen enter; it was an angel.

The Stripping of the Altars.—After the Mass on Holy Thursday, the stripping of the altars takes place. The missal, the cards, the linens, cloths, and other ornaments are successively taken away, and then the candles are extinguished. The afflicted Church recalls to us by this ceremony the stripping to which Our Lord submitted, to expiate the fault of our first parents. Let us think then of Jesus Christ despoiled of everything, His garments, His glory, and His friends.

4. GOOD FRIDAY.

The altar stripped of its ornaments, the silence of the

bells, the vestments of mourning in the sanctuary, the sadness upon each face, say to us that this day is the anniversary of a great sorrow. The anniversary of the death of a father unites all his children around his tomb. Faithful Christians hasten on Good Friday around the cross and the sepulchre of Jesus Christ. Only the unnatural child is lacking to this fraternal meeting of love and gratitude.

The morning office is divided into four parts: the Lessons, the Prayers, the Adoration of the Cross, and the Mass of the Presanctified.

The Lessons.—Before mounting the altar-steps the priest prays, prostrate, with his face on the earth. On this day, more than on any other, the altar seems to his faith like a new Calvary. But Our Lord, before consummating His sacrifice there, watered with His blood in sorrowful agony the Garden of Gethsemani. The gospel shows Him to us in this anguish, prostrate, His brow in the dust. The humiliated position of the priest recalls to us this first act of the great drama of the passion. The office begins by the reading of certain passages taken from the prophets, Exodus, and the gospel. The Church places before the eyes of her children the history of the great Victim of the human race. The prophets have announced long in advance His sufferings, His humiliations; Exodus, in the sacrifices of the Jewish law, has figured the different circumstances of His death; then the gospel gives us the simple and sublime story of that bloody immolation.

The Prayers.—The reading of the passion finished, the spouse of Jesus Christ, in tears prostrates herself at the foot of the cross, and prays for all the needs of her numerous family. No one is forgotten. Even for the Jews she has a prayer. Only, with the intention of imprinting a stigma upon the ironical genuflections of the prætorium and Calvary, she suppresses that act of adoration when she prays for the deicidal race.

The Unveiling of the Cross.—The ceremony known as the unveiling of the cross represents the preaching and the triumph of a crucified God. It is begun by detaching the portion of the veil which covers the top of the cross, and uncovering it as far as the arm.

It is raised a little, while in a medium voice are chanted the words: "*Ecce lignum crucis.*" And those present, or rather the entire world, are invited to come and adore: "*Venite adoremus.*" This first unveiling and the medium tone express the first preaching of the cross which the apostles made among themselves; they did not speak of the mystery of the redemption but with the disciples of Jesus, fearing otherwise to call the attention of the Jews. The cross receives, at the same time, the first homage of adoration, in reparation for the outrages which the Saviour received in the house of Caiphas.

The sacred ministers have gone further into the sanctuary, and uncovered the right arm of the cross. It is then raised higher, and in a louder voice than before is chanted again: "*Ecce lignum crucis.*" This second unveiling, accompanied with louder tones than the first, represents the preaching of the mystery of the cross to the Jews, after Pentecost; and the adoration which it receives for the second time is a reparation for the injuries of the prætorium.

Then the cross, entirely uncovered, is raised higher

than before, and the chant, become nearly triumphant, repeats: "*Ecce lignum crucis.*" The solemnity of this last unveiling recalls the preaching of the mystery of the cross in the entire world, and by the third adoration the Church wishes to repair the blasphemies, the genuflections, and the cruelties of Calvary. (Guéranger, *Holy Week.*)

The Adoration of the Cross.—The cross, entirely uncovered, is shown to the pious and recollected crowd. For many days they have not seen the crucifix; in this moment they contemplate the head crowned with thorns, the hands and feet pierced with nails, the side opened by the iron of the lance, and all, kings and pontiffs, old men and children, rich and poor, come to adore the redeeming wood. Would it not seem as if they were weeping children admitted to the death-chamber of the head of the family, where he was exposed upon his bed, and presenting themselves with respectful grief to kiss his beloved remains?

Under the influence of one of those sweet illusions so familiar to sorrow and love, the faithful son sees in this moment but Calvary and its sorrowful road; out of respect for its dust empurpled with the divine blood, and in reparation for the falls of the Redeemer, he removes his shoes, and three times he bends his knee and bows his head.

Mass of the Presanctified.—Properly speaking there is no Mass on Good Friday. The ceremony which takes its place is called the Mass of the Presanctified; *Mass*, because some of the rites of the Mass are preserved; *of the Presanctified*, that is to say, gifts consecrated before, because the celebrant there offers to the adoration of the people, and consumes himself, the host consecrated in the Mass of Holy Thursday. The clergy go to bring from the repository the host reserved in the chalice. The altar-candles are lighted to receive the Blessed Sacrament. The absence of lights in the preceding ceremonies recalls to us the darkness which accompanied the death of our God. In this Mass the Church omits that which has direct connection with the mysteries of Calvary, and all the prayers in which mention is made of the communion of the faithful, or that under the species of wine, both of which have no place in this day. (Gav. p. iv. tit. 9.)

The elevation at the *Pater* is made with the right hand only, to distinguish it from the ordinary form; nothing, on this sorrowful day, must resemble other days. The prayer *Libera nos* is to-day said aloud, to celebrate the descent of Jesus Christ into Limbo, and the deliverance of the souls which were detained there. (*Rational*, l. iv. c. 49.)

Vespers, recited in a grave and mournful voice, end the office of the morning.

5. HOLY SATURDAY.

To understand the different parts of the office of this day, let us recall three facts: first, that this office, celebrated now in the morning, was formerly said in the night of Easter; secondly, that in this night the catechumens were baptized; thirdly, that the Mass was said in the dawn of the very day of the resurrection.

Blessing of the New Fire.—The lamps of the sanctuary, extinguished during these days, should have reminded us that the divine Light has, in a sense, extinguished and eclipsed Himself in the night of the tomb; the blessing of the new fire will represent to us His glorious return. In this ceremony the Church wears purple, the color of mourning; the joys of the Resurrection have not yet rejoiced the heart of the sorrowing spouse. However, it is no longer, like yesterday, black; hope has allowed some sweet rays to fall into her soul; her Beloved will soon be restored to her. For the blessing of the fire, the clergy go outside the church, following the steps of the holy women who had to go out of Jerusalem to reach the sepulchre. The celebrant, taking a stone, strikes from it a new fire. The stone is an emblem of Jesus Christ: though stricken by death at the hands of the Jews, He has none the less become, by His resurrection, the sacred fire which enlightens and warms the world. This glorious life, of which the sepulchre was as the cradle, Jesus Christ has not received; it was in Himself; the Church wishes to figure this mystery of the power of the Saviour raising Himself when she commands that the new fire shall not be taken from a fire already existing. The grains of incense, blessed with the new fire, recall to us the aromatic herbs brought to the sepulchre by Magdalen and her pious companions.

The Triangular Candle.—After blessing the new fire, the clergy enter again the holy place. The deacon carries a rod surmounted by a candle in three branches. This rod and triple candle symbolize Jesus Christ in His two natures: one the human nature with its weakness; the other the divine nature all resplendent with the glories of the Holy Trinity. One of the branches of this candle is lighted in the door of the church, and the deacon, showing it, says: "*Lumen Christi*"—"Behold the light of

Christ "; and the response is made with genuflection: "*Deo gratias*"—"Thanks be to God." The second branch and then the third is lighted and shown to the people, with the same words said in louder tone. This triple manifestation of the light marks for us the preaching by the Incarnate Word of the divinity of the Father, Son, and Holy Ghost; and this tone, gradually raised, expresses the word, heard in the first instance like a faint murmur in the little circle of the apostles, and later resounding like the violent wind which symbolized it on the day of Pentecost, and that the voice of the Lord has dominated by its power the thunder of angry waters. (Ps. xxviii. 3; Guéranger; Gavantus.) As to the deacon clothed in white, delegated to be the messenger of the good tidings, he recalls to us the angel shining in light who announced to the holy women the resurrection of Jesus Christ.

Blessing of the Paschal Candle.—It is the duty of the deacon to fulfil this function of the liturgy in the presence of the priest and even of the bishop. Jesus Christ arisen appeared first to the holy women, and then to the disciples at Emmaus, and then to the apostles reunited in the upper chamber of the last supper. Because of this fact in the Gospel, the inferior in the hierarchy has been preferred for the blessing of the paschal candle over the bishops and priests, successors of the disciples and the apostles.

As preliminaries of this ceremony the Gospel of the Mass is said; then the deacon, immediately, without saying *Dominus vobiscum*, to better express the agitation of the Church at the tidings of the Resurrection, intones the *Exultet*, that sublime chant which celebrates

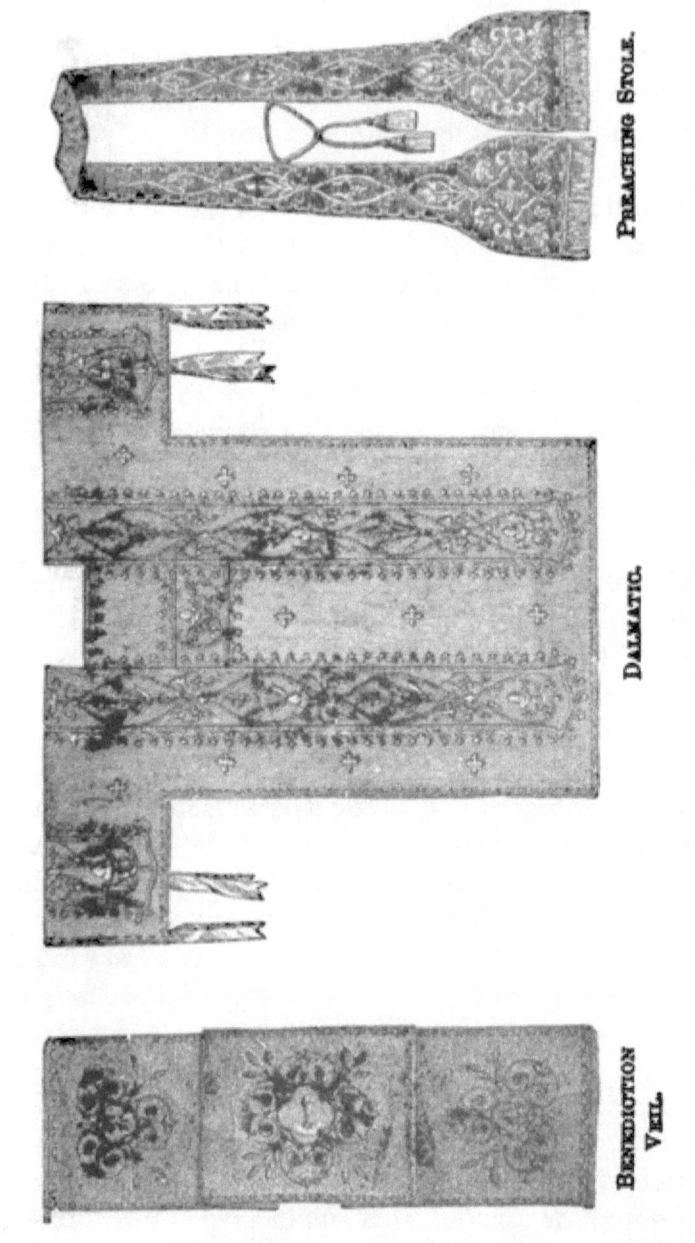

xxvii.

the victory over hell and death. The immortal Conqueror is there before our eyes, figured by the paschal candle. This, not yet lighted, recalls Jesus Christ stricken by death, and the five grains of incense, His embalming. The embalmed candle is lighted by the new fire, and then with its light and its five grains of incense it appears to us as a magnificent symbol of the Saviour, preserving after His resurrection His glorious wounds, the sight of which alone is a prayer full of tenderness and grace before His Father. (Guéranger, *The Liturgical Year.*)

From the paschal candle the other candles and the sanctuary lamp are lighted, as it is Jesus Christ from whom the apostles, the true torches of the world, received their light, destined to enlighten the universe. During the forty days consecrated to the honor of the mysteries of the risen Saviour the paschal candle lights the offices of the Church; it disappears on Ascension-day after the reading of the Gospel.

The Lessons.—We have said that in the night of Easter the catechumens were solemnly baptized. While they were gathered in the church porch the priests gave them the preparatory rites of baptism. To keep the assembly attentive, passages of the Scriptures were read relative to the circumstances, and divided by prayers and canticles. The number of the Lessons reminded the catechumens of the twelve apostles, to whom, after God, they owed the blessing of faith. (*Gem. animæ*, l. iii. c. 108.) At the prayer which accompanies each one of these lessons the knee is bent, except at the last one. This retraces the history of the three young Hebrews who preferred to suffer the fires of the furnace rather than give idolatrous homage to the statue of Nabuchodonosor. The Church omits the genuflection to honor the beautiful example of fidelity to God given to all ages, and also to publicly condemn idolatry in the presence of the catechumens, taken, for the most part, from the darkness of paganism.

Blessing of the Water.—The Lessons finished, the clergy go to the sacred fonts ; the celebrant there blesses the water destined for regeneration, following a rite religiously preserved by the Church, which we are about to explain. The priest, after having implored the divine intervention, touches the water thrice with his hand. The first time he divides it in the form of a cross, to show that, by virtue of the cross, the waters have received their power to regenerate souls. The second time he touches it with his hand to imprint this virtue upon it, that it may vivify and purify. The third time, after dividing it, he throws it towards the four points of the compass, to signify that all nations from the north and the south, the east and the west, are called to the grace of baptism.

Thrice also the priest breathes upon the water in the form of a cross, to call upon the matter of baptism, by the merits of Jesus Christ crucified, the fruitful intervention of the three divine Persons.

The water, prepared from the beginning of the world to become the powerful instrument of mercies, received all its virtue in the Jordan from the contact with the divine flesh of Jesus Christ. The Church expresses this mystery by plunging into the water the paschal candle, symbol of the Saviour. Its triple immersion figures the three immersions of baptism. But the regeneration of man is pre-eminently the work of the Holy Spirit; this is why the priest at the same time prays Him to descend upon the waters of baptism and pour out upon them His fruitful grace; also, to represent this merciful intervention, he breathes again upon the water, making this time with his breath the Greek letter ψ, the first of the word *spirit* in the language of the Hellenes; then he pours into it the oil of catechumens and holy chrism, sacred gifts become since Holy Thursday the repositories of divine graces.

At this moment was begun the immersion of catechumens. This solemn baptism on Holy Saturday is no longer customary; only the aspersion of water upon the assistants after the blessing is a souvenir of it. The new Christians then re-entered the church, and saluted their new brothers of heaven by the chant of the litanies. (Guér., Gav.)

Mass of Holy Saturday.—The altar, stripped and bare during these last days, is to-day re-clad with white linens and its rich ornaments, to represent to us the glories of the Resurrection.

Dawn begins to tinge the horizon, the commemorative hour of the Resurrection has arrived; the bells, uniting their sweet voices, celebrate it in a unanimous concert. For many long days the Alleluia has been banished from the liturgy; in the sorrows of exile, fallen man could not repeat it, but to-day heaven is opened to us; before we taste the joys of eternity let us repeat the sweetest of its canticles: "Alleluia, Alleluia!" At the Gospel incense is carried, but not candles. Again an allusion to the events of this morning. The holy women have come to the tomb with perfumes, but their souls were not illumined with the light of faith. Did they not expect to find in the sepulchre Him Who had promised to rise again on the third day? (*Rational*, l. vi. c. 81.) "There was in them all the ardor of love," says Alcuin, "but faith was extinct."

The Credo is not sung; it is the symbol of the faith preached by the apostles, and they had not yet believed in the resurrection of their Master. (Gavantus, p. iv. tit. 10.)

There is no Offertory at this Mass. The faithful, presenting as they did the bread and wine intended for the sacrifice, and the number of those intending to communicate, and consequently offer, being great, the length of this ceremony would have added still more to the fatigues of the night. For these reasons of charitable condescension the Offertory was omitted. The same thoughtfulness has made the Vespers of this day chosen from the shortest of all the psalms. Sung in the place of the anthem of the Communion, they are like a canticle of thanksgiving of the newly baptized, admitted for the first time to the banquet of the Lamb. Our Lord not having given peace to His apostles until the evening of His resurrection, the Kiss of Peace, and the *Agnus Dei*, which speaks of peace, are suppressed in the Mass of Holy Saturday.

CHAPTER V.—PASCHAL TIME AND PENTECOST.

1. PASCHAL TIME.

The Feast of Easter.—Christmas is the feast of love, but Easter is the feast of hope. "This solemnity," says St. Gregory the Great, "snatches us from earth to transport us into the delights of heaven." (*Homil. xxii., In Evangel.*) On this day which our fathers so well named "the day of days," we celebrate the resurrection of Jesus Christ, but we salute also with transports of unspeakable joy the dawn of our own resurrection. The paschal solemnity comes to say to man: "Thou shalt not die: the tomb shall be to thy flesh, stricken by the breath of sorrow or of time, as the earth is to the grain confided to her; there it shall germinate in the silence of centuries, to burst forth glorious and immortal. To the pure soul everything speaks of resurrection. Nature, which seems to sleep through the days of winter, clothes herself again with verdure and joy; upon the branches, yesterday so dry, bloom to-day the loveliest flowers, and everything has a voice to say to us: "If God so clothe the grass of the field, which to-day is, and to-morrow is cast into the oven, shall He not much more clothe you, O ye of little faith?" (St. Matt. vi. 30.)

The sun, which until now was wrapped in a sombre mantle of fog and clouds, appears to us all resplendent with new fires; in this more radiant sun the Christian will find a pledge of hope: one day in glory his risen flesh shall seem "like to it." (St. Matt. xiii. 43.)

And in the holy place the Church, in all the forms which tenderness suggests to her, recalls to her children the consoling dogma. Ornaments of joyous colors have replaced the signs of mourning; rich embroideries adorn the altars; the bells ring out their most solemn peals, and in the sanctuary a chant from heaven rises in all voices: "Alleluia, Alleluia, Alleluia."

Pasch in Hebrew means *passage*. This name alone

awakens in the Christian soul the greatest memories. *Pasch:* it is the passage of the angel of death in the midst of Egypt. *Pasch:* it is the passage of the Hebrews through the waves of the Red Sea. *Pasch:* it is the passage of Jesus Christ from death to life. *Pasch.* it is the passage of the souls of the just from Limbo to heaven. *Pasch:* it is the passage of the catechumens from unbelief to the light of the faith. *Pasch:* it is for us the passage from sin to grace, from the dust of the tomb to the glory of the resurrection. The Church makes mention of these different mysteries in the liturgy of this day, but she seems to prefer to occupy herself with the joys of the Resurrection and of Baptism.

Easter Eggs.—The egg was regarded as a symbol of the resurrection of the body. (St. Augustine, *Serm.* cv.) In the tomb of several martyrs have been discovered marble eggs, like hen's eggs, or even the shells of natural eggs. For the Christian the egg is an image of the tomb; he remains there, without movement and without life, until He Who has vouchsafed to compare His tenderness to that of a hen gathering her chickens beneath her wings comes to break the chains which hold him the captive of death. It is to this eminently religious origin that the Easter egg can be traced. In some churches to this day an ostrich-egg is hung in the middle of the sanctuary as a pledge of hope, and at the domestic hearth blessed eggs are eaten before any other food on Easter, which is called, for this reason, pasch of the egg. (*Dict. des Antiq. Chrét.;* Godard, *Archéol.*)

Symbolism of Paschal Time.—Now the days of penitence are fled. No more tears, no more mourning in the liturgy. The Church, opening out the vast horizons of eternity, transports us to them on the wings of hope, to show us that after the sufferings of this life a shining crown will be laid upon the brow of the victor, and he will rejoice in the boundless joys of the vision of God. Catholic worship translates this consoling thought during the paschal time. This embraces a period of fifty days. The jubilee year, which falls every fifty years, has stamped this number with a joyful character. "And as the number forty is taken for the punishment of penitence, this is the figure of recompense and rest," says St. Gregory. (*Mor.* l. i. c. 15.)

Throughout all the paschal time the first Christians prayed standing. St. Justin, asking himself the reason of such a custom, answers: "It is to place unceasingly before our eyes the blessing of our resurrection. The humiliation of our bodies during the other periods is a symbol of our fall by sin, but the position which we assume during these days which belong to the Lord is a sign of the resurrection of Jesus Christ, Who has delivered us from the chains of sin and of death." (*Quæst. ad Orthod. Resp.* cxv.) The Council of Nice raised this custom into a canonical law. (*Canon ult.*) It has been retained, as we have already said, during the paschal time for the recitation of the Regina Cœli, and on Sundays for the Angelus.

Quasimodo Sunday opens the series of five Sundays that belong to the paschal time. The first words of the Introit give it the name which it bears. It was the eve of the day when the newly baptized laid off their white robes; this made it also called Sunday *in albis depositis*.

Procession of St. Mark, 25th of April.—Under the

pontificate of Pelagius, in 589, the swollen waters of the Tiber rose to the summit of the temple of Nero. In subsiding they left such an infectious deposit that there resulted a violent plague. To turn away the divine wrath the Pope ordered a general procession. But God demanded an illustrious victim: Pelagius was taken away by the contagion, in the very procession, with seventy other persons. St. Gregory the Great, his successor, ordered a second procession, at the head of which was carried the picture of the Blessed Virgin painted by St. Luke. Before this venerated relic the plague disappeared. When they had come to the castle of Adrian (now the castle of San Angelo) St. Gregory saw an angel sheathing a sword wet with blood. It was the signal of pardon. As a thanksgiving the Church renews this procession each year. (We have seen in a preceding chapter that the Regina Cœli was said by angels on this occasion.)

According to several authors, the pagans had a procession on the 25th of April to call down the blessings of the gods on the fruits of the earth. They carried a statue of Ceres, the goddess of the harvest. The Church probably chose this day for the procession of which we have spoken in order to interest the pagans themselves in the prescribed prayers for the cessation of the plague.

Processions and Rogations.—Plagues, ceaselessly recurring, desolated the Church in Vienne: droughts, earthquakes, fires, and the ravages of wild beasts. St. Mamertus, to appease heaven, ordered prayers, or *rogations*, sanctified by fasting and accompanied by a solemn procession. Copying those of the Ninivites, they

ANTEPENDIUM.

Hangings or Panels for the front of the Altar.

xxviii.

were three days in duration, and the three days immediately preceding the feast of the Ascension were chosen. Is it not the Gospel of the last Sunday after Easter which says: "Ask and you shall receive"? St. Mamertus remembered this, and put under the protection of this solemn promise his celebrated institution, which the entire Church soon adopted. "It seemed," says Bossuet, "that the Church wished to lay upon Jesus Christ ascending into heaven all her desires, as the true Mediator for man with God." (*Catech. des Fêtes.*)

In the processions of the rogation-days, as in that of St. Mark, the Church prays for the fruits of the earth. Not to join therein is to affect a stupid independence: the rich as well as the poor, and more than the poor, because His domains are vaster; the city man as well as he who tills the fields, need God. (See what has been said of processions in general, page 89.)

The Ascension.—The fortieth day following His resurrection, Our Lord appeared a last time to His disciples, ate with them, led them to the Mount of Olives, and there, toward noon, arose into heaven in their presence: this is the mystery celebrated on this day. The paschal candle is extinguished after the gospel, to indicate that Jesus Christ, the true light, has left the earth.

The Finding of the Holy Cross, May 3d.—We borrow from the Roman breviary the story of this marvellous event. "After the signal victory which the Emperor Constantine won over Maxentius, thanks to the divine sign revealed by heaven, Helena, his mother, admonished in a dream, went to Jerusalem, to discover the sacred tree of our redemption. In the first place she threw down the marble statue which paganism, to efface all vestige of the passion, had raised to Venus on the very spot of the crucifixion. By her orders were also destroyed the statues of Adonis and Jupiter on the Saviour's cradle and the tomb of the Resurrection. Then they proceeded to the excavations on Calvary. Three crosses were found at a great depth; the inscription placed above the Saviour's head was discovered on another side. It was important to know which of these three crosses had been consecrated by the blood of the adorable Victim. God dissipated all doubts by a miracle. Macarius, bishop of Jerusalem, prayed fervently to heaven, and had the crosses brought to the bedside of a lady who was dangerously ill. The first two had no effect, but the third restored her instantly to health.

"In the place where she had found the cross, the pious empress built a magnificent church, where was religiously preserved, in a silver case, a part of the holy relic; the other part was sent to Constantine at Rome, who placed it in the church called 'the Holy Cross of Jerusalem.'"

The feast of the Finding of the Holy Cross was in the beginning celebrated in the temple built by St. Helena on Calvary; it spread through the Catholic world with the fragments of the true cross. Each church enriched by this precious treasure wished to celebrate the anniversary of its miraculous discovery, which took place on May 3d in the year 326. If we would enter into the spirit of this feast, let us think that the cross is to many Christians lost and hidden. In sufferings they murmur, or revolt, or blaspheme; but suffering is a treasure, a precious stone, a crown. Whence comes such conduct? The cross is not known; let us ask God, for ourselves and our brethren, that we may discover this rich treasure.

2. PENTECOST TIME.

The Feast of Pentecost.—Jesus Christ has given us part of all that He possessed. As God He had a Father; He gave Him to us when He taught us to pray "Our Father Who art in heaven." As man He had a mother; she became ours on Calvary. In the Incarnation His Divinity was clothed with a body and soul; He presents us with them in the Eucharist, with His divine nature, that they may become our food. King of heaven, He has gone there to prepare a place for us. What has Jesus Christ that man has not possessed in his turn? His Spirit; and behold, He gives Him to us in the great solemnity of Pentecost.

On this day Our Lord put the last touch to the work of our redemption. The perfect alliance of God with man, promised for forty centuries, was then accomplished. That which the jubilee year, or the fiftieth year, was to the Jews, the fiftieth day was to the disciples of Jesus Christ and the entire world. The jubilee brought liberty to all; Pentecost has given it to the earth; for, says St. Paul, "where the Spirit of the Lord is, there is liberty." (II. Cor. iii. 17.)

The Church, as a mother full of wisdom, wishes that the joys of which her Spouse has made her the repository should be the recompense to Christians for their prayers and their desires. Advent has prepared us for the joys of the crib; Lent for those of the Resurrection; paschal time for those of Pentecost.

Blessing of the Fonts.—On the eve of Pentecost the fonts are blessed, as on Holy Saturday. This ceremony was formerly followed by the solemn administration of baptism to those who had not been able to receive it at Easter. Different motives pointed out this day to the choice of the Church: the descent of the Holy Ghost upon the apostles had been announced as being to them a second baptism (Acts i.); the apostles baptized three thousand Jews on Pentecost; the regeneration of the soul by baptism is the first operation of the Holy Spirit.

Symbolism of Pentecost Time.—Pentecost is the memorable day of the birth of the Church, in the upper room of the last supper; the days which are to follow to Advent recall to us her life of pilgrimage across the centuries. As the liturgic time of Pentecost rolls away, the days become shorter and colder, image of life and of the world; the light of charity and of faith fades little by little; scarcely will it show its feeble rays at the coming of the Sovereign Judge.

The gospel of the last Sunday after Pentecost unfolds before our eyes the judgment, the supreme drama in the world's existence; then the Church militant will enter into the joy of beatitude and rest. Filled with the Spirit from on high, the laborers of the Father of the family went after Pentecost to water with their sweat or their blood the divine heritage, and for the Church began the labors of her spiritual harvest. Green, which is worn in this liturgic period, symbolizes well the harvest which sprouts and which increases.

Feast of the Holy Trinity.—This feast, placed at the beginning of the Pentecost season, recalls to us that the

Paschal Time and Pentecost.

apostles, after the descent of the Holy Ghost, haste
to preach the mystery of the Holy Trinity. The Chu[rch]
has already honored by a special feast each one of
divine Persons: Christmas was for the Father, Ea[ster]
for the Son, Pentecost for the Holy Ghost. But
this day the liturgy unites them in the same feast
order to chant the great dogma of the Unity in
Trinity.

Corpus Christi.—After His ascension, Jesus Ch[rist]
has willed to remain in the tabernacle, to be the stre[ngth]
of His spouse in the combats of her pilgrimage. [The]
grateful Church has instituted a feast to celebrate [the]
greatness of a God humbled and concealed under the [Eu]charistic veils: it is Corpus Christi, or the feast of J[esus]
Christ in the Eucharist. Corpus Christi was not alw[ays]
celebrated in the Church. A venerable religious ho[spi]taller, Juliana of Mont-Corneillou, of the city of Li[ege]
learned from Our Lord in a revelation that He des[ired]
the institution of a feast to honor the sacrament of
love. The plan received the approbation of Urban [IV,]
but the death of the Pontiff delayed its execution. [The]
glory of definitely establishing this solemnity was [re]served to a French pope. It was Clement V., in [a]
general Council held at Vienne in 1311.

Feast of the Sacred Heart.—A humble religious na[med]
Margaret Mary Alacoque, of the Order of the Visita[tion]
was in adoration during the octave of Corpus Ch[risti]
when Our Lord appeared to her and expressed the d[esire]
to see the Friday after the octave of Corpus Christi [con]secrated to the celebration of a particular feast in h[onor]
of His Heart, to repair the outrages which He rec[eives]
in the Sacrament of the Altar.

The pious maiden, treated as a visionary, saw a violent storm arise around her, but Jesus Christ watched over her, and with a look calmed the tempest. We will not repeat all the divers phases through which this devotion has passed. The institution of the new feast was not obtained until the pontificate of Clement XIII., in 1765, and did not become general till the time of Pius IX., in 1857. There is now no part of the Catholic world where the devotion to the Sacred Heart of Jesus is not established.

Nativity of St. John the Baptist, June 24th.—This feast, one of the oldest in the liturgy, was for a long time preceded by a fast-day and a Lent of three weeks, in memory of the penitent life of the holy Precursor. An angel had announced that "many should rejoice at His birth." (St. Luke i. 14.) This joy flowed down through the Christian world from the mountains of Hebron. The fires which are lighted upon the heights in the evening of this day are a souvenir of the joy brought by this feast to all Christian hearts.

Feast of Sts. Peter and Paul, June 29th.—In the year 67 of the Christian era, and the 29th day of June, Saint Peter and Saint Paul left the damp cell in the Mamertine prison to be led to execution. The former was to be crucified; but the latter, because his title of Roman citizen gave him the right to a more honorable death, was to be decapitated by the sword. At a little distance from Rome, on the Ostian Way, the two apostles separated.

"Peace be with thee, head of the Church, shepherd of all Christ's lambs," said St. Paul.

"Go in peace, herald of heavenly joys, guide of the just in the way of salvation," responded St. Peter.

The veneration of centuries has carved these words on the pediment of the Church of the Farewells, built on the spot of the separation, and there they are still to be read.

The procession divided. St. Peter, taken to the Janiculum, the place of common executions, was scourged, and crucified head downwards. Two Christian women remained at the foot of the cross, like the women on Calvary; they gathered up in linen cloths the blood of the glorious martyr.

St. Paul continued on the Ostian Way. The patrician lady Plautilla, a new Veronica, weeping, accompanied the mournful procession. Upon the place of martyrdom she took off her veil at St. Paul's request, and gave it to him to bandage his eyes, according to the Roman custom. After a fervent prayer he offered himself to the executioners. His head bounded thrice upon the ground, and where it came in contact with the earth three fountains burst forth, which are to be seen at this day.

Visitation of the Blessed Virgin Mary, July 2d.—This is the feast commemorative of the visit of Mary to St. Elizabeth in the mountains of Hebron. "Blessed art thou among women, and blessed is the fruit of thy womb," cried the spouse of Zachary at the sight of the august Virgin whose divine maternity had been revealed to her by the Holy Spirit. The beautiful canticle of the Magnificat was the response of the humble Mary.

This feast was established because of a great schism in the West. The Church had striven for a long time to put an end to these deplorable divisions; the charity shown by Mary in her visit to her cousin prompted Pope Urban VI. to place under the protection of the mystery of the Visitation such an important enterprise. He hoped by the intercession of the Mother of Beautiful Love to lead these two parties to give each other the kiss of peace; his hope was not deceived, as history shows us.

If Mary unites the sad divisions of the Church, let us have recourse to her, begging her to bring into the pale of unity those who live separated from it. Many sheep have been stolen from the fold of Christ by schism; let us pray this tender shepherdess to lead them back to the Church's sheepfold.

Perhaps more than one reader has asked himself why the Visitation is celebrated on July 2d. In the beginning of April Mary left Nazareth to go to Hebron; it would seem that the date of the feast should have been then. Some churches, it is true, at first chose that period, but generally it was preferred to transfer the celebration because of Holy Week, with which it often would have collided. It was thought then that there was no better time to select than July 2d, anniversary of Mary's return. She passed three months in Elizabeth's house, remaining in Hebron till the octave of the birth of St. John the Baptist, the day of his circumcision; but the next day, July 2d, she set out for Nazareth.

Our Lady of Mount Carmel, July 16th.—From the heights of Carmel Elias had the vision of the mysterious little cloud which, changing into rain, brought blessed fruitfulness upon the sterile fields.

This cloud, according to the doctors, prophesied Mary. And Elias and his disciples honored on Mount Carmel

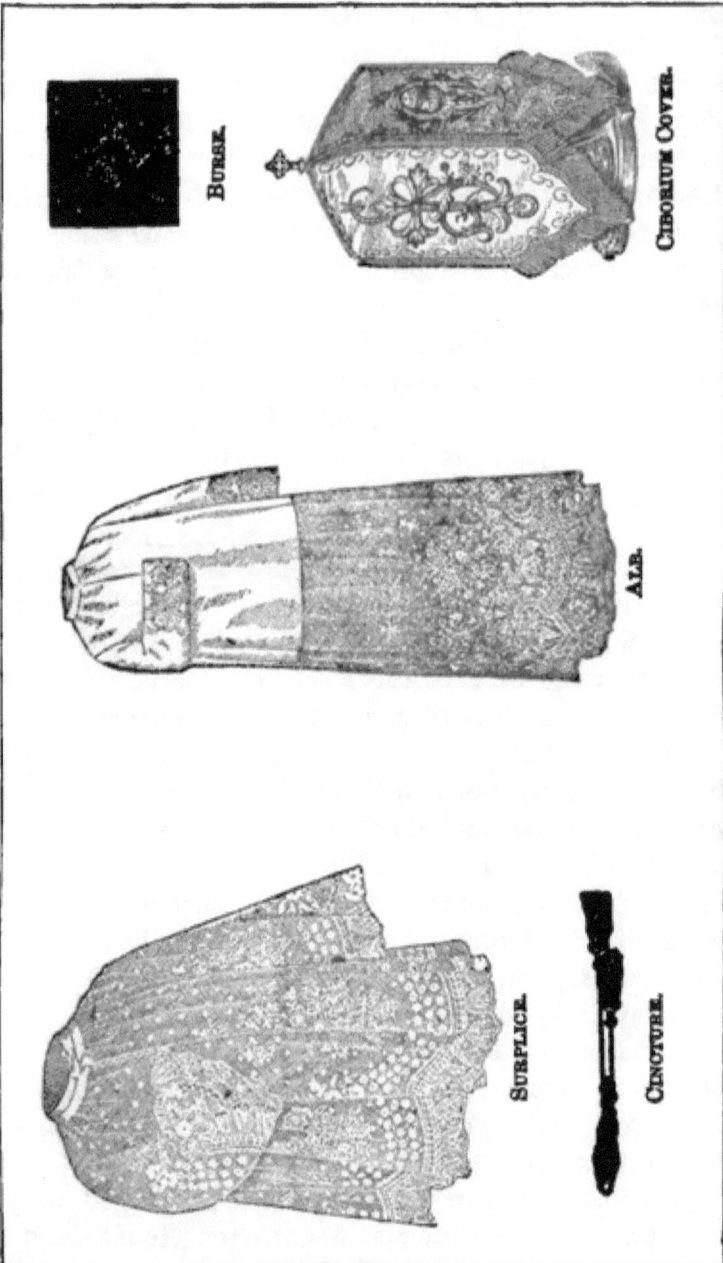

xxix.

her who was to be in the course of ages the blessed Mother of the Redeemer. Mary, long before her birth, was already the Lady of Mount Carmel.

The delicious solitudes of this mountain, and, still more, its great memories, drew there many Christians. It is even believed that a chapel in Mary's honor was raised there during her life, in the very place where the prophet had seen the mysterious cloud. Thus Carmel was the first place on earth to be solemnly dedicated to Mary, where the powerful name of the Advocate of the Church was invoked. As heirs of the devotion of the prophets and the first Christians, in the twelfth century some religious took Our Lady of Mount Carmel for their founder and superior, and called themselves Brothers of Our Lady of Mount Carmel, or simply Carmelites. The Holy See authorized them to celebrate an annual feast, to solemnize the dedication of the first oratory built on Carmel and to recognize the graces which the Blessed Virgin had poured forth from there so abundantly. This solemnity was fixed for the 16th of July, in memory of a signal favor shown their order on that day. Mary appeared to Simon Stock, general of the Carmelites, accompanied by a multitude of heavenly spirits, and holding in her hand a scapular, a little brown woollen habit. She told him that she would be favorable to all who associated themselves with the Congregation of Carmel by wearing this holy habit; that she would consider them as her children, protect them in dangers, and assist them in the hour of their death to escape the eternal flames. Fifty years later the Blessed Virgin appeared to Pope John XXII., and promised especial assistance on the Saturday following their death to the members of the Confraternity of the Scapular condemned to purgatory, provided that during their life they had observed the three following conditions : 1st, to carefully wear the scapular even to their death ; 2d, to guard inviolate chastity, each according to his state ; 3d, to recite each day the Little Office of the Blessed Virgin, or, if they could not read, to fast on the days commanded by the Church, and abstain every Wednesday and Friday of the year, except on Christmas, or during illness, or when prevented by some other valid reason. The bull in which John XXII. accorded these favors bears the name of *Sabbatine*, or of Saturday, and from this the promise of Mary to her faithful servants of consolation on the Saturday after their death is called the *Sabbatine indulgence*.

Our Lady of the Snow, August 5th.—The sanctuary the dedication of which the Church celebrates to-day bears different names. It is called the Liberian basilica, after Pope Liberius, its founder. Later it was dedicated to the Blessed Virgin, and enriched by the precious gift of the crib of Our Lord, whence it took its name of Santa Maria ad Præsepe, and also Santa Maria Maggiore, or major, the greatest, for, as Peter the Venerable says, after the basilica of the Lateran, dedicated to Our Saviour, this of which we speak is the most celebrated, not in Rome only, but throughout the entire world. (Lib. ii., *De Miracul.*)

This church owes its renown above all to the miraculous event which gave it its name of Our Lady of Snows. Under the pontificate of Liberius, a patrician named John and his wife, being childless, had consecrated all their goods to the Blessed Virgin. By fervent prayers they supplicated her to show them the use to which they should put their riches. On August 5th, when the heat is greatest at Rome, the Esquiline hill was whitened by a fall of snow during the night. At the same time these pious people received in a dream the answer of the Blessed Virgin to their request, who ordered them to build a temple on the spot which they should find covered with snow. The tidings were carried to Pope Liberius, who had the same dream. The people went to the Esquiline in procession, and all were witnesses to the event, the memory of which is perpetuated through the ages by the feast of this day.

Assumption of the Blessed Virgin, August 15th.—A death without suffering, a tomb without corruption, the anticipated resurrection of a glorious body, this is the triple mystery solemnized under the name of the Assumption of the Blessed Virgin.

The God Who from all ages had exempted her who was to be His mother from the corruption of Adam's sin, would not suffer the pure body from which the body of Jesus Christ was formed to see corruption in death. She was taken up into heaven to be crowned the Queen of angels, and to be man's advocate and help in his struggle to reach the eternal goal. The Introit of this day gives us the key to the Church's feeling; and what should be our own when we think that our mother and advocate is seated at the right hand of her Son in bliss eternal! "Let us all rejoice in the Lord, while we celebrate this festival in honor of the Blessed Virgin Mary, for whose assumption the angels rejoice and praise the Son of God."

Nativity of the Blessed Virgin, September 8th.—For

the third time the Church unites her children around a cradle. If the first two were surrounded with glory, this one is enveloped with veils of silence. We find nothing in the Gospel of the different circumstances which must have accompanied the birth of the Blessed Virgin. Who were her father and her mother? What place saw her birth? The Scriptures do not tell us. The humble Virgin had no wish that she should be spoken of in those pages which retraced the life of Jesus Christ. All that we know has been transmitted by tradition. Her father was called Joachim, and was of the race of the kings of Juda. Anne, her mother, descended from the high-priest Aaron. She was born at Nazareth, on the 8th of September, and the name of Mary was given her, which means queen, and star of the sea.

Several authors tell us that the establishment of this feast is owing to a miraculous event. A holy religious every year heard during the night concerts of angels who celebrated a feast in heaven. He asked God to show him the reason for this joy, and it was revealed to him that the celestial choirs honored the birth of Mary, which took place on that day. This being laid before the Holy See, the feast was established. To-day is the feast of the birth of our mother; let us offer her a bouquet of those flowers which she best loves, and among them the flower which she looks upon with the keenest pleasure, humility. If our birth be humble, let us never blush for it; if it be illustrious, let us avoid speaking of it. May this resolution, laid at the feet of Mary, be our birthday bouquet!

Feast of the Holy Name of Mary.—This feast is appointed for the Sunday following the Nativity of the

Blessed Virgin. Established in Spain in the year 1513, it became universal toward the year 1683, under Innocent XI., in gratitude for the protection of Mary during the siege of Vienna. The Christians, strong in the help of her who is "terrible as an army in battle array," forced the Turks to raise the siege. If this bulwark of Christianity had fallen into their power, one trembles at the thought of the evils which would have been poured over Europe. This name, given by God Himself, according to tradition, to her who should be His Mother, signifies Star of the sea, Ocean of bitterness, and Illuminator. "Thou art," says one of her pious servants, "an ocean of bitterness to the demons, a shining star to those who sail through this poor world, a radiant light for those who are plunged in darkness, and even for the angels who rejoice in heaven." (*Fasciculus precum Cathol.*)

Exaltation of the Holy Cross, September 14th.—
When Jesus Christ went up to Calvary laden with His cross, He met upon His way only insult and contempt; according to the Jewish law a curse covered with its anathema the man condemned to this infamous execution. Who would then have dared say that this insulted cross would one day be glorious and venerated, that it would become as a shining throne from which Jesus Christ would receive the homage of people and kings? Yet even then a few hours had scarcely elapsed when already the voice of entire nature proclaimed the triumph of the cross. The murderers beat their breasts; one of the thieves crucified beside the Saviour recognized Him as his God. This was the first exaltation of the cross. Jesus Christ crucified received then the homage of sor

rowing nature and of the repentant murderers. Miraculously recovered by the care of the Empress Helena, the cross had become the object of holy veneration to the Christians. But at the end of the sixth century, Khosru, king of Persia, having taken possession of Jerusalem, carried into his states the wood of the true cross. The Emperor Heraclius made offers for the ransom of this precious relic; the barbarous king accepted them, on the condition that the Romans would renounce their religion and adore the sun. The negotiations were broken off, and a campaign entered upon. Khosru was vanquished, and put to death by his son, who accepted the conditions of peace imposed upon him by the victor. The cross was returned, and Heraclius himself wished to bear it upon his shoulders to Calvary. Six centuries after this event, the memory of which is for ever consecrated by the feast of this day, St. Louis of France came to receive at the gates of Paris the cross and the instruments of the passion, presents from Baldwin, emperor of Constantinople; the king, denuded of all royal apparel and barefooted, bore them upon his shoulders to the holy chapel, which he had built to receive these sacred relics. This was on the 14th of September, 1241. It must be said, however, that God had not waited for Heraclius and St. Louis to exalt the cross in the world. Since Constantine it had been shining on the pediments of public monuments, on the standards of armies. This was the second exaltation of the cross: Jesus Christ received the homage of power and of courage; He called to Himself every grandeur.

But another, more complete and more solemn triumph is promised to the cross: on the last day it will judge the world. When it shines forth, luminous upon the clouds of heaven, all heads will bow before it, the angels and the demons, the elect and the reprobate. This is the supreme exaltation of the cross which will receive then the homage of all generations. May all these great memories excite in our hearts sentiments of respect for the instrument of our salvation! Let us give it a place of honor in our houses; let us form the holy habit of wearing it religiously on our hearts; let us salute it with love when we meet it in our way. And let us not forget that there are infidel countries where the cross does not yet shine; the missionary has the pang of seeing it trodden under foot. Let us pray that soon it will arise, like a luminous star, in the midst of the pagan countries of the far East.

Our Lady of the Rosary.—This feast, instituted by Pope St. Pius V., recalls to us the victory won by the Catholic army over the Turks at Lepanto on October 7, 1571. The triumph was obtained through the prayers of the Confraternity of the Holy Rosary, and bore its name. The suitability of the chant of the *Ave Maris Stella* on this feast is striking; the Church sings it at Vespers, at the hour when the sea beheld the triumph of the Christian fleet protected by Mary.

The devotion to the rosary is older than the feast which bears its name. Under its actual form it dates from St. Dominic, but its origin goes back much further. The anchorites of the first centuries, in order not to interrupt the work of their hands, learned certain prayers, principally psalms, and repeated them each day a definite number of times. For those who could not read it was the Lord's Prayer, or other formulas short and easy to remember. That they might not forget one, they had under the skirts of their vestments a number of little stones corresponding to the number of prayers which had been imposed upon them, and they threw away one for each prayer recited.

In the eleventh century we learn from William of Malmesbury (*De Pontif.*, l. iv. c. 4) that Godiva, wife of Count Leofric, had the habit of rolling in her fingers a circle of precious stones strung upon a cord, and of reciting a prayer as she touched each gem, that she might not omit any. Some years later, Peter the Hermit, to make the means of prayer easier to those crusaders who could not read, put into their hands the chaplet properly so called. St. Dominic then followed and gave this devotion its definite form.

The word chaplet and the word rosary signify a crown of roses. Each of its beads is like a flower serving to make the crown of the Queen of heaven, whom the Church calls the Mystical Rose.

All Saints, November 1st.—The liturgic year is the life of the human race. With its four weeks Advent figures the four thousand years of prayers and sighs before the coming of the Messias. From Christmas to the Ascension we kneel by turns at the foot of the crib, the cross, the sepulchre, and, filled with the rich blessings of Jesus ascending into heaven, we wait prayerfully the coming of the Holy Ghost into our souls. Then begins, as we have seen, the life of pilgrimage of the Church. To raise his courage the traveller loves to turn his eyes toward that side of the horizon where his hopes lie. Now, in her pilgrimage, the goal toward which the Church aspires is heaven. This is why we keep the feast

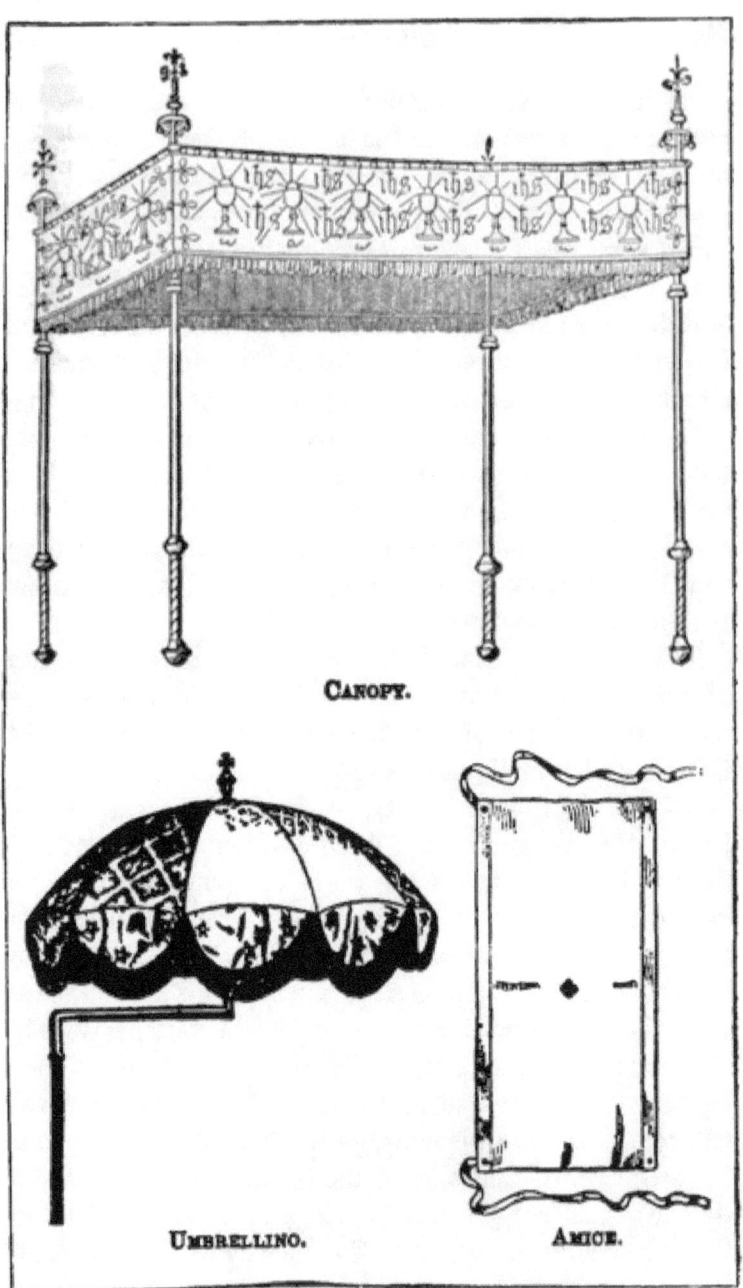

CANOPY.

UMBRELLINO. AMICE.

of heaven at this period. It was introduced into the liturgy in the seventh century. Pope Boniface IV. in 610, having obtained the Pantheon for a church, dedicated it to the Blessed Virgin and all the martyrs, which gave this monument the name of Holy Mary of the Martyrs. In the following century Gregory III. consecrated, in the church of St. Peter, a chapel in honor of all the saints. By degrees, because of the intimate connection of this solemnity with the preceding one, the two feasts formed but one, and their celebration was fixed for November 1st. The saints are classed by the Church in different orders: the apostles, martyrs, confessors, virgins, and holy women. None of these terms, except confessor, needs explanation; we will speak of this here. In the primitive Church the name of confessor was given to any Christian who, after having confessed the faith of Jesus Christ openly before his judges, was condemned to another punishment than death. The name of martyr was reserved for those who suffered the extreme penalty. The era of persecution passed, and the title of confessor was given to the just who, after having lived in the practice of all the virtues, died in the odor of sanctity. Have they not also given testimony to the religion of Christ by the splendor of their works? Have they not, by strong combat with vice, confessed Our Lord?

All Souls, November 2d.—Nature has taken care to prepare our hearts for the sadness of this day. For the joyous feast of the Eucharist she had her bluest sky, her sweetest flowers; on the day of All Souls she is clad in mourning. This is the first harmony which springs from this feast. But there are more. To man, forgetful of his last end, God has been pleased to constantly recall the inexorableness of death. Each of the days which make up our short existence he has made an image of our life. Dawn is youth, so fleeting; its glow lasts but a little time. Scarcely has the sun arisen than it descends to the horizon, and no sooner has man attained the strength of maturity, of intelligence, than he leans toward the decline of his days. Evening is old age, and night is death; its silence, its obscurity, the abandonment of creatures, are they not a faithful image of the tomb? The year in its turn places before our eyes these great reminders, annoying to the majority. The smile of springtime figures the graces of early youth, and icy winter—winter with its mantle of snow, winter from which we seek to flee—does it not remind us of that dreaded age when cold will numb our vigor, our hair will whiten, when we shall find but empty spaces around our hearth? The wise man, then, sees around him the twilight of eternity.

The Church, in choosing this season for the celebration of All Souls, has, as always, given proof of her profound wisdom. What a delicate thought to choose for it the day after All Saints, and even to begin it on the evening of that solemnity! In doing this she has wished to show us that All Saints is the true feast of the Church triumphant, the Church militant, and the Church suffering. The canticles of joy, interrupted by the plaintive accents of the *De Profundis*, tell us that the three sisters have joined hands to help one another to reach supreme happiness.

The feast or the commemoration of the dead was originally a holy-day, like Sunday; then it was reduced to a half-holyday which ended at noon, and for this reason it has no second Vespers.

Feast of the Dedication.—Our churches are the tents of the God of the Eucharist. He remains therein perpetually, to be the strength and the support of humanity in its combats. To this temple sanctified by the prayers of the Church, and by the presence of the thrice-holy God, a feast has been consecrated to recall the grandeur of our edifices, and to thank God for the graces which He gives us there each day. This feast, under the name of the Dedication, is celebrated in France on the Sunday which follows the Octave of All Saints. The liturgic period, which represents the pilgrimage of the Church throughout the centuries, draws to a close. Soon the last gospel of Pentecost time will recount the history of the Last Day. This date is not far distant; this is why the spouse of Jesus Christ, raising her eyes toward heaven, considers there the eternal temple which will replace that built by man to the Lord : Jesus Christ is its altar ; the elect are its stones ; the apostles its foundation. This heavenly Jerusalem is the object of the divine chants of this solemnity.

Presentation of the Blessed Virgin, November 21st.— Tradition says that Mary, at the age of three years and two months, was offered to God in the Temple at Jerusalem by her pious parents. It is commonly believed that this was done in fulfilment of a vow made to the Lord. For many years childless, they had promised to consecrate to Jehovah the child which should be given them. This child of miracle was Mary. Her first years literally passed in the shadow of the Lord's wings, in the part of the Temple destined to receive Israel's young maidens. Prayer, the study of the Scriptures, and work divided her moments. This is all that we know of the eleven years that the Blessed Virgin passed in the Temple. The feast of the Presentation, celebrated in the East from all antiquity, was introduced into the West toward 1372. Avignon, then the residence of the popes, had the glory of first celebrating the new solemnity.

Patron Feast.—The Church, in her solicitude for the salvation of her children, has given a protector to each kingdom, each diocese, each parish, each confraternity. to each Christian. This protector, chosen among the saints in heaven, is honored under a name which expresses the affection of a father for his family: the name of patron.

In the first centuries the churches were not distinguished from each other but by a title which bore directly upon God, under the invocation of a mystery Thus there were churches dedicated to Our Saviour, Christ, the Trinity, the Paraclete, the Transfiguration, etc. But as a temple was never built but on the burial place of some saint, or upon his relics, the custom soon spread of giving the sacred edifice the name of this saint, although the temple was always consecrated to God only. It happened that certain churches took for patrons saints whose relics and tombs they did not possess; a particular devotion fixed their choice. The patronage most often claimed was without question that of the Blessed Virgin; it is necessary but to look around us to be convinced of this. When several altars can be erected in the same church there is always one to the Mother of God.

Formerly the patron feast of the diocese was of obligation, like Sunday; that of the parish was only obligatory to those who belonged to it. This celebration is now transferred to the following Sunday.

Sundays after Pentecost.—There cannot be between Pentecost and Advent less than twenty-three Sundays nor more than twenty-eight. The office of the twenty-fourth is always said on the Sunday before Advent. If between the twenty-third and the last Sunday there is but one Sunday, the Mass of the sixth Sunday after Epiphany is said. If there are two, the Masses of the fifth and sixth are said. If there are three, those of the fourth, fifth, and sixth are said; and if there are four, those of the third, fourth, fifth, and sixth.

THE ORDINARY OF THE MASS.

IN nomine Patris, et Filii, et Spiritus Sancti. Amen.
Ant. Introibo ad altare Dei.
R. Ad Deum, qui lætificat juventutem meam.

IN the name of the Father, and of the Son, etc. Amen.
Ant. I will go in to the altar of God.
R. To God, Who rejoiceth my youth.

PSALM XLII.

P. Judica me, Deus, et discerne causam meam de gente non sancta: ab homine iniquo et doloso erue me.

R. Quia tu es, Deus, fortitudo mea, quare me repulisti, et quare tristis incedo dum affligit me inimicus?

P. Emitte lucem tuam et veritatem tuam: ipsa me deduxerunt, et adduxerunt in montem sanctum tuum, et in tabernacula tua.

R. Et introibo ad altare Dei: ad Deum qui lætificat juventutem meam.

P. Confitebor tibi in cithara, Deus, Deus meus: quare tristis es, anima mea? et quare conturbas me?

R. Spera in Deo, quoniam adhuc confitebor illi: salu-

P. Judge me, O God, and distinguish my cause from the nation that is not holy: from the unjust and deceitful man deliver me.

R. Since Thou, O God, art my strength, why hast Thou rejected me; and why do I go sorrowful whilst the enemy afflicteth me?

P. Send forth Thy light and Thy truth; they have conducted and brought me unto the holy mount, and into Thy tabernacles.

R. And I will go in to the altar of God: to God Who rejoiceth my youth.

P. I will praise Thee on the harp, O God, my God: why art thou sorrowful, O my soul? and why dost thou disturb me?

R. Hope in God, for Him will I still praise: He is my

tare vultus mei, et Deus meus.

P. Gloria Patri, et Filio, et Spiritui Sancto.

R. Sicut erat in principio, et nunc, et semper, et in sæcula sæculorum. Amen.

P. Introibo ad altare Dei.

R. Ad Deum qui lætificat juventutem meam.

P. Adjutorium nostrum in nomine Domini.

R. Qui fecit cœlum et terram.

P. Confiteor Deo omnipotenti, etc.

R. Misereatur tui omnipotens Deus, et dimissis peccatis tuis, perducat te ad vitam æternam.

P. Amen.

R. Confiteor Deo omnipotenti, beatæ Mariæ semper virgini, beato Michaeli Archangelo, beato Joanni Baptiste, sanctis apostolis Petro et Paulo, omnibus sanctis, et tibi Pater, quia peccavi nimis cogitatione, verbo, et opere, mea culpa, mea culpa, mea maxima culpa. Ideo precor beatam Mariam semper virginem, beatum Michaelem Archangelum, beatum Joannem Baptistam, sanctos apostolos Petrum et Paulum, omnes sanctos,

God, and the Saviour I look for.

P. Glory be to the Father, and to the Son, etc.

R. As it was in the beginning, is now, and ever shall be, world without end. Amen.

P. I will go in to the altar of God.

R. To God Who rejoiceth my youth.

P. Our help is in the name of the Lord.

R. Who made heaven and earth.

P. I confess to Almighty God, etc.

R. May Almighty God be merciful to thee, and, forgiving thee thy sins, bring thee to everlasting life.

P. Amen.

R. I confess to Almighty God, to the blessed Mary ever virgin, blessed Michael the Archangel, blessed John the Baptist, the holy apostles Peter and Paul, to all the saints, and to you, Father, that I have sinned exceedingly in thought, word, and deed, through my fault, through my fault, through my most grievous fault. Therefore I beseech the blessed Mary ever virgin, blessed Michael the Archangel, blessed John the Baptist, the holy apostles Peter and Paul, and all the saints, and you, O Father

et te, Pater, orare pro me ad Dominum Deum nostrum.

P. Misereatur vestri omnipotens Deus et dimissis peccatis vestris, perducat vos ad vitam æternam.

R. Amen.

P. Indulgentiam, absolutionem, et remissionem peccatorum nostrorum, tribuat nobis omnipotens et misericors Dominus.

R. Amen.

P. Deus, tu conversus vivificabis nos.

R. Et plebs tua lætabitur in te.

P. Ostende nobis, Domine, misericordiam tuam.

R. Et salutare tuum da nobis.

P. Domine, exaudi orationem meam.

R. Et clamor meus ad te veniat.

P. Dominus vobiscum.

R. Et cum spiritu tuo.

to pray to the Lord our God for me.

P. May Almighty God be merciful unto you, and, forgiving you your sins, bring you to life everlasting.

R. Amen.

P. May the almighty and most merciful Lord grant us pardon, absolution, and remission of our sins.

R. Amen.

P. O God, Thou being turned toward us, wilt enliven us.

R. And Thy people will rejoice in Thee.

P. Show us, O Lord, Thy mercy.

R. And grant us Thy salvation.

P. O Lord, hear my prayer.

R. And let my cry come unto Thee.

P. The Lord be with you.

R. And with thy spirit.

The Priest going to the Altar, says:

Take away from us our iniquities, we beseech Thee, O Lord, that we may be worthy to enter, with pure minds, into the Holy of holies: through, etc. Amen.

Bowing down, he says:

We beseech Thee, O Lord, by the merits of Thy saints whose relics are here, and of all the saints, that Thou wouldst vouchsafe to forgive me all my sins. Amen.

BANNER.

Whilst he reads the Introit, say:

Let the name of the Lord be blessed both now and for ever. From the rising to the setting of the sun all praise is due to the name of the Lord. Who is like the Lord our God, Who dwells on high, and looks on all that is humble both in heaven and earth? Glory be to the Father, etc.

THE KYRIE.

P. Kyrie eleison.	*P.* Lord have mercy on us.
R. Kyrie eleison.	*R.* Lord have mercy on us.
P. Kyrie eleison.	*P.* Lord have mercy on us.
R. Christe eleison.	*R.* Christ have mercy on us.
P. Christe eleison.	*P.* Christ have mercy on us.
R. Christe eleison.	*R.* Christ have mercy on us.
P. Kyrie eleison.	*P.* Lord have mercy on us.
R. Kyrie eleison.	*R.* Lord have mercy on us.
P. Kyrie eleison.	*P.* Lord have mercy on us.

GLORIA IN EXCELSIS.

Gloria in excelsis Deo, et in terra pax hominibus bonæ voluntatis. Laudamus te; benedicimus te; adoramus te; glorificamus te. Gratias agimus tibi propter magnam gloriam tuam, Domine Deus, Rex cœlestis, Deus Pater omnipotens. Domine Fili unigenite, Jesu Christe. Domine Deus, Agnus Dei, Filius Patris, qui tollis peccata mundi, miserere nobis. Qui tollis peccata mundi, suscipe deprecationem nos-

Glory be to God on high, and on earth peace to men of good will. We praise Thee; we bless Thee; we adore Thee; we glorify Thee. We give Thee thanks for Thy great glory. O Lord God, heavenly King, God the Father Almighty. O Lord Jesus Christ, the only-begotten Son. O Lord God, Lamb of God, Son of the Father, Who takest away the sins of the world, have mercy on us. Who takest

tram. Qui sedes ad dexteram Patris, miserere nobis. Quoniam tu solus sanctus. Tu solus Dominus. Tu solus altissimus, Jesu Christe, cum Sancto Spiritu in gloria Dei Patris. Amen.

away the sins of the world. receive our prayers. Who sittest at the right hand of the Father. have mercy on us. For Thou only art the Lord. Thou only art holy. Thou only, O Jesus Christ, together with the Holy Ghost, art most high in the glory of God the Father. Amen.

Turning towards the people, he says:

P. Dominus vobiscum.
R. Et cum spiritu tuo.

P. The Lord be with you.
R. And with thy spirit.

AT THE COLLECTS.

We humbly beseech Thee, O almighty and eternal God, mercifully to give ear to the prayers of Thy servant, which he offers to Thee in the name of Thy Church, and on behalf of us Thy people: accept them to the honor of Thy name, and the good of our souls, and grant us all those blessings that may contribute to our salvation: through, etc. Amen.

AT THE EPISTLE.

Be Thou, O Lord, eternally praised and blessed, for having communicated Thy Spirit to Thy holy prophets and apostles, disclosing to them admirable secrets, redounding to Thy glory and our great good. We firmly believe their word, because it is Thine. Give us, we beseech Thee, the happiness to understand their instructions, and so conform our lives thereto, that, at the hour of death, we may merit to be received by Thee into the mansions of eternal bliss.

At the end of the Epistle the Clerk answers:

Deo gratias.   Thanks be to God.

DURING THE GRADUAL OR TRACT.

How wonderful, O Lord, is Thy name through the whole earth! I will bless the Lord at all times; His praise shall be ever in my mouth. Be Thou my God and protector; in Thee alone I put my trust; oh, let me never be confounded!

BEFORE THE GOSPEL.

Cleanse my heart and my lips, O Almighty God, Who didst cleanse the lips of the prophet Isaias with a burning coal; and vouchsafe, through Thy gracious mercy, so to purify me, that I may worthily attend to Thy holy Gospel: through Christ our Lord. Amen.

May the Lord be in my heart, and on my lips, that I may worthily, and in a becoming manner, attend to His Gospel. Amen.

P. Dominus vobiscum.
R. Et cum spiritu tuo.
P. Sequentia (*vel* initium) sancti Evangelii secundum, etc.
R. Gloria tibi, Domine.

P. The Lord be with you.
R. And with thy spirit.
P. The continuation (*or* the beginning) of the holy Gospel according to, etc.
R. Glory be to Thee, O Lord.

DURING THE GOSPEL.

Be Thou ever adored and praised, O Lord, Who, not content to instruct us by Thy prophets and apostles, hast even vouchsafed to speak to us by Thy only Son, Our Saviour Jesus Christ, commanding us by a voice from heaven to hear Him: grant us, merciful God, the grace to profit by His divine and heavenly doctrine. All that is written of Thee, divine Jesus, in Thy Gospel, is truth itself; manifesting infinite wisdom in Thy actions; power and goodness in Thy miracles; light and instruction in Thy maxims. With Thee, sacred Redeemer, are the words of eternal life; to whom shall we go but to Thee, eternal Fountain of Truth? I firmly believe, O God, all Thou teachest; give me only grace to practise what Thou commandest, and command what Thou pleasest.

At the end of the Gospel, answer:

R. Laus tibi, Christe.   *R.* Praise be to Thee, O Christ.

Then add with the Priest in a low voice:

May our sins be blotted out by the words of the Gospel.

THE NICENE CREED.

Credo in unum Deum, Patrem omnipotentem, factorem cœli et terræ, visibilium omnium et invisibilium.

Et in unum Dominum Jesum Christum, Filium Dei unigenitum; et ex Patre natum ante omnia sæcula. Deum de Deo; Lumen de lumine; Deum verum de Deo vero; genitum, non factum; consubstantialem Patri, per quem omnia facta sunt. Qui propter nos homines, et propter nostram salutem, descendit de cœlis, et incarnatus est de Spiritu Sancto, ex Maria Virgine, *et homo factus*

I believe in one God, the Father Almighty, Maker of heaven and earth, and of all things visible and invisible.

And in one Lord Jesus Christ, the only-begotten Son of God ; and born of the Father before all ages. God of God; Light of light; true God of true God; begotten, not made; consubstantial to the Father, by Whom all things were made. Who for us men, and for our salvation, came down from heaven, and became incarnate by the Holy Ghost of the Virgin Mary, *and was made man.*

est. Crucifixus etiam pro nobis sub Pontio Pilato, passus et sepultus est. Et resurrexit tertia die secundum Scripturas. Et ascendit in cœlum, sedet ad dexteram Patris. Et iterum venturus est cum gloria judicare vivos et mortuos: cujus regni non erit finis.

Et in Spiritum Sanctum, Dominum et vivificantem, qui ex Patre Filioque procedit: qui cum Patre et Filio simul adoratur, et conglorificatur: qui locutus est per prophetas. Et unam sanctam Catholicam et Apostolicam Ecclesiam. Confiteor unum baptisma in remissionem peccatorum. Et expecto resurrectionem mortuorum, et vitam venturi sæculi. Amen.

P. Dominus vobiscum.
R. Et cum spiritu tuo.
Oremus.

He was crucified also for us, suffered under Pontius Pilate, and was buried. And the third day He rose again according to the Scriptures. And ascended into heaven, sitteth at the right hand of the Father; and He is to come again with glory to judge the living and the dead, of Whose kingdom there shall be no end.

And in the Holy Ghost, the Lord and Giver of Life, Who proceedeth from the Father and the Son: Who, together with the Father and the Son, is adored and glorified: Who spoke by the prophets. And one holy Catholic and Apostolic Church. I confess one baptism for the remission of sins. And I expect the resurrection of the dead, and the life of the world to come. Amen.

P. The Lord be with you.
R. And with thy spirit.
Let us pray.

AT THE OFFERTORY.

O my God, I sincerely offer myself and all I have to Thee, to do and suffer whatever Thou commandest or permittest. Receive my offering, and cleanse me from my sins, that through the infinite merits of the victim about to be presented to Thy divine Majesty I may become acceptable in Thy sight.

OBLATION OF THE HOST.

Accept, O holy Father, almighty and eternal God, this unspotted host, which I, Thy unworthy servant, offer unto Thee, my living and true God, for my innumerable sins, offences, and negligences, and for all here present; as also for all faithful Christians, both living and dead, that it may avail both me and them unto life everlasting. Amen.

When the Priest pours the wine and water into the chalice.

O God, Who in creating human nature hast wonderfully dignified it, and still more wonderfully reformed it, grant that, by the mystery of this water and wine, we may be made partakers of His divine nature, Who vouchsafed to become partaker of our human nature, namely, Jesus Christ our Lord, Thy Son, Who with Thee, in the unity of, etc. Amen.

OBLATION OF THE CHALICE.

We offer unto Thee, O Lord, the chalice of salvation, beseeching Thy clemency that it may ascend before Thy divine Majesty as a sweet odor, for our salvation, and for that of the whole world. Amen.

When the Priest bows before the altar.

Accept us, O Lord, in the spirit of humility and contrition of heart, and grant that the sacrifice which we offer this day in Thy sight may be pleasing to Thee, O Lord God.

When he blesses the bread and wine.

Come, O almighty and eternal God, the Sanctifier, and bless this sacrifice, prepared for the glory of Thy holy name.

Washing his fingers, he says Ps. xxv.

Lavabo inter innocentes manus meas, et circumdabo altare tuum, Domine.	I will wash my hands among the innocent; and will compass Thy altar, O Lord.
Ut audiam vocem laudis, et enarrem universa mirabilia tua.	That I may hear the voice of Thy praise; and tell of all Thy wondrous works.
Domine, dilexi decorem domus tuæ, et locum habitationis gloriæ tuæ.	The beauty of Thy house I have loved, O Lord, and the place where Thy glory dwelleth.
Ne perdas cum impiis animam meam, et cum viris sanguinum vitam meam.	Take not away my soul with the wicked; nor my life with bloody men.
In quorum manibus iniquitates sunt; dextera eorum repleta est muneribus.	In whose hands are iniquities; their right hand is filled with gifts.
Ego autem in innocentia mea ingressus sum: redime me, et miserere mei.	But I have walked in my innocence; redeem me, and have mercy on me.
Pes meus stetit in directo: in ecclesiis benedicam te, Domine.	My foot has stood in the direct way; in the churches I will bless Thee, O Lord.
Gloria Patri, etc.	Glory be to the Father. etc.

Bowing before the Altar, he says.

Receive, O holy Trinity, this oblation which we make to Thee, in memory of the passion, resurrection, and ascension of Our Lord Jesus Christ, and in honor of the blessed Mary, ever virgin, the blessed John the Baptist, the holy apostles Peter and Paul, and of all the saints, that it may be available to their honor and our salvation; and may they vouchsafe to intercede for us in heaven whose memory we celebrate on earth. Through the same Christ Our Lord. Amen.

Turning towards the people, he says:

P. Orate fratres, ut meum ac vestrum sacrificium acceptabile fiat apud Deum Patrem omnipotentem.

R. Suscipiat Dominus sacrificium de manibus tuis, ad laudem et gloriam nominis sui, ad utilitatem quoque nostram, totiusque Ecclesiæ suæ sanctæ.

P. Brethren, pray that my sacrifice and yours may be acceptable to God the Father Almighty.

R. May the Lord receive the sacrifice from thy hands, to the praise and glory of His name, and to our benefit, and that of His entire holy Church.

AT THE SECRET PRAYER OR PRAYERS.

Mercifully hear our prayers, O Lord, and graciously accept this oblation, which we Thy servants present to Thee; that as we offer it to the honor of Thy name, so it may be to us here a means of obtaining Thy grace, and hereafter eternal happiness. Through, etc.

P. Per omnia sæcula sæculorum.
R. Amen.
P. Dominus vobiscum.
R. Et cum spiritu tuo.
P. Sursum corda.
R. Habemus ad Dominum.
P. Gratias agamus Domino Deo nostro.
R. Dignum et justum est.

P. World without end.
R. Amen.
P. The Lord be with you.
R. And with thy spirit.
P. Lift up your hearts.
R. We have lifted them up to the Lord.
P. Let us give thanks to our Lord God.
R. It is meet and just.

THE PREFACE.

Vere dignum et justum est, æquum et salutare, nos tibi semper et ubique gratias agere, Domine sancte, Pater omnipotens, æterne Deus; per Christum Dominum nostrum. Per quem majestatem tuam laudant angeli, adorant dominationes, tremunt potestates. Cœli cœlorumque virtutes ac beata seraphim, socia exultatione concelebrant. Cum quibus et nostras voces ut admitti jubeas deprecamur, supplici confessione dicentes:

Sanctus, sanctus, sanctus, Dominus Deus Sabaoth. Pleni sunt cœli et terra gloria tua. Hosanna in excelsis. Benedictus qui venit in nomine Domini. Hosanna in excelsis.

It is truly meet and just, right, and available to salvation, that we should always, and in all places, give thanks to Thee. O holy Lord, Father Almighty, eternal God. Through Christ our Lord: by Whom the angels praise Thy Majesty, the dominations adore it, the powers tremble before it, the heavenly virtues and blessed seraphim with common jubilee glorify it. Together with whom we beseech Thee, that we may be admitted to join our humble voices, saying:

Holy, holy, holy, Lord God of Sabaoth. Heaven and earth are full of Thy glory. Hosanna in the highest. Blessed is he that cometh in the name of the Lord Hosanna in the highest.

THE CANON OF THE MASS.

We therefore humbly pray and beseech Thee, most merciful Father, through Jesus Christ Thy Son, our Lord, that Thou wouldst vouchsafe to accept and bless these gifts, these presents, these holy unspotted sacrifices, which in the first place we offer Thee for Thy holy Catholic Church, to which vouchsafe to grant peace; as also to preserve, unite, and govern it throughout the world: together with Thy servant N. our Pope, N. our Bishop, as also all orthodox believers and professors of the Catholic and Apostolic Faith.

AT THE COMMEMORATION OF THE LIVING.

Be mindful, O Lord, of Thy servants, men and women, N. and N. (*The Priest prays silently for those he wishes to pray for.*) And of all here present, whose faith and devotion are known unto Thee, for whom we offer, or who offer up to Thee, this sacrifice of praise for themselves, their families, and friends: for the redemption of their souls, for the health and salvation they hope for, and for which they now pay their vows to Thee, the eternal, living, and true God.

Communicating with, and honoring in the first place, the memory of the ever-glorious Virgin Mary, Mother of our Lord and God Jesus Christ; as also of the blessed apostles and martyrs, Peter and Paul, Andrew, James, John, Thomas, James, Philip, Bartholomew, Matthew, Simon and Thaddeus, Linus, Cletus, Clement, Xystus, Cornelius, Cyprian, Lawrence, Chrysogonus, John and Paul, Cosmas and Damian, and of all Thy saints; by whose merits and prayers grant that we may be always defended by the help of Thy protection. Through the same Christ our Lord. Amen.

Spreading his hands over the Oblation, he says.

We therefore beseech Thee, O Lord, graciously to accept this oblation of our servitude, as also of Thy whole family; dispose our days in Thy peace, preserve us from eternal damnation, and rank us in the number of Thine elect. Through Christ our Lord. Amen.

Which oblation do Thou, O God, vouchsafe in all respects to bless, approve, ratify, and accept; that it may be made for us the body and blood of Thy most beloved Son Jesus Christ our Lord.

Qui pridie quam pateretur, accepit panem in sanctas ac venerabiles manus suas; et elevatis oculis in cœlum, ad te Deum, Patrem suum omnipotentem, tibi gratias agens, benedixit, fregit, deditque discipulis suis, dicens: Accipite et manducate ex hoc omnes: *Hoc est enim corpus meum.*

Simili modo postquam cœnatum est, accipiens et hunc præclarum calicem in sanctas ac venerabiles manus suas; item tibi gratias agens benedixit, deditque discipulis suis, dicens: Accipite, et bibite ex eo omnes: *Hic est enim calix sanguinis mei, novi et æterni testamenti;* mysterium fidei; qui pro vobis, et pro multis effundetur in remissionem peccatorum. Hæc quotiescunque feceritis, in mei memoriam facietis.

AT THE ELEVATION.

While the priest pronounces the words of consecration, do you contemplate in silence the wonders that pass before you. Your God, your Saviour, and your Judge descends on the altar; hail His sacred presence by the most lively sentiments of respect, confidence, and love.

O Victim of salvation! Eternal King! Incarnate Word! sacrificed for me and all mankind! Precious body of the Son of God! Sacred flesh, torn with nails, pierced with a lance, and bleeding on a cross for us poor sinners! Amazing goodness! infinite love! Oh let that tender love plead now in my behalf: let all my iniquities be here effaced, and my name written in the Book of Life. I believe in Thee; I hope in Thee;

love Thee. To Thee be honor, praise, glory, and benediction, forever and ever. Amen.

O sacred blood, flowing from the wounds of Jesus Christ, and washing away the sins of the world! cleanse, sanctify, and preserve my soul, that nothing may ever separate me from Thee. Behold, O eternal Father, Thy only-begotten Son, and look upon the face of Thy Christ, in Whom Thou art well pleased. Hear the voice of His blood crying out to Thee, not for vengeance, but for mercy and pardon. Accept this divine oblation, and through the infinite merits of all the sufferings that Jesus endured on the cross for our salvation, be pleased to look upon us, and upon all Thy people, with an eye of mercy.

We most humbly beseech Thee, Almighty God, command these things to be carried by the hands of Thy holy angels to Thy altar on high, in the sight of Thy divine Majesty, that as many as shall partake of the most sacred body and blood of Thy Son at this altar may be filled with every heavenly grace and blessing, through the same Christ Our Lord. Amen.

AT THE COMMEMORATION OF THE DEAD.

Be mindful also, O Lord, of Thy servants N. and N., who are gone before us with the sign of faith, and rest in the sleep of peace.

Here particular mention is made of such of the dead as are to be prayed for.

To these, O Lord, and to all that sleep in Christ, grant, we beseech Thee, a place of refreshment, light, and peace, through the same Christ our Lord. Amen.

The Ordinary of the Mass.

Here, striking his breast, the Priest says:

Also to us sinners, Thy servants, confiding in the multitude of Thy mercies, vouchsafe to grant some part and fellowship with Thy holy apostles and martyrs; with John, Stephen, Matthias, Barnabas, Ignatius, Alexander, Marcellinus, Peter, Felicitas, Perpetua, Agatha, Lucy, Agnes, Cecilia, Anastasia, and with all Thy saints: into whose company we beseech Thee to admit us, not in consideration of our merits, but of Thy own gratuitous pardon, through Christ our Lord.

By Whom, O Lord, Thou dost always create, sanctify, enliven, bless, and give us all these good things. By Him, and with Him, and in Him, is to Thee, God the Father Almighty, in the unity of the Holy Ghost, all honor and glory.

P. Per omnia sæcula sæculorum.

R. Amen.

Oremus.

Præceptis salutaribus moniti, et divina institutione formati, audemus dicere:

Pater noster, qui es incœlis, sanctificetur nomen tuum; adveniat regnum tuum; fiat voluntas tua sicut in cœlo, et in terra. Panem nostrum quotidianum, da nobis hodie; et dimitte nobis debita nostra, sicut et nos dimittimus debitoribus nostris. Et ne nos inducas in tentationem.

R. Sed libera nos a malo.
P. Amen.

P. Forever and ever.

R. Amen.
Let us pray.

Being instructed by Thy saving precepts, and following Thy divine directions, we presume to say:

Our Father, Who art in heaven: hallowed be Thy name: Thy kingdom come: Thy will be done on earth as it is in heaven. Give us this day our daily bread: and forgive us our trespasses, as we forgive them that trespass against us. And lead us not into temptation.

R. But deliver us from evil.
P. Amen

Deliver us, we beseech Thee, O Lord, from all evils, past, present, and to come: and by the intercession of the blessed and ever-glorious Virgin Mary, Mother of God, and of the holy apostles Peter and Paul, and of Andrew, and of all the saints, mercifully grant peace in our days: that through the assistance of Thy mercy we may be always free from sin, and secure from all disturbance, through the same Jesus Christ Thy Son, Our Lord Who with Thee and the Holy Ghost liveth and reigneth, God.

P. Per omnia saecula saeculorum.
R. Amen.
P. Pax Domini sit semper vobiscum.
R. Et cum spiritu tuo.

P. World without end.
R. Amen.
P. May the peace of the Lord be always with you.
R. And with thy spirit.

At his breaking and putting part of the Host into the chalice, say:

May this mixture and consecration of the body and blood of Our Lord Jesus Christ be to us that receive it effectual to eternal life. Amen.

Then bowing and striking his breast, he says:

Agnus Dei, qui tollis peccata mundi, miserere nobis.

Agnus Dei, qui tollis peccata mundi, miserere nobis.

Agnus Dei, qui tollis peccata mundi, dona nobis pacem.

Lamb of God, Who takest away the sins of the world, have mercy upon us.

Lamb of God, Who takest away the sins of the world, have mercy upon us.

Lamb of God, Who takest away the sins of the world, give us peace.

In Masses for the Dead, he says twice, Give them rest; and lastly, eternal rest. The following prayer is also omitted:

Lord Jesus Christ, Who saidst to Thy apostles, My peace I leave you, regard not my sins, but the faith of Thy Church; and grant her that peace and unity which is agreeable to Thy will, Who livest, etc. Amen.

Lord Jesus Christ, Son of the living God, Who, according to the will of Thy Father, through the co-operation of the Holy Ghost, hast, by Thy death, given life to the world: deliver me by this Thy most sacred body and blood from all my iniquities and from all evils: make me always adhere to Thy commandments, and never suffer me to be separated from Thee: Who livest and reignest with God, the Father, in the unity of, etc. Amen.

Let not the participation of Thy body, O Lord Jesus Christ, which I, though unworthy, presume to receive, turn to my judgment and condemnation: but through Thy mercy may it be a safeguard and remedy both of soul and body. Who with God the Father, in the unity of the Holy Ghost, livest and reignest one God, forever and ever. Amen.

Taking the Host in his hands he says:

I will take the bread of heaven and call upon the name of the Lord.

Striking his breast, he repeats three times:

Lord, I am not worthy that Thou shouldst enter under my roof: say but the word, and my soul shall be healed.

On receiving the sacred Species, he says:

May the body of Our Lord Jesus Christ preserve my soul to life everlasting. Amen.

Taking the chalice in his hands, he says:

What return shall I make the Lord for all He has given to me? I will take the chalice of salvation, and call upon the name of the Lord. Praising I will call upon the Lord, and shall be saved from my enemies.

Receiving the blood of Our Saviour, he says:

May the blood of Our Lord Jesus Christ preserve my soul to everlasting life. Amen.

During the Ablutions and Post Communion make a Spiritual Communion, as follows:

O my divine Saviour! I fervently adore Thee in this sacred and venerable sacrament; I love Thee with all the affections of my heart, and I hope with confidence in that infinite goodness which induces Thee to remain among us. Oh, that I could this moment enjoy the happiness of really communicating! Oh, that I could this day receive that precious body which was once sacrificed for my love, and that adorable blood which flowed from Thy sacred veins to wash away the sins of the world! But, alas! I am most unworthy of so great a favor. I do not deserve to receive Thee, O God of all sanctity! Yet I ardently desire to do so, and I humbly conjure Thee to accept this desire, and to give Thyself to me by the influence of Thy all-powerful grace. Come, O my God! my only good! come to me, for I now offer Thee my whole heart, most ardently desiring that it should belong to Thee for Whose love it was created, and Whose love can alone make it truly happy. I now consecrate and present to Thee all my thoughts, words, and actions, from this moment to the happy day of my next communion, in union with Thy infinite merits, and as a preparation for that great happiness. O my God, I already look forward to it with joy, and I beg of Thee most earnestly to grant me such purity of heart, and such fervent dispositions in approaching Thy holy table, that each communion may produce in my soul an increase of Thy fear and love, and strengthen me to perform the exalted duties of a true Christian, in whatever situation of life Thy providence shall hereafter place me.

P. Dominus vobiscum.
R. Et cum spiritu tuo.
P. Ite missa est (*vel* Benedicamus Domino).
R. Deo gratias.

P. The Lord be with you.
R. And with thy spirit.
P. Go, you are dismissed (*or* Let us bless the Lord).
R. Thanks be to God.

In Masses for the Dead.

P. Requiescant in pace.
R. Amen.

P. May they rest in peace.
R. Amen.

Bowing before the Altar, the Priest says:

Let the performance of my homage be pleasing to Thee, O Holy Trinity: and grant that the sacrifice which I, though unworthy, have offered in presence of Thy Majesty, may be acceptable to Thee, and through Thy mercy be a propitiation for me and all those for whom it has been offered. Through, etc. Amen.

Turning toward the people he gives them his blessing, saying:

May Almighty God the Father, Son, and Holy Ghost bless you. Amen.

P. Dominus vobiscum.	P. The Lord be with you.
R. Et cum spiritu tuo.	R. And with thy spirit.
P. Initium sancti Evangelii secundum Joannem.	P. The beginning of the Gospel according to St. John.
R. Gloria tibi, Domine.	R. Glory be to Thee, O Lord.

THE LAST GOSPEL.

In principio erat Verbum, et Verbum erat apud Deum, et Deus erat Verbum. Hoc erat in principio apud Deum. Omnia per ipsum facta sunt: et sine ipso factum est nihil, quod factum est: in ipso vita erat, et vita erat lux hominum: et lux in tenebris lucet, et tenebræ eam non comprehenderunt. Fuit homo missus a Deo, cui nomen erat Joannes. Hic venit in testimonium, ut testimonium perhiberet de lumine, ut omnes crederent per illum. Non erat ille lux, sed ut testimonium perhiberet de lumine. Erat lux vera, quæ illuminat omnem hominem venientem in hunc mundum. In mundo erat, et mundus per ipsum factus est, et mundus eum non cognovit. In propria venit, et sui eum non receperunt;

In the beginning was the Word, and the Word was with God, and the Word was God. The same was in the beginning with God. All things were made by Him, and without Him was made nothing that was made. In Him was life, and the life was the light of men: and the light shineth in darkness, and the darkness did not comprehend it. There was a man sent from God whose name was John. This man came for a witness, to give testimony of the light, that all men might believe through him. He was not the light, but was to give testimony of the light. That was the true light which enlighteneth every man that cometh into this world. He was in the world, and the world was made by Him,

quotquot autem receperunt eum, dedit eis potestatem filios Dei fieri, his, qui credunt in nomine ejus : qui non ex sanguinibus, neque ex voluntate carnis, neque ex voluntate viri, sed ex Deo nati sunt. *Et Verbum caro factum est*, et habitavit in nobis ; et vidimus gloriam ejus, gloriam quasi unigeniti a Patre, plenum gratiæ, et veritatis.

R. Deo gratias.

and the world knew Him not. He came into His own, and His own received Him not. But as many as received Him, He gave them power to be made the sons of God, to them that believe in His name : who are born not of blood, nor of the will of the flesh, nor of the will of man, but of God. *And the Word was made flesh*, and dwelt among us : and we saw His glory, the glory as it were of the only-begotten of the Father, full of grace and truth.

R. Thanks be to God.

VESPERS FOR SUNDAYS.

Pater noster, etc. Ave Maria, etc.
P. Deus, in adjutorium meum intende.
R. Domine, ad adjuvandum me festina.
V. Gloria Patri, et Filio, * et Spiritui Sancto.

R. Sicut erat in principio, et nunc, et semper, * et in sæcula sæculorum. Amen. Alleluia.
In Lent. Laus tibi, Domine, Rex æternæ gloriæ.

Our Father, etc. Hail Mary, etc.
P. Incline unto my aid, O God.
R. O Lord, make haste to help me.
V. Glory be to the Father, and to the Son, and to the Holy Ghost.

R. As it was in the beginning, is now, and ever shall be, world without end. Amen. Alleluia.
In Lent. Praise be to Thee, O King of eternal glory.

PSALM 109

Dixit Dominus Domino meo : * sede a dextris meis,

Donec ponam inimicos tuos * scabellum pedum tuorum.

Virgam virtutis tuæ emittet Dominus ex Sion ; * dominare in medio inimicorum tuorum.

Tecum principium in die virtutis tuæ, in splendoribus

The Lord said to my Lord : Sit Thou at My right hand,

Until I make Thy enemies Thy footstool.

The Lord will send forth the sceptre of Thy power out of Sion : rule Thou in the midst of Thy enemies.

With Thee is the principality, in the day of Thy

*sanctorum: * ex utero ante luciferum genui te.

Juravit Dominus, et non pœnitebit eum: * tu es sacerdos in æternum, secundum ordinem Melchisedech.

Dominus a dextris tuis: * confregit in die iræ suæ reges.
Judicabit in nationibus, implebit ruinas: * conquassabit capita in terra multorum.
De torrente in via bibet: * propterea exaltabit caput.

Gloria Patri, etc.

strength, in the brightness of the saints: from the womb before the day-star I begot Thee.

The Lord hath sworn, and He will not repent: Thou art a priest forever according to the order of Melchisedech.

The Lord at Thy right hand hath broken kings in the day of His wrath.
He shall judge among nations, He shall fill ruins: He shall crush the heads in the land of many.
He shall drink of the torrent in the way: therefore shall He lift up the head.

Glory be to the Father, etc.

PSALM 110.

Confitebor tibi Domine in toto corde meo: * in concilio justorum, et congregatione.

Magna opera Domini: * exquisita in omnes voluntates ejus.
Confessio et magnificentia opus ejus: * et justitia ejus manet in sæculum sæculi.
Memoriam fecit mirabilium suorum, misericors et miserator Dominus: * escam dedit timentibus se.

Memor erit in sæculum testamenti sui: * virtutem operum suorum annunciabit populo suo,

I will praise Thee, O Lord, with my whole heart: in the council of the just, and in the congregation.

Great are the works of the Lord, sought out according to all His wills.

His work is praise and magnificence, and His justice continueth forever and ever.

He hath made a remembrance of His wonderful works, being a merciful and gracious Lord: He hath given food to them that fear Him.

He will be mindful forever of His covenant: He will show forth to His people the power of His works,

Ut det illis hæreditatem Gentium; * opera manuum ejus veritas et judicium.

Fidelia omnia mandata ejus, confirmata in sæculum sæculi, * facta in veritate et æquitate.

Redemptionem misit populo suo ; * mandavit in æternum testamentum suum.

Sanctum et terribile nomen ejus : * initium sapientiæ timor Domini.

Intellectus bonus omnibus facientibus eum: * laudatio ejus manet in sæculum sæculi.

Gloria Patri, etc.

That He may give them the inheritance of the Gentiles : the works of His hands are truth and judgment.

All His commandments are faithful, confirmed forever and ever, made in truth and equity.

He hath sent redemption to His people: He hath commanded His covenant forever.

Holy and terrible is His name: the fear of the Lord is the beginning of wisdom.

A good understanding to all that do it: His praise continueth forever and ever.

Glory, etc.

PSALM 111.

Beatus vir, qui timet Dominum: * in mandatis ejus volet nimis.

Potens in terra erit semen ejus: * generatio rectorum benedicetur.

Gloria et divitiæ in domo ejus: * et justitia ejus manet in sæculum sæculi.

Exortum est in tenebris lumen rectis: * misericors, et miserator, et justus.

Jucundus homo qui miseretur et commodat, disponet sermones suos in judicio: * quia in æternum non commovebitur.

Blessed is the man that feareth the Lord : he shall delight exceedingly in His commandments.

His seed shall be mighty upon earth: the generation of the righteous shall be blessed.

Glory and wealth shall be in his house: and his justice remaineth forever and ever.

To the righteous a light has sprung up in darkness: he is merciful, and compassionate, and just.

Acceptable is the man that showeth mercy and lendeth: he shall order his words with judgment : because he shall not be moved forever.

In memoria æterna erit justus: ab auditione mala non timebit.

Paratum cor ejus sperare in Domino, confirmatum est cor ejus: * non commovebitur, donec despiciat inimicos suos.

Dispersit, dedit pauperibus: justitia ejus manet in sæculum sæculi: * cornu ejus exaltabitur in gloria.

Peccator videbit, et irascetur, dentibus suis fremet et tabescet: * desiderium peccatorum peribit.

Gloria Patri, etc.

The just shall be in everlasting remembrance: he shall not fear the evil hearing.

His heart is ready to hope in the Lord, his heart is strengthened: he shall not be moved until he look over his enemies.

He hath distributed, he hath given to the poor: his justice remaineth forever and ever, his horn shall be exalted in glory.

The wicked shall see, and shall be angry; he shall gnash with his teeth and pine away: the desire of the wicked shall perish.

Glory, etc.

PSALM 112.

Laudate pueri Dominum:* laudate nomen Domini.

Sit nomen Domini benedictum, * ex hoc nunc et usque in sæculum.

A solis ortu usque ad occasum,* laudabile nomen Domini.

Excelsus super omnes gentes Dominus,* et super cœlos gloria ejus.

Quis sicut Dominus Deus noster, qui in altis habitat,* et humilia respicit in cœlo et in terra?

Suscitans a terra inopem,*

Praise the Lord, ye children: praise ye the name of the Lord.

Blessed be the name of the Lord, from henceforth, now and forever.

From the rising of the sun unto the going down of the same, the name of the Lord is worthy of praise.

The Lord is high above all nations, and His glory above the heavens.

Who is as the Lord our God, Who dwelleth on high, and looketh down on the low things in heaven and in earth?

Raising up the needy from

et de stercore erigens pauperem;

Ut collocet eum cum principibus, cum principibus populi sui.

Qui habitare facit sterilem in domo,* matrem filiorum lætantem.

Gloria Patri, etc.

the earth, and lifting up the poor out of the dung-hill;

That He may place him with princes, with the princes of His people.

Who maketh a barren woman to dwell in a house, the joyful mother of children.

Glory, etc.

PSALM 113.

In exitu Israel de Ægypto * domus Jacob de populo barbaro,

Facta est Judæa sanctificatio ejus,* Israel potestas ejus.

Mare vidit, et fugit; * Jordanis conversus est retrorsum.

Montes exultaverunt ut arietes; * et colles sicut agni ovium.

Quid est tibi, mare, quod fugisti?* et tu Jordanis, quia conversus es retrorsum?

Montes exultastis sicut arietes?* et colles sicut agni ovium?

A facie Domini mota est terra,* a facie Dei Jacob.

Qui convertit petram in stagna aquarum,* et rupem in fontes aquarum.

Non nobis, Domine, non nobis;* sed nomini tuo da gloriam.

When Israel went out of Egypt, the house of Jacob, from a barbarous people:

Judea was made his sanctuary, Israel his dominion.

The sea saw and fled: Jordan was turned back.

The mountains skipped like rams: and the hills like the lambs of the flock.

What aileth thee, O thou sea, that thou didst flee? and thou, O Jordan, that thou wast turned back?

Ye mountains, that ye skipped like rams; and ye hills like the lambs of the flock?

At the presence of the Lord the earth was moved, at the presence of the God of Jacob.

Who turned the rock into pools of water, and the stony hills into fountains of waters.

Not unto us, O Lord, not unto us, but to Thy name give glory

Super misericordia tua, et veritate tua; * ne quando dicant Gentes: ubi est Deus eorum?

Deus autem noster in cœlo; * omnia quæcumque voluit fecit.

Simulacra Gentium argentum et aurum,* opera manuum hominum.

Os habent, et non loquentur; * oculos habent, et non videbunt.

Aures habent, et non audient; * nares habent, et non odorabunt.

Manus habent, et non palpabunt; pedes habent, et non ambulabunt; * non clamabunt in gutture suo.

Similes illis fiant qui faciunt ea; * et omnes qui confidunt in eis.

Domus Israel speravit in Domino: * adjutor eorum et protector eorum est.

Domus Aaron speravit in Domino; * adjutor eorum et protector eorum est.

Qui timent Dominum, speraverunt in Domino; adjutor eorum et protector eorum est.

Dominus memor fuit nostri: * et benedixit nobis.

Benedixit domui Israel; * benedixit domui Aaron.

Benedixit omnibus qui ti-

For Thy mercy and for Thy truth's sake; lest the Gentiles should say, Where is their God?

But our God is in heaven; He hath done all things whatsoever He would.

The idols of the Gentiles are silver and gold, the work of the hands of men.

They have mouths and speak not; they have eyes and see not.

They have ears and hear not; they have noses and smell not.

They have hands and feel not; they have feet and walk not, neither shall they cry out through their throats.

Let them that make them become like unto them; and such as trust in them.

The house of Israel hath hoped in the Lord; He is their helper and their protector.

The house of Aaron hath hoped in the Lord; He is their helper and their protector.

They that fear the Lord have hoped in the Lord; He is their helper and their protector.

The Lord hath been mindful of us; and hath blessed us.

He hath blessed the house of Israel; He hath blessed the house of Aaron.

He hath blessed all that

ment Dominum, * pusillis cum majoribus.

Adjiciat Dominus super vos; * super vos, et super filios vestros.

Benedicti vos a Domino; * qui fecit cœlum et terram.

Cœlum cœli Domino; * terram autem dedit filiis hominum.

Non mortui laudabunt te, Domine: * neque omnes qui descendunt in infernum.

Sed nos qui vivimus, benedicimus Domino; * ex hoc nunc et usque in sæculum.

Gloria Patri, etc.

fear the Lord, both little and great.

May the Lord add blessings upon you and upon your children.

Blessed be you of the Lord, Who made heaven and earth.

The heaven of heavens is the Lord's: but the earth He hath given to the children of men.

The dead shall not praise Thee, O Lord: nor any of them that go down to hell.

But we that live bless the Lord, from this time now and forever.

Glory, etc.

Instead of 118, *Psalm* 116 *is often sung.*

PSALM 116.

Laudate Dominum omnes Gentes; * laudate eum omnes populi.

Quoniam confirmata est super nos misericordia ejus; * et veritas Domini manet in æternum.

Gloria Patri, etc.

Praise the Lord, all ye nations; praise Him, all ye people.

Because His mercy is confirmed upon us, and the truth of the Lord remaineth forever.

Glory, etc.

THE CAPITULUM.

Benedictus Deus et Pater Domini nostri Jesu Christi, Pater misericordiarum, et Deus totius consolationis,

Blessed be the God and Father of Our Lord Jesus Christ, the Father of mercies, and the God of all com-

qui consolatur nos in omni fort, Who comforteth us in tribulatione nostra. all our tribulations.
 R. Deo gratias! *R.* Thanks be to God!

Here is usually sung a hymn appropriate to the season of the year.

HYMN FOR SUNDAY.

Lucis Creator optime,	O great Creator of the light,
Lucem dierum proferens,	Who, from the darksome womb of night,
Primordiis lucis novæ,	Broughtst forth new light at nature's birth,
Mundi parens originem.	To shine upon the face of earth.
Qui mane junctum vesperi,	Who, by the morn and evening ray,
Diem vocari præcipis;	Hast measured time and called it day,
Illabitur tetrum chaos,	Whilst sable night involves the spheres,
Audi preces cum fletibus.	Vouchsafe to hear our prayers and tears.
Ne mens gravata crimine,	Lest our frail mind, with sin defiled,
Vitæ sit exul munere;	From gifts of life should be exiled,
Dum nil perenne cogitat,	Whilst on no heavenly thing she thinks,
Seseque culpis illigat.	But twines herself in Satan's links.
Cœleste pulset ostium:	Oh! may she soar to heaven above,
Vitale tollat præmium.	The happy seat of light and love;
Vitemus omne noxium:	Meantime all sinful actions shun,
Purgemus omne pessimum.	And purge the foul ones she hath done.
Præsta, Pater piissime,	This prayer, most gracious Father, hear.

Patrique compar unice,	Thy equal Son incline His ear,
Cum Spiritu Paraclito,	Who, with the Holy Ghost and Thee,
Regnans per omne sæculum. Amen.	Doth live and reign eternally. Amen.

THE MAGNIFICAT,

or the Canticle of the Blessed Virgin Mary.

Magnificat * anima mea Dominum.	My soul doth magnify the Lord:
Et exultavit spiritus meus * in Deo salutari meo.	And my spirit hath rejoiced in God my Saviour.
Quia respexit humilitatem ancillæ suæ; * ecce enim ex hoc beatam me dicent omnes generationes.	Because He hath regarded the humility of His handmaid: for behold from henceforth all generations shall call me blessed.
Quia fecit mihi magna qui potens est; * et sanctum nomen ejus.	For He that is mighty hath done great things to me; and holy is His name.
Et misericordia ejus a progenie in progenies, * timentibus eum.	And His mercy is from generation to generation, to them that fear Him.
Fecit potentiam in brachio suo; * dispersit superbos mente cordis sui.	He hath showed might in His arm; He hath scattered the proud in the conceit of their heart.
Deposuit potentes de sede, * et exaltavit humiles.	He hath put down the mighty from their seat, and hath exalted the humble.
Esurientes implevit bonis; * et divites dimisit inanes.	He hath filled the hungry with good things; and the rich He hath sent away empty.
Suscepit Israel puerum suum, * recordatus misericordiæ suæ.	He hath received Israel His servant, being mindful of His mercy.
Sicut locutus est ad patres	As He spoke to our fathers,

nostros, * Abraham, et semini ejus in sæcula.
Gloria Patri, etc.

to Abraham, and to his seed forever.
Glory, etc.

For the *Magnificat* Pope Leo XIII. granted an indulgence of 100 days, to be gained by reciting it devoutly and with contrite heart, once a day. (September 20, 1879.)

Then follows the Prayer, which is different every day.

P. Dominus vobiscum.
R. Et cum spiritu tuo.
P. Benedicamus Domino.
R. Deo gratias!
P. Fidelium animæ, per misericordiam Dei, requiescant in pace.
R. Amen.

P. The Lord be with you.
R. And with thy spirit.
P. Let us bless the Lord.
R. Thanks be to God!
P. May the souls of the faithful, through the mercy of God, rest in peace.
R. Amen.

Then is sung one of the following Anthems, according to the time.

FROM ADVENT TO THE PURIFICATION.

Alma Redemptoris mater, quæ pervia cœli,
Porta manes, et stella maris, succurre cadenti,
Surgere qui curat populo, tu quæ genuisti,
Natura mirante, tuum sanctum genitorem,
Virgo prius ac posterius: Gabrielis ab ore,
Sumens illud ave, peccatorum miserere.

Mother of Jesus, heaven's open gate,
Star of the sea, support the fallen state
Of mortals: thou whose womb thy Maker bore,
And yet, strange thing, a virgin as before:
Who didst from Gabriel's hail this news receive,
Repenting sinners by thy prayers relieve.

In Advent.

P. Angelus Domini nuntiavit Mariæ;
R. Et concepit de Spiritu sancto.

P. The angel of the Lord declared unto Mary;
R. And she conceived of the Holy Ghost.

P. Oremus.

Gratiam tuam quæsumus, Domine, mentibus nostris infunde; ut qui, angelo nuntiante, Christi filii tui Incarnationem cognovimus, per passionem ejus et crucem, ad resurrectionis gloriam perducamur. Per eundem Christum Dominum nostrum.

R. Amen.

P. Let us pray.

Pour forth, we beseech Thee, O Lord, Thy grace into our hearts, that we, to whom the Incarnation of Christ, Thy Son, has been made known by the message of an angel, may, by His passion and cross, be brought to the glory of His resurrection. Through the same Christ our Lord.

R. Amen.

After Advent.

P. Post partum virgo inviolata permansisti.

R. Dei genitrix, intercede pro nobis.

P. Oremus.

Deus, qui salutis æternæ beatæ Mariæ virginitate fœcunda humano generi præmia præstitisti; tribue quæsumus, ut ipsam pro nobis intercedere sentiamus, perquam meruimus Auctorem vitæ suscipere Dominum nostrum Jesum Christum Filium tuum.

R. Amen.

P. After childbirth thou didst remain a pure virgin.

R. Mother of God, intercede for us.

P. Let us pray.

O God, Who, by the fruitful virginity of the Blessed Virgin Mary, hast given to mankind the rewards of eternal salvation: grant, we beseech Thee, that we may be sensible of the benefits of her intercession, by whom we have received the Author of life, Our Lord Jesus Christ, Thy Son.

R. Amen.

FROM THE PURIFICATION TILL EASTER.

Ave, Regina cœlorum!
Ave, Domina angelorum!
Salve, radix! salve, porta!

Hail, Mary, queen of heavenly spheres!
Hail, whom the angelic host reveres!
Hail, fruitful root! hail, sacred gate!

Vespers for Sundays.

Ex qua mundo lux est orta.	Whence the world's light derives its date.
Gaude, Virgo gloriosa,	O glorious Maid, with beauty blest,
Super omnes speciosa,	May joys eternal fill thy breast!
Vale, O valde decora,	Thus, crowned with beauty and with joy,
Et pro nobis Christum exora.	Thy prayers with Christ for us employ.
P. Dignare me laudare te, Virgo sacrata.	*P.* Vouchsafe, O sacred Virgin, to accept my praises.
R. Da mihi virtutem contra hostes tuos.	*R.* Give me power against thy enemies.
P. Oremus.	*P.* Let us pray.
Concede misericors Deus, fragilitati nostræ præsidium; ut qui sanctæ Dei genitricis memoriam agimus, intercessionis ejus auxilio a nostris iniquitatibus resurgamus. Per eundem Christum Dominum nostrum.	Grant us, O merciful God, strength against all our weakness; that we, who celebrate the memory of the holy Mother of God, may, by the help of her intercession, rise again from our iniquities. Through the same Christ our Lord.
R. Amen.	*R.* Amen.

FROM EASTER TILL TRINITY SUNDAY.

Regina cœli, lætare, Alleluia.	O Queen of heaven, rejoice, Alleluia.
Quia quem meruisti portare, Alleluia.	For He Whom thou didst deserve to bear, Alleluia.
Resurrexit, sicut dixit, Alleluia.	Is risen again, as He said, Alleluia.
Ora pro nobis Deum, Alleluia.	Pray for us to God, Alleluia.
P. Gaude et lætare, Virgo Maria, Alleluia.	*P.* Rejoice and be glad, O Virgin Mary, Alleluia.
R. Quia surrexit Dominus vere, Alleluia.	*R.* Because Our Lord is truly risen, Alleluia.
P. Oremus.	*P.* Let us pray.
Deus qui, per resurrecti-	O God, Who, by the res-

onem Fil.. tui, Domini nostri Jesu Christi, mundum lætificare dignatus es, præsta, quæsumus, ut per ejus genitricem Virginem Mariam perpetuæ capiamus gaudia vitæ. Per eundem Christum Dominum nostrum.

R. Amen.

urrection of Thy Son, Our Lord Jesus Christ, hast been pleased to fill the world with joy: grant, we beseech Thee, that, by the Virgin Mary, His Mother, we may receive the joys of eternal life. Through the same Christ our Lord.

R. Amen.

FROM TRINITY SUNDAY TILL ADVENT.

Salve, Regina, mater misericordiæ, vita, dulcedo, et spes nostra salve.

Hail to the Queen who reigns above,
Mother of clemency and love!

Ad te clamamus, exules filii Evæ. Ad te suspiramus, gementes et flentes in hac lacrymarum valle.

Hail, thou our hope, life, sweetness! We,
Eve's banished children, cry to thee.
We, from this wretched vale of tears,

Eia ergo, advocata nostra, illos tuos misericordes oculos ad nos converte.

Send sighs and groans unto thy ears;
Oh then, sweet advocate, bestow
A pitying look on us below!

Et Jesum benedictum fructum ventris tui nobis post hoc exilium ostende.

After this exile let us see
Our blessed Jesus, born of thee.

O clemens, O pia, O dulcis Virgo Maria!

O merciful, O pious Maid,
O gracious Mary, lend thy aid!

P. Ora pro nobis, sancta Dei Genitrix!
R. Ut digni efficiamur promissionibus Christi.

P. Pray for us, O holy Mother of God!
R. That we may be made worthy of the promises of Christ.

P. Oremus.
Omnipotens, sempiterne

P. Let us pray.
Almighty and eternal God,

Deus, qui gloriosæ Virginis Matris Mariæ corpus et animam, ut dignum Filii tui habitaculum effici mereretur, Spiritu Sancto cooperante, præparasti; da, ut cujus commemoratione lætamur ejus pia intercessione ab instantibus malis, et a morte perpetua liberemur. Per eundem Christum Dominum nostrum.

R. Amen.
P. Divinum auxilium maneat semper nobiscum.
R. Amen.

Who, by the cooperation of the Holy Ghost, didst prepare the body and the soul of the glorious Virgin Mother Mary, that she might become a worthy habitation for Thy Son: grant that, as with joy we celebrate her memory, so, by her pious intercession, we may be delivered from present evils and eternal death. Through the same Christ our Lord.

R. Amen.
P. May the divine assistance always remain with us.
R. Amen.

BENEDICTION OF THE BLESSED SACRAMENT.

O SALUTARIS.

O SALUTARIS Hostia!
Quæ cœli pandis ostium :

Bella premunt hostilia :

Da robur, fer auxilium.

Uni trinoque Domino,

Sit sempiterna gloria ;

Qui vitam sine termino,

Nobis donet in patria.

O SAVING Host, that heaven's gate
Laid'st open at so dear a rate :
Intestine wars invade our breast ;
Be Thou our strength, support, and rest.
To God the Father, and the Son,
And Holy Spirit, three in one,
Be endless praise : may He, above,
With life eternal crown our love.

TANTUM ERGO.

Tantum ergo sacramentum,

Veneremur cernui,

Et antiquum documentum
Novo cedat ritui :
Præstet fides supplementum

Sensuum defectui.

To this mysterious table now
Our knees, our hearts, and sense we bow ;
Let ancient rites resign their place
To nobler elements of grace,
And faith for all defects supply,
While sense is lost in mystery.

Benediction of the Blessed Sacrament.

Genitori, Genitoque
Laus et jubilatio,
Salus, honor, virtus, quoque
Sit et benedictio;
Procedenti ab utroque
Compar sit laudatio. Amen.

P. Panem de cœlo præstitisti eis.
R. Omne delectamentum in se habentem.

Oremus.

Deus qui nobis sub sacramento mirabili passionis tuæ memoriam reliquisti, tribue, quæsumus, ita nos corporis et sanguinis tui sacra mysteria venerari, ut redemptionis tuæ fructum in nobis jugiter sentiamus. Qui vivis et regnas Deus in sæcula sæculorum. Amen.

To God the Father, born of none,
To Christ, His co-eternal Son,
And Holy Ghost, Whose equal rays
From both proceed, one equal praise,
One honor, jubilee, and fame,
Forever bless His glorious name. Amen.

P. Thou hast given them bread from heaven.
R. Replenished with all sweetness and delight.

Let us Pray.

O God, Who hast left us in this wonderful sacrament, a perpetual memorial of Thy passion, grant us, we beseech Thee, so to reverence the sacred mysteries of Thy body and blood that we may continually find in our souls the fruit of Thy redemption, Who livest and reignest, etc.

When the priest gives the benediction with the Blessed Sacrament, bow down, and profoundly adore your Saviour there present. Give Him thanks for all His mercies; offer your whole self to Him, to be His for ever; and earnestly beg His blessing upon you and yours, and upon His whole Church.

PRINTED BY BENZIGER BROTHERS, NEW YORK.

www.ingramcontent.com/pod-product-compliance
Lightning Source LLC
Chambersburg PA
CBHW031850220426
43663CB00006B/569